P9-DNF-377

CONTENTS

AVON

Building the World's Premier Company for Women

LAURA KLEPACKI

WILEY

JOHN WILEY & SONS, INC.

ISBN-13 978-0-471-78723-5
ISBN-10 0-471-78723-X

10   9   8   7   6   5   4   3   2   1

AVON

FOREWORD

Every day, I am inspired in some small way by the story of Avon—by the company's rich history of empowering women and its belief in the importance of social responsibility to make the world a better place. These are core values that have been passed down and nurtured since the company's founding more than a century ago. We saw this book as a wonderful opportunity to share the story of this extraordinary company—"The Company for Women"—and the role it has played in improving women's lives.

It all started back in 1886 when the company's founder, an entrepreneur named David McConnell, recruited women to sell perfume door-to-door. This was considered quite revolutionary at the time because women virtually never worked outside the home and would not win the right to vote for another 34 years. Nonetheless, Avon's commitment to create economic opportunities for women took hold, not only in the United States, but all around the world.

Today Avon is a $7.7 billion company with almost five million representatives in over 100 countries. Our Avon sales representatives remain the heart and soul of the company. These smart, savvy, thoughtful businesswomen are my role models. Their ambition and work ethic is unparalleled. It takes a special kind of courage to run your own business, and I am filled with admiration for their extraordinary accomplishments. Everything we do is about helping to make their job easier.

I am very privileged to lead Avon at this important moment in the company's history. We have transformed a brand that was always well respected, but now is recognized as truly world class. We have improved the Avon selling experience and created greater earning opportunities for our representatives. We're proud that each year women earn close to $3 billion selling Avon. We also run our business more efficiently and profitably than ever, increasing the value for Avon's shareholders.

But none of these accomplishments compare to the gratitude I feel knowing that Avon is changing women's lives for the better—not only through their earning opportunity, but also through the philanthropic efforts of the Avon Foundation to eradicate breast cancer and end domestic violence, two issues that concern women everywhere. And our corporate profile reflects our focus on equal opportunities for women. Today, we have more women managers than any other Fortune 500 company. Our president and chief operating officer is a woman, as are half the members of our board of directors.

Thanks to the original vision of our founder and to the power of the company's mission—which is fully embraced by our millions of representatives and associates around the world—Avon has emerged as a true force for good, forever changing the social and economic landscape for women and lighting the way for future generations. It is a legacy of which all of us at Avon are the proud stewards. And it is a legacy that guides us to see even greater possibilities for tomorrow.

Andrea Jung
Chairman and Chief Executive Officer
Avon Products, Inc.

INTRODUCTION

Two hundred and sixty Avon sales representatives, with family members in tow, took their seats in the cordoned off VIP section at New York's Governors Island, a spot providing a clear view across New York Harbor to Liberty Island. They were seated in the grandstand near international dignitaries including First Lady Nancy Reagan and French President Francois Mitterrand. Among the glittering crowd were such entertainment legends as Elizabeth Taylor, Gregory Peck, Henry Winkler, Helen Hayes, and Mikhail Baryshnikov. Clearly, it was an event fit for royalty.

It was the evening of July 3, 1986, a date marked by unseasonably chilly temperatures and gusty winds. Nancy Reagan kept a red shawl around her shoulders; others shivered under blankets. All were gathered for the opening ceremony of a four-day festival to celebrate the magnificent centennial of the Statue of Liberty. The occasion also marked the completion of the landmark's $87 million head-to-toe restoration. This was to be her official unveiling.

President Ronald Reagan wowed the crowd with the push of a button that tripped off a cascade of lights bathing the statue in red, white, and blue. There were speeches and musical performances, along with the presentation of the Medal of Liberty to 12 naturalized citizens for their contributions to the nation, including scientist Albert Sabin and architect I. M. Pei.

This Liberty Weekend extravaganza was staged by Hollywood producer David Wolper, known for his film epics *Roots* and *North and South*. It featured music by composer John Williams of *Star Wars* fame. The patriotic colored, nautical-style uniforms worn by the hostesses guiding invited guests were designed and donated by Avon, which helped to sponsor Liberty Weekend and the restoration efforts leading up to it. Inviting some of its representatives to be a part of this awe-inspiring event was just one of many perks the company treated its top performers to that year in recognition of their efforts in going door-to-door, selling a variety of products, and making women around the world both more beautiful and financially independent.

In what would be a prophetic slogan for the company itself, in the months before the festivities, the company ran advertisements showing work being done on the Statue of Liberty with a banner reading: "A Monumental Makeover: Avon Helping to Keep the Face of America Beautiful." Indeed, just 15 years later, Avon would undergo a transformation of its own—one that would make it one of the biggest and most powerful global powerhouse companies in the world.

It was only natural that Avon should lend a hand to this event. After all, like the Statue, the company was commemorating its own 100th anniversary. What's more, as Lady Liberty herself, Avon had long heralded the independence of women.

It was in 1886, nearly three decades before women in the United States had the right to vote, that company founder David Hall McConnell first gave housewives a chance to earn a living at a time when few other options were available. Since then, the company famous for ringing customer doorbells and offering in-home service, has operated under the same founding principles originally set forth by McConnell—a man described by Avon's current chairman and chief executive officer, Andrea Jung, as being ahead of his time in fashioning a business with an exclusively female sales force. "What McConnell did was heretical" for the period, says Jung, who broke stereotypes herself when she became Avon's first female CEO in 1999.

Unusual, yes, but McConnell's formula was an instant hit from the start.

Avon's corporate philosophy called for providing "an earning opportunity in support of a person's well-being and happiness," to make only the "highest quality products," and to "render service that is outstanding."

Additionally, McConnell decreed that management always recognize its employees and representatives "on whom the company's success depends," and that they share the rewards of that success. Furthermore, the company must contribute to society and "maintain and cherish the friendly spirit" it conveyed.

A former door-to-door book salesman, McConnell started Avon from the ground up, almost by accident, with one sweet-natured, middle-aged saleswoman. He likened his company's graceful expansion to that of an "acorn into an oak."

The Avon of today is more robust than ever. Functioning in a world where competition for the sales of beauty products is anything but pretty, the company has, with a few trial-and-error exceptions, stuck to its original formula and flourished by leveraging its distinctive person-to-person selling system.

Avon is not only a giant in the beauty business, it is also the largest direct-selling company of any kind on the planet. Although the company is best known for its various cosmetics products—from lipstick to anti-aging cream—it now offers everything from vitamins to weight-control products to meet the growing needs of its customers. Avon's time-tested methods of operation are the model to which other direct-selling companies aspire to emulate.

In the United States, where the majority of women no longer stay home during the day, the actual door-to-door approach is falling by the wayside in lieu of more productive avenues to connect with customers, such as workplace selling and the Internet. But the original high-touch model remains in full force in more than 143 countries around the globe. In fact, of Avon's 4.9 million representatives, more than 75 percent now reside outside of America.

One of the crucial keys to Avon's good fortune has been its ability to inspire and motivate its sales representatives. As McConnell recognized from the start, without their commitment and dedication, his operation would falter.

Avon: Building the World's Premier Company for Women provides an "insider's" view of the development and expansion of an incredible company. For the first time, you'll be there through every step of its growth and discover how it greatly differs from almost every other traditional consumer products company. At Avon, the sales representatives (often referred to as simply the "reps") run the show, and everything the company does centers around supporting them. This means providing reps with a nurturing and encouraging environment, while working up slate after slate of new products designed to keep their customers coming back.

In the pages ahead, you'll get a colorful and nostalgic look at Avon's journey to the top, which hasn't been seamless. Over the years, the company has endured more than its share of management turnover and failed initiatives, though in each case it came back stronger than ever. You will learn how this empire was built, discover the management techniques that guide the company, and get the exclusive details on what the current management team, under CEO Andrea Jung, has done to reinvigorate the company to the delight of both Wall Street and Avon's ever-growing sales force.

What's more, you'll examine the company's unique and fast-paced business structure, which has been designed around meeting its two- to four-week selling cycles to keep products turning over on a regular basis. To sustain this repetitive system, Avon has developed one of the most prolific product development departments in the beauty industry. You'll learn exactly how Avon is able to meet the requirements imposed by this demanding arrangement, and how it has managed to replicate this winning formula in even the most remote areas of the world.

While Avon has a soft and warm exterior, science and technology have always played an important behind-the-scenes role in keeping the company running. In this book, you'll discover how the company is increasingly using computer technology and automated systems to make selling cosmetics—and virtually everything else—easier and more profitable.

Throughout its history, Avon has gone through multiple transitions, resulting in its metamorphosis from a one-man business to the global conglomerate it is today. By selling woman-to-woman, one small order at a time, Avon has evolved into one of the most widely known, respected, and ubiquitous brands in the world. It conducts 1.6 billion customer transactions each year, and is the largest fragrance manufacturer around the globe—selling another one of its famous lipsticks every three seconds.

Avon: Building the World's Premier Company for Women tells the story of one company's drive to provide women with an opportunity for financial independence. It also takes a closer look at the innovative selling techniques and recruitment methods used by those entrepreneurial Avon ladies who have been turning kitchen tables and basements into business offices for decades.

By the end of the story, you'll understand how one man's simple business idea blossomed into a powerhouse beauty company that, over the course of time, has provided limitless opportunities to millions of women around the world. You'll also benefit by uncovering the key tenets by which the company operates—lessons you can use to bolster your own business, regardless of what industry you're in. Avon serves as a model for how to run a great company, and its operating practices are applicable to any fledgling entrepreneur in every part of the world.

CHAPTER 1

GIVE THEM WHAT THEY WANT

David Hall McConnell was a hard worker from the start. The second of six children, as a young boy he rolled up his sleeves and helped run the family farm in Southwest Oswego, New York, a rural locale on the north central border of the state where Lake Ontario separates the United States from Canada. It is a place noted for its severe winters, with average snowfalls of 141 inches per year.

His parents, James and Isabella Hall McConnell, had emigrated from County Cavan, Ireland, in 1856. Like so many others, they came to the United States hoping to find a better life for their family. The couple already had one son, William, who was born in 1855. David arrived three years later on July 18, 1858. In succession, Joseph, Margaret Ann, George, and Hattie followed.

David McConnell was a sturdy youth who didn't allow the heavy fieldwork to distract him from his education. He became a diligent student at the "little red school," as the town's public school was known. Afterward, he continued his studies at the Oswego Normal School, a training college for teachers.

Together, he felt the outdoor work and solid schooling had made him rugged. When he set out as a young man to seek his fortune, McConnell said that his hardy upbringing gave him a "positive advantage" over others with less life experience.

An intelligent lad, McConnell liked school. As he progressed through his grades, he even taught some classes as well. He had long imagined a career for himself as a mathematics instructor and the experience was considered good preparation.

SELLING BOOKS

But McConnell was a boy willing to try new things. One summer, during a brief recess from school, he stepped outside his familiar routine and took a temporary job as a book salesman with the New York office of Union Publishing House. Little did he know that this brief encounter with business would ultimately lure him away from academics and change his life forever.

It was through this experience, which required him to peddle goods door-to-door, that the onetime farm boy discovered he had an aptitude for selling—and was intrigued by the world of commerce. He immediately took to the challenges of it, and from the start wanted to continually find better ways to approach and engage potential customers.

After his first brief taste of this business, McConnell gladly returned to work with the publisher the following year. Once again, he found the experience to be rewarding. It didn't take much convincing after that for McConnell to throw himself into the venture full force. In 1878, he said goodbye to his studies and to his family in Oswego and set out to work full-time as a book canvasser.

McConnell's ascent was rapid and he soon became the firm's leading salesperson. He then moved into the publisher's Chicago headquarters where his successes continued to mount.

Within two years, he was promoted from canvasser to general traveling agent, a role that would take McConnell on trips to almost every state east of the Rocky Mountains. In this management position, he recruited and trained other agents. In the process, he honed his own selling skills and learned how to motivate others. For a time, he led the company's southern district headquartered in Atlanta.

The experiences with his customers and colleagues, he wrote, "gave me good insight into human nature."

So accomplished was McConnell at the book-selling trade that he swiftly proceeded to buy out the publishing firm from his boss. Soon after, he moved the operation to New York City.

THE SWEET SMELL OF SUCCESS

When he moved back East, McConnell wasn't alone. He had met his wife, Lucy Hays, while working in Chicago. The two were married in a quiet ceremony at the home of Lucy's sister on March 31, 1885. Lucy also helped McConnell with the business. In the ensuing years, the couple had three children: David Hall Jr., Edna, and Dorys.

It was now 1886 and McConnell had been selling books for some eight years. His enchantment with the book business was diminishing, and he was also anxious to expand his operation into new areas. But he wasn't quite sure how.

He and his employees steadily peddled the books and, as always, he continuously sought new and different ways to engage their customers. A chemist friend had mixed up some perfume samples, which McConnell handed out to housewives in order to win them over and then draw their attention to his books.

But it didn't take long for the savvy salesman to recognize that the small fragrance vials were delighting the women far more than his books were. It was a eureka moment for McConnell. By chance, he had stumbled on the new business opportunity he had been searching for—perfume!

Perfume may have caught McConnell's attention by happenstance, but from then on his venture was guided by strategic planning. Before stepping into the fragrance business, he first fully researched its potential. After evaluating the competition posed by other door-to-door enterprises, McConnell concluded that there was a high likelihood for success not only in perfumes, but also in expanding into various grooming items.

"The starting of the perfume business was the result of the most careful and thorough investigation, guided by the experience of several years' successful operation in the book business—that is, in selling goods direct to the consumer or purchaser," McConnell said. "In investigating this matter, nearly every line of business was gone over, and it seemed to me then, as it has since been proved, that the perfume business in its different branches afforded the very best possible opportunity to build up a permanent and well-established trade."

While the company was always based in New York City, glowing descriptions of California and air scented from fields of wildflowers peppered McConnell's conversations with his close friend and former boss, Charles L. Snyder, from whom he had acquired the book business. McConnell credits Snyder, who was living in San Francisco at the time, with helping to come up with the name for this new venture.

With five single note fragrances—lily of the valley, violet, heliotrope, white rose, and hyacinth—McConnell launched the California Perfume Company in 1886 at 126 Chambers Street in Manhattan. (As a reminder of its origins, large black and white photographs of each of the flowers hang on the lobby walls of the company's U.S. headquarters at 1251 Avenue of the Americas in Manhattan and at its global offices a few blocks north.) The first product was named the Little Dot Perfume Set and it contained a selection of the five scents.

From the start, McConnell was committed to creating quality products and immediately issued a money-back guarantee to aid in the marketing. That pledge still appears on every brochure distributed by the company around the world. His instinct was to focus on using the best ingredients on the formulas, while not spending much on packaging. He later learned that packaging was important, too, and the company soon began to upgrade the appearance of its products. Through his catalogs, McConnell made sure that customers knew he used only the finest ingredients. His scents, he stressed, were derived from natural essences and were as good as any French perfume.

For several years, he maintained the book business while, at the same time, expanding the perfume operation. But with beauty showing robust promise, McConnell finally abandoned the book business forever in 1892. Despite his early accomplishments with book selling, McConnell expressed no regrets about the way his life changed course.

"The book business was not congenial to me, although I was, in every sense, successful in it," he later said. "But there were many things that were not pleasant."

Like many who happen into the glamorous world of the beauty business, McConnell developed a taste for its aspirational nature and whimsy and set out to learn how to mix product formulas himself. He took earnestly to the task in his homemade lab for several years.

It was a trial-and-error process at the start. "I did much experimental work in making these odors, and the selling price of the first batch of perfumes I made did not cover one-half the actual cost of the goods," he observed.

MARKETING WOMAN-TO-WOMAN

McConnell made a pragmatic decision in shifting his operation from books to beauty. Still lauded today as a progressive thinker, McConnell saw business advantages in having women sell to other women for their ability to add a personal and understanding touch to the exchange. It was during his days on the road as a bookseller that he encountered women who needed a way to make money for themselves. Wrote a nephew in 1962, "As he was canvassing, he was moved by the way women were struggling 'to makes ends meet.'"

It was therefore no surprise that McConnell tapped one of his best booksellers, Mrs. Persis Foster Eames Albee of Winchester, New Hampshire (P. F. E. Albee) as the first official salesperson for his newly minted California Perfume Company. Her title was "general agent." Born in 1836, the mother of two—Ellery and Ellen—she was 50 years old when she started her new job.

Through the California Perfume Company, McConnell provided earning opportunities to women at a time when other employment options were few. Even while peddling his books and only contemplating the creation of a new business, he had always imagined women would be part of the plan.

Albee and her husband, Ellery Albee, an attorney who served as New Hampshire state senator from the Ninth District from 1869 to

1871, operated a variety store together from their home in Winchester. Because the store also possessed the town's public phone, many people had an additional reason to stop by. Not wanting to miss an opportunity to gain attention for the California Perfume Company's wares, Mrs. Albee prepared an attractive display of the samples in her store.

The Albees' home, a two-story colonial structure located near the center of town on the banks of a narrow river, was close to the railroad station. "It was white . . . all landscaped . . . it was a beautiful house," remembered a childhood neighbor.

For many families, making ends meet can be challenging. The Albees were no different. Town records show times when property bills weren't met and warnings were issued to the family that ownership of their home on Depot Street (now 9 Elm Street) was in jeopardy.

Through her work with the California Perfume Company, Albee, a Sunday school teacher, was able to help with her family's income. To sell her wares, she traveled by horse and buggy and by train to distribute the California Perfume Company product line. After several months, McConnell promoted her to "depot manager." In her new, elevated role, she began recruiting other women to sell.

Albee's business grew and she earned a reputable name for herself as having "unfailing integrity." It was said that Albee "was as good an employer as she was her own businesswoman. She helped those who helped the business prosper," according to an article in New Hampshire's *The Banner* newspaper.

McConnell was very public in recognizing the contributions of Albee. Noting that Albee had been the company's first general agent and had also secured several good workers, "It is only befitting," wrote McConnell, "that we give her the honorary title of 'Mother of the California Perfume Company,' for the system that we now use for distributing our goods is the system that was put in practical operation by Mrs. Albee."

With Albee's help, the California Perfume Company's growth was brisk from the start. The company's first home on 126 Chambers Street had blossomed from a 20- by 25-square foot space containing shipping, manufacturing, and office functions to occupy the building's full six floors by 1894. The original staff included one stenographer; Albee as the sole general agent; McConnell as the self-proclaimed manufacturing chemist, shipping clerk, and office boy; and his wife Lucy.

Then, as now, the company's sales were closely aligned with the rise and fall of the size of the sales force. So Albee began to bring more sales agents into the fold. As she did, sales volume climbed. To keep new and old customers coming back, the California Perfume Company ratcheted up research and development efforts to maintain a flow of enticing new products. Before long, the company outgrew its Manhattan workspace.

MOVING TO SUFFERN

McConnell had relocated his family from Brooklyn to the Rockland County Village of Suffern, a 2.1-square-mile enclave where the railroad came early (circa 1848) luring settlers. Situated in a valley surrounded by the lush rolling hilltops of the Ramapo Mountains, it was also a popular retreat for summer visitors escaping the heat of New York City. In its 1889 pamphlet "Suburban Homes on the Picturesque Erie," the New York and Erie Railroad described Suffern as a "choice picture of natural beauty." The train ride to Manhattan took about an hour.

Two years after he moved his family in, McConnell relocated the research and development and manufacturing operations of the California Perfume Company to Suffern in 1895. The headquarters stayed in Manhattan (where it remains today, albeit it at a different location).

McConnell had a heavy hand in the development of Suffern. In addition to being a leading businessman in the area, he was a founder of the Suffern Presbyterian Church and the Suffern National Bank and Trust Company. He also served as superintendent of schools and treasurer of the Rockland County Republican Committee. During World War I, he was chairman of the Rockland County Selective Service Board.

With a progressive eye toward his community and business, in 1896 McConnell was among a group of Suffern leaders who passed out fliers and lobbied for the village's incorporation. The measure was approved by a resident vote of 206 to 19. The empowered status gave Suffern more autonomy from Ramapo Township and hastened the start of vast capital improvement projects such as street lighting and road building. Better services, of course, improved business opportunities. And while Suffern enjoyed rail service, in the 1890s, it still had no paved streets or sidewalks, no street lights or water system, and no formal police or fire protection.

The first California Perfume Company facility in Suffern was a 1,600-square-foot temporary space. This was quickly replaced by a three-story wooden structure in 1897 at Fair and Division streets, strategically located on the Erie train line. The building provided 3,000 square feet of working space and was outfitted with a full laboratory.

By then, the company was growing so rapidly, McConnell was personally being stretched, dividing his time among product manufacturing, distribution, and his sales team. After creating the product line himself for 10 years, in 1896 he hired a perfumer—Adolph Goetting—to lead that area. Goetting was a naturalized German immigrant with 25 years experience in the fragrance industry.

GROWING THE BUSINESS

Meanwhile, the representative ranks were escalating. By 1898, there were 5,000 agents. Two years later, that number climbed to 6,100. Altogether, the representative force produced sales of $200,000 annually.

After setting out with simple perfumes, the product portfolio blossomed to include shampoo cream, witch hazel cream, almond cream balm, and household items such as toothbrushes, tooth powder, and cleansers. By 1906, the collection had some 117 items, 600 when individual sizes and varieties were taken into account. Fragrances remained a mainstay with new scents and ancillary items being added regularly. As early as 1914, a scent for children was introduced. The first was the Little Folks Set that combined fragrances in packages with pretty illustrations.

Cosmetics were not part of the starting lineup. But nearly 20 years after its launch, customers were clamoring for some color. "Numerous requests have been made by our Depot Managers for a cosmetic or rouge," reported the company in a newsletter. "After duly experimenting, we have decided to manufacture a rouge in both liquid and powder form . . . Our rouge is now ready for delivery."

As recognized by turn-of-the-century writer Ella Adelia Fletcher, societal mores were changing. "It is not so very long ago that there existed a certain prejudice—a sort of aftermath of Puritan influence against the endowment of physical beauty," she wrote in 1901. Paying attention to personal care, "is now considered necessary, without being charged with the heinous crime of vanity."

As the business flourished, more and more capacity was needed. The California Perfume building in Suffern was expanded and remodeled again, so that by 1903 it boasted 17,200 square feet of working space.

Accustomed from his life as a book agent to travel extensively, McConnell didn't hesitate to expand his new beauty products into more and more neighborhoods. Women worked out well as the firm's representative base. The concept was to have women sell within their own neighborhoods, where they were known. McConnell was aware of the changes in society as his perfume and toiletries business developed. He continued to believe that having women sell personal items to women in the privacy of their homes was the most beneficial approach for this product line.

McConnell's decision to take his goods directly to consumers was a planned and deliberate one. He later claimed that, even while selling books, he was devising a business plan for marketing and manufacturing a line of consumer goods that could be sold direct to the customer via a general agent. But he was determined to come up with a line of consumable items, so that repeat purchases would be necessary.

To support this personal selling method, California Perfume Company was a charter member of the National Association of

Agency Companies, now known as the Direct Selling Association, a trade group devoted to supporting the operations of direct sellers.

When drugstores or other retailers inquired about selling California Perfume Company's products, McConnell had a prepared and diplomatic response ready. The real answer of course was "no." But the inquiring merchants were always encouraged to buy products for themselves or to direct their customers to one of the California Perfume Company's agents directly. The sales model has become ingrained in the company's culture. Throughout the years, when other distribution methods have been tested, frequently an outcry erupts from some faction or another against tampering with the decades' old, tried-and-true model.

Sales offices to help develop representatives were starting to sprout across the country with sites in San Francisco, California; Davenport, Iowa; Dallas, Texas; and Luzerne, Pennsylvania. A Kansas City, Missouri, site would later consolidate the operations of Dallas and Davenport. In 1914, Albee died and was buried in Evergreen Cemetery in Winchester, the town in which she had lived most of her adult life. Thanks to her efforts in growing the sales force, by that year the company reached northward into Canada opening up an office in Montreal.

As testament to the progress it had made, in 1915 the California Perfume Company won the prestigious Gold Medal Award at the Panama-Pacific Exposition in San Francisco for its products and packaging. The medal's winning stamp was soon applied to all packaging.

By 1916, the California Perfume Company had displaced the Suffern area's two leading employers—the New York and Erie Railroad and the Ramapo Iron Works—as the region's largest provider of jobs. Although its ranks have slimmed in recent years because of shifts in its manufacturing operations, the company has remained a leading corporate citizen in Suffern and primary employer in Rockland County.

"Many, many people here have worked at [the company]," confirms 90-year-old Gardner Watts, a lifelong Suffern resident and the village's historian. "People here are keen about [the company] and their work." McConnell, he notes, "was the big person in Suffern for decades."

In 1920, sales hit the $1 million mark. Over the next six years, the volume more than doubled to $2.2 million as some 25,000 representatives were going door-to-door.

The product line continued to branch into new areas. In 1927, the first skin care collection was unveiled, starting with the Gertrude Recordon Facial Treatment, named for the skin care expert who helped create it.

In 1931, there was another reason to exult: The California Perfume Company's products had been granted the Good Housekeeping Seal of Approval.

CHANGING FOR THE BETTER

McConnell lived to preside over his business for 50 years. During his leadership, there were some major overhauls in its operations. For one, the selling cycle switched from monthly orders to three-week campaigns. While the move seems against logic, given that it occurred in 1932 during the Depression when few had money to spend, the change yielded astounding results—with sales jumping 70 percent. At this time, the company also introduced specially priced items—that is *sale* items. These bargains have since become an expected feature in the company's brochures.

Four years later, the company began a program that would be its boilerplate sales model for at least four decades—the creation of sales territories. Under the plan, each representative was assigned a district and had exclusive authority for all sales in that area.

By the time it completed its first half-century, the California Perfume Company had sales of $4.2 million and its Suffern-based manufacturing and research and development plant had ballooned to 127,000 square feet. McConnell took a paternalistic approach to his company and his community and was constantly concerned with the well-being of each.

His longtime home, "The Ridge," built on a hillside at what is now the crossroad of Lafayette Street and Oakdale Manor, afforded easy access to the plant set near the center of town. As expected of one of the town's most successful businessmen, McConnell lived on one of the premier properties. It was conveniently located and also offered a grand view.

Being in close proximity to his plant was something that appealed to McConnell, who favored a hands-on manner. This enabled him to conveniently stop in at his laboratories to check on product developments. He would spend almost an hour a day conversing with the chemist before heading to the company's offices in Manhattan or going to other business appointments.

Visiting the labs and checking production lines is a habit that persisted throughout his lifetime. Even in his late seventies, McConnell continued to make his rounds. Tom Ford, who started his career at California Perfume Company in 1936 and retired in 1980 as the director of purchasing in Suffern, recalls "he would come every day."

McConnell's impact on the community in which he lived and on the business that he ran there remains in the memory of longtime Suffern residents.

The McConnell family heavily supported the Suffern Presbyterian Church, where the perfume marketer would sit on the right side in the third pew. The original building still stands as part of the church complex that has been considerably expanded since being built in 1903. The McConnell family donated three of the sanctuary's eight stained glass windows, and a new wing built in the 1960s with donations from McConnell's descendants was named in his honor.

There are recollections, too, of a power struggle at the church in the late 1930s, chronicled in church documents. That's when its pastor, Reverend Henry Watts—Gardner's father—was forced out. Apparently a difference of opinion arose on the merits of the Reverend's sermons—in particular, the length of his orations. A powerful segment of the church membership used salary restrictions to encourage him to leave. McConnell was among the group seeking Watts' departure.

Jean Forsberg, now 86 and living in Maine, was a little girl at the time but remembers the McConnell family. Forsberg's father had succeeded McConnell as superintendent of the church's Sunday school. Soon after, McConnell wrote him a letter commending one of his new programs, recounts Forsberg, who kept the letter for years until it was lost in a recent move.

"They [the California Perfume Company] were well known," she says. "They were the basis of carrying it through the Depression. They kept the jobs going for Suffern. It would have been tragic without the McConnells."

KEEPING A SENSE OF FAMILY

From humble beginnings, McConnell took to the road and built a powerful business. Yet, he always tried to impart a family feeling to his operation. The employee newsletter was named, "The Family Album"; he tried to know as many sales representatives as he could, and he always offered his personal suggestions.

McConnell frequently wrote about his life experiences. His musings revealed a self-confidence and visionary spirit. As the California Perfume Company grew, he would continuously pen letters and memos offering suggestions and tips to guide and inspire the firm's growing legion of sales agents.

Always projecting a healthy opinion of his product line, McConnell possessed an earnest belief that in the selling of it, women were provided opportunities for personal self-fulfillment beyond the benefits of financial empowerment.

"Deep down in the heart of every person there lingers a spark of hope—secret longing to be, or to have, something more," McConnell wrote in an instruction of how to recruit a new agent. "If you can only show a prospect how our work opens the door of oportunity to the realization of this hope, there is never an objection [that] cannot be countered or a difficulty that cannot be overcome."

In a brief history of the company, penned in 1903, McConnell wrote, "The growth of the California Perfume Company only emphasizes what energy and fair dealings with everyone can accomplish. We propose first to be fair with our customers—your customers—by giving them the very best goods that can be made for the money; we propose to be fair and just, even liberal, with you who form the bone and sinew of our business."

On the occasion of McConnell's 75th birthday, every single sales representative submitted an order—be it for a large or small amount—during that sales campaign. This was done in McConnell's honor. It's a feat that, as any direct-selling firm will attest, is almost never achieved—especially by the entire sales force.

When McConnell died at the age of 78 on the morning of January 20, 1937, his death was front-page news in the next issue of *The Ramapo Valley Independent*: "D.H. McConnell, Prominent Local Citizen, Passed Away at Suffern Home Wednesday," read the headline. The story, above the fold and left of center, bore a larger typeface than an article on a national event that also occurred that day: the swearing in of President Franklin Delano Roosevelt to a second term in office. In a bolded block providing an abbreviated list of McConnell's civic and business affiliations, the newspaper declared him to be, "One of [the] Community's Outstanding Men."

In addition to his business associations, McConnell had been socially connected as well, and held memberships in three country clubs: the Houvenkopf in Suffern, the Arcola in New Jersey, and the Ormond Beach in Florida. He was also a member of the Union League in New York and of the Masonic Order.

Yet, in the annals of powerful cosmetics families—Mary Kay, Estée Lauder, Max Factor, Helena Rubinstein, Elizabeth Arden, and Revlon (named after Charles Revson)—the McConnell name remains relatively unknown.

Family members and descendants of McConnell have been adept at keeping their lives private, acknowledges Hays Lawrence (Larry) Clark, a great grandson who opted for a career in oceanography rather than cosmetics. "It just wasn't my thing," he simply states.

Clark's father, Hays Lawrence Clark Sr., is now in his eighties. He was the last family member to be employed by the company. The senior Clark is the son of W. Van Alan Clark and Edna McConnell Clark, McConnell's daughter.

"There is a family modesty," Clark admits. "My grandfather and father would say they were a cog in the wheel. The growth of the company depended on the work of a lot of people more so than themselves, so the credit wasn't really theirs."

BECOMING AVON

What remains clear to Clark are family stories on how the company's name was ultimately changed to the one it is known by today.

During a trip to England in 1928, David Hall McConnell Sr. was taken by the beauty of Stratford-Upon-Avon, home of William Shakespeare. In fact, he thought it was reminiscent of his own hometown of Suffern.

Always looking for ways to make the California Perfume Company's products more interesting and novel, he took to applying the Avon name to a collection of items when he returned home. A new logo was designed for the packaging that featured a sketch of Anne Hathaway's cottage. But that was as far as the name progressed for more than 10 years.

After his death, David Hall McConnell Jr., the founder's son, took over the company as president. A 1923 graduate of Princeton University, the younger McConnell had worked in his father's company as a young boy after school. "He was interested in everything. As soon as he was big enough, he asked to be allowed to do something," wrote Ann Meany, the senior McConnell's longtime secretary. "By the time he graduated college, he had a splendid knowledge of his father's business." David H. McConnell Jr. first joined the company in 1931 and was named executive vice president. As president, he recognized that times were changing. After all, the company was selling products in 48 states. The attachment to California was just too limiting.

Recalling his father's affection for Avon, and believing the name exotic, two years later, the younger McConnell formally changed the company's name. On October 6, 1939, Avon Products, Inc. was born.

CHAPTER 2

STAY FOCUSED

With little head-on competition to stand in its way, Avon used its novel direct-selling method to slowly but steadily infiltrate small towns, farm communities, and big cities across America. Its image as an affordable, family-friendly beauty and grooming brand was being formed one household at a time as thousands of freshly anointed saleswomen knocked on the doors of friends and families in their neighborhoods. In short order, Avon evolved into nothing less than a virtual cash-making machine.

Using a system that cuts out the middleman, Avon posted comfortable profits, even from its very outset. The depot managers, now known as sales representatives, were pocketing healthy commissions, too. In 1901, the company reported sales of $200,000. Of that, Avon representatives were paid $80,000, or 40 percent of the total.

McConnell favored the person-to-person sales method because it was, he wrote, "the most economical way" to get products into the hands of consumers. The customer, he contended, got "the benefit of this enormous saving in an infinitely superior quality [product], not otherwise possible at the price."

As noted by Ann Meany, McConnell's longtime secretary, "The profits were immediate. The business paid for itself." According to Meany's memoir, McConnell once told her, "No man ever had to put himself, even $1, into the California Perfume Company," which was now widely known as Avon.

Sticking with its tried-and-true business model, Avon's sales were on a steady climb. In 1940, three years after the founder's death, sales doubled from $4.2 million to $8.4 million.

The younger McConnell now in charge of running the company was a handsome man with wavy black hair and a charming smile. He led the charge for Avon's fast-paced growth. David H. McConnell Jr.'s tenure, however, was abruptly cut short on August 4, 1944, with his untimely death at the age of 42. He passed away at his home in East Hampton, New York. Newspaper articles published at the time said only that he died after a brief illness. A company newsletter reported the ailment as coronary thrombosis. Married three times, he left behind a third wife and two sons from his first marriage, neither of whom ever joined Avon.

GOING PUBLIC

Graduating from a well-run but modest-sized family business, Avon became a public corporation in 1946. By then its sales had more than doubled again to $17.2 million, with a net profit of just over $1 million.

In 1950, Avon posted sales of $31.2 million. During the decade, sales skyrocketed, multiplying more than five-fold, hitting $168 million in 1960, with net earnings of $17.6 million.

The company's ambition was stoked and, in 1954, it began on an international expansion plan, breaking first into Venezuela and Puerto Rico. Domestically, manufacturing and distribution centers, along with branch sales offices, were sprouting in Pasadena, California; Morton Grove, Illinois; Atlanta, Georgia; and Newark, Delaware. By the end of the decade, in addition to Canada, Avon had international facilities in Puerto Rico, Cuba, and Mexico City. Many more would soon open.

Avon evolved into a veritable cosmetics juggernaut. The company experienced another growth spurt in the 1960s, ending the decade with sales of $759 million. In 1972, sales broke the $1 billion mark, with earnings of $124.9 million. Three years later, one-third of all lipsticks sold in the United States were made by Avon. By 1977, at least one-half of all households in the United States bought Avon one or more times during the year, according to the company.

DEBT-FREE OPERATIONS

Throughout its history, Avon has operated nearly debt-free. Because of this luxury, Avon's once male-dominated management team gained a reputation for enjoying two-hour martini lunches and epitomizing the country club lifestyle. Since the company was flush with cash, there was little concern about spending. As corporate facilities started cropping up around the world, they were lavish, to say the least.

In the lakes region of northern Italy, for instance, Avon constructed a magnificent edifice on the banks of beautiful Lake Como in 1966. The fact that its business was really centered in the southern region of the country was of little concern. The region's manager, who helped build up Avon's operation in Italy, desired a villa on Lake Como, along with an expansive office appointed with marble tables and teak inlay.

There was a feeling of invincibility on the part of management, as if the party would never stop. "Talk about being fat and happy," recalls James E. Preston, who joined the company in 1964 and retired in 1999 as chairman. "Avon had always made so much money."

IGNORING THE WARNINGS

Yet, something was happening outside of Avon's corporate walls—then at 9 West 57th Street—where it occupied 25 floors above the Manhattan skyline. The company also leased an additional two floors in another New York skyscraper. It was the 1970s, the era of leisure suits and mood rings. Society was in an experimental mode and a one-size-fits-all product line was becoming a thing of the past.

Women, meanwhile, were being driven into the workplace. Times were clearly changing. Avon sales representatives discovered that many of the doorbells they rang went unanswered. It was a two-edged sword for the company. Avon found it more difficult to recruit new sales representatives because women were being offered other attractive work opportunities. At the same time, there were fewer customers at home to buy. In response, Avon began to spend more money on recruitment and training efforts only to lure people who were less productive.

A study was commissioned by Avon management in the early 1970s to look into the potential impact of women moving into the workplace. Results came back with a forecast of what the landscape was expected to look like over the next five years. The findings: There would be an increase in both the number of women expected to move into the workforce and in the number of female customers that Avon had begun referring to as the "not at homes." Indeed, this trend was already starting to happen, even though the company wasn't immediately ready to admit it.

At the same time, Revlon had a bestseller on its hands with Charlie, a new fragrance that extolled the lifestyle of the independent working woman, marketed using advertisements that featured a woman in a pantsuit. It was during this same period that Barbara Walters became television's first network news anchorwoman, further advancing this overall notion.

Rather than instituting programs to offset emerging changes in its marketplace, Avon management was told to ignore this prophetic report. This information, it was feared, would only scare the organization. At the time, Avon still possessed a healthy share of the U.S. beauty market—about 15 percent—and it was decided there was really nothing to worry about.

In its 1978 annual report, the company instead glowed over Avon's sterling stock dividend history. "A cash dividend has been paid in each quarter of the past 33 years, and there has been a dividend increase every year since 1953," wrote David W. Mitchell, the company's then chairman and chief executive officer. But this assuring statement didn't tell the whole story. It neglected to point out that Wall Street was having doubts about Avon's future. The stock price had taken a mighty tumble from its high of $140 in 1972, when it had been one of Wall Street's "Nifty Fifty" stocks, to the $20 to $30 range.

A NEW WORLD APPROACH

Avon was being pressured to diversify. Mitchell, who had risen through the ranks at Avon, wasn't prepared to run a multifaceted operation. He stepped down in 1983, after the company's earnings fell for three straight years. Waiting in the wings was Hicks Waldron, who had been appointed to the board in 1980. He was being bypassed for the top job at RJ Reynolds and was ready to take on a CEO position elsewhere.

Waldron brought on two other outsiders: John Chamberlin, who became president and chief operating officer, and Robert Pratt, who was initially appointed to evaluate new retail strategies. The two were to help Waldron redirect the future of Avon. All three had worked at General Electric at one time and shared a consumer products marketing background.

The new management team ushered in a new company philosophy. Instead of devising ways to adjust the core business model to not only survive, but possibly even thrive in the new way society was taking shape, Avon's direct-sales operation was looked at as a "no growth" or at best "slow growth" business. In fact, Waldron and his men had little regard for the established door-to-door style operation and were all but certain the future of that form of direct selling was dead.

Promising shareholders their investment would remain secure and that healthy dividend payments would continue, the company told investors it would move into fast-growing, fat-margin businesses. As strange as it might sound today, the health care industry was at the top of the company's list.

Avon thus got caught up in the frenzy of the high-flying 1980s, when everybody did deals and discussions of leveraged buyouts (LBOs) and corporate takeovers became part of everyday conversation. Beginning in 1979, and for the next 10 years, Avon wheeled and dealed, buying and selling businesses with fervor.

Avon's old guard, a group that still believed there was life in its direct-selling beauty business, stood by in disbelief as the newcomers tampered with and even showed disdain for Avon's core business—its once sacred cow. More insulting was that the cash churned by the beauty business was being siphoned off and used to fuel these new initiatives that ultimately were expected to replace it. The company also started to borrow money, something it had never done before.

Avon's legacy management was kept to look over the beauty business, while the newly hired executives and those brought on board through acquisitions tended to the new operations. Both sides had a tough road ahead of them. The lack of focus on the cash cow was proving costly to the company. With little money being reinvested in Avon's core beauty operation, combined with shifts in workplace demographics, business was sputtering. And the new acquisitions proved to be more of a distraction than anything else.

"It certainly was something to live through," remembers Susan Kropf, today the company's president and chief operating officer. Avon's once monolithic structure turned into a three-ring circus. And on every stage was a juggling act.

FIRST CAME TIFFANY

If there was an early indication that the mentality at Avon was changing, it was signaled with the purchase of the Tiffany Company on April 25, 1979. Management thought the high-priced, prestigious retailer of fine jewelry and gifts would transfer some of its upscale imagery onto Avon—and that Avon would enable Tiffany to broaden its customer base beyond the affluent. It was an awkward bond from the start, despite the fact that Tiffany's sales rose in the first two years under Avon's wing.

Tiffany added specialty items from noted sculptor Charles O. Perry. Its New York store was expanded to increase the design area and backroom services. Space at the Beverly Hills store doubled. Tiffany also operated shops in Atlanta, Chicago, Houston, and San Francisco. Additionally, there were Tiffany salons in the Mitsukoshi department stores in Tokyo and Honolulu.

The company reported that sales of its jewelry, silverware, and other merchandise reached record levels in 1980. But as quickly as Tiffany rose, it fell.

By 1984 Avon had lost patience with Tiffany. Avon management concluded it was a capital-intensive, slow-growth industry and not a strategic fit for the company. Tiffany was the first of many businesses that would come and go quickly under the Avon fold during the 1980s. Tiffany was sold to an investment group led by William Chaney, an Avon executive who had been put in charge of the business after its acquisition in 1979 for $105 million in stock. Tiffany was sold for $135 million, giving Avon a $30 million premium on the deal. Other such ventures would not be as profitable for the company.

MOVING ON TO OTHER VENTURES

Avon seemed open to trying just about anything. There was especially considerable support behind expanding into direct-marketing ventures, which appeared to be a natural extension of the company.

Geni, which sold plastic housewares through at-home parties, was bought by Avon and quickly sold. Family Fashions, a direct-mail apparel business later renamed Avon Fashions, turned a profit after a couple of slow years before its sales reversed. The hope was that, through Family Fashions, Avon would gain a bigger customer base for its cosmetics line. That never happened and Family Fashions was soon jettisoned as well.

In addition, Avon brought some other catalog operations into the fold. James River Traders, for one, offered better quality men's apparel. Bright's Creek, meanwhile, carried children's clothing. Avon also bought the Great American Magazine Company, through which it sold magazine subscriptions for several publishing companies. But because all of these various operations either did not make money or were too difficult to operate, one by one they were sold off. By 1987, Avon had divested itself of each of these ventures.

THE HEALTH CARE TRIAGE

While direct-marketing companies were a diversion, Avon had really put the focus of its attention on the health care industry. Health care was supposed to be the company's savior, entering it into what was expected to be a high-reward, high-margin segment. After all, the population was aging and health care needs were on the rise, according to demographers and statisticians.

It was on March 8, 1982, that Avon officially entered the health care business with the acquisition of Mallinckrodt, Inc., a St. Louis-based firm that made medical diagnostic equipment and other health care products, specialty chemicals, and flavors and fragrances. It possessed 30 plants and reported net sales of $494 million in 1981 with earnings of $39.7 million. Raymond Bentele, the president and chief executive officer of Mallinckrodt, became an executive vice president of Avon and retained his titles at Mallinckrodt as well.

The photography on the cover of Avon's 1982 annual report said it all. Along with a jar of Avon Nurtura Replenishing Cream, a perfume bottle, a folded blouse, a makeup compact, and lipstick sat a bottle of MD-76 Diatrizoate Meglumine and Diatrizoate Sodium Injection. The label on the bottle noted it was for intravascular use. It was definitely an odd sight to behold.

Entering the health care industry took Avon into what was then assessed as a $50 billion health care and specialty chemical market, providing many opportunities for growth, at least in the eyes of some in management.

And so the piecemeal construction of Avon as a health care provider began. Next came Foster Medical, a business operating outpatient home health care services, in 1984. Although Avon was challenged by investors about the high price it paid for Foster, the company decreed it was well worth the premium price. It was said to be part of a dynamic business and not capital intensive. It offered an above-average return on investment and, alas, was a "strategic fit," or so management wrote in a report to shareholders at the time.

Yet, it wasn't as easy as it looked. In 1985, Mallinckrodt was sold at a loss after only three years in Avon's possession. Avon posted a loss of $59.9 million from this experience. A letter to shareholders dated February 28, 1985, written by then chairman and chief executive officer Hicks Waldron, captured the essence of the moment. "This is an exciting time at Avon, and I am pleased to be a part of it," he said. "This is also an awkward time. We are not what we have been. Neither are we what we will be."

In the meantime, the business that had been put on the backburner was starting to boil again. After a six-year decline, sales at

Avon's beauty business rebounded. All the while, beauty was still carrying the load at the company. By 1986, it represented more than 70 percent of sales and 80 percent of the profits.

Nevertheless, Avon was determined to make health care work. The same year the company declared a rebound in beauty, it bought The Mediplex Group, a firm operating nursing homes, alcohol/substance abuse clinics, and retirement facilities. It also purchased Retirement Inns of America, a company that ran 11 retirement facilities in California and Utah. Avon's plan was to roll out the Inns concept nationwide.

Waldron theorized that these businesses all fit into the company's "culture of caring" which, he wrote in the 1985 Annual Report, was a "hallmark of the company since its founding in 1886."

Not long after acquiring Foster Medical, the firm's sales grew 64 percent to $260.3 million and its operating profit shot up from $22.3 million to $51.2 million. It seemed Avon might have finally hit on something. That success, however, was short-lived. The company soon after warned that changes in government health care reimbursement programs could be forthcoming, possibly having an adverse affect on its results going forward. The following year Foster's profits dropped by $30 million. On January 18, 1988, Avon signed an agreement to sell Foster Medical, too.

Waldron blamed Foster's failure on the federal government. "A changed government reimbursement environment turned a simple and attractive business into a difficult and far less profitable business," he maintained. Later that year Avon also sold Mediplex, prompting the company to post an $800 million pretax loss as a result of its failed health care operations. Retirement Inns was pushed out of the portfolio and sold for $10.8 million, also at a loss, in 1989. It had been acquired just three years earlier for nearly three times that amount. This final sale closed Avon's chapter on health care with one last bitter pill.

GOING RETAIL

While direct selling was thought of as passé by Avon's leadership, there was an interest in breaking into the traditional retail market.

As the company noted, 80 percent of all beauty products are sold in retail outlets, so it was too important a market to ignore.

The company wouldn't sell its core Avon brand in retail stores, for that could anger and alienate the sales representatives. But it felt it could safely experiment with non-Avon beauty brands.

Avon's first foray was into department and specialty stores. To do this, it began buying up and forging deals with prestigious fragrance brands. Avon kicked off the proposition with a joint venture with designer Liz Claiborne to create a fragrance and cosmetics line. The items were made available in 2,000 stores. About this same time, Avon aligned itself with actress/model Catherine Deneuve, for a new fragrance jointly developed with a France-based business called Parfums Phenix.

Then, in 1987, Avon struck a deal with the hottest fragrance purveyor of the day—Giorgio Beverly Hills. Owners Fred and Gayle Hayman were divorced and the business was on the block. Avon snapped the company up and took possession of Giorgio, one of the decade's most popular scents. It then expanded the business with Red, another stunning seller. Along the way, Avon gathered the Louis Feraud designer scents and the Parfums Stern business, which possessed the Oscar de la Renta, Valentino, and Perry Ellis brands.

Avon truly struck gold at points with some of these bustling brands. Yet, the timing was not right for the company to try to integrate, learn, and build new businesses—even if they were beauty related.

This was all about to put Avon into a cash crunch. Before long, the retail beauty pieces the company picked up would have to go, too.

A CHANGE IN DIRECTION

In April 1988, James Preston was named as Avon's president and chief operating officer, succeeding Chamberlin who resigned. A few months later Preston was elevated to chief executive officer. Waldron, then chairman, was retiring at year-end. Early the following year, Preston, who had all but been counted out as ever getting the top job when Waldron and Chamberlin came on board, was also named chairman.

Preston says he learned a lot from Waldron, but they did not share a vision. For those Avon employees who had been with the company awhile, "It was hurtful, quite honestly, to keep hearing from these new people that Avon's best days were behind it," Preston says. "The first thing we needed to do was get back to basics. We had to get back to business, as we knew and loved and understood it, and get rid of all the noncore businesses." Preston declared that there would be a return to direct selling and beauty, the heart of the business. He called it Avon's "heritage and strength."

As noted, by 1989 the remaining pieces of Avon's health care business had been dismantled and sold. The retail pieces of beauty were also being shed. The only possession still in hand was Giorgio. Waiting until it got the right price, Avon held on longer than it wanted to. Eventually, Procter & Gamble came through with a sufficient offer, and Giorgio was signed over in 1994 at a $25 million loss from Avon's initial investment.

"Though painful and costly, withdrawing from health care was the right thing to do, ending a diversification strategy into health care services that began five years ago," wrote Preston in the company's 1988 annual report. "The irony is that in the final analysis, Avon didn't need to diversify into health care," he now reflects. "Today, worldwide beauty and direct selling are healthy and provide ample opportunities for the company."

By then the beauty business had been restored and was firing on all cylinders. Even so, Avon's future was not at all clear. When the moving and shaking was all said and done, Preston was left holding $1.2 billion debt. On top of that, the company realized its cash flow situation was worse than it ever thought.

FACING A STARK REALITY

On January 23, 1989, James Preston presided over a meeting of Avon management that sent shockwaves throughout the organization. "Welcome to what is undoubtedly the most important meeting this management team will ever have," he started off.

Preston, a motivator and people person, had previously presided over the Avon division and led a turnaround of the beauty business. In the previous three years, Avon's beauty sales had increased 50 percent to $3 billion in 1988.

With the health care and other businesses on their way out, there was every reason to believe that through hard work and diligence the company could pay off its debt and glide smoothly into the future. "Three years ago, the 'industry' experts had written off direct selling in the U.S.," he told the group. "Today, the viability of direct selling is no longer a question."

But there was more to Avon's story, and Preston was there to prepare his troops for what could be the battle of their lives. Even he was shocked to learn the harsh reality of the company's true financial state. He turned the podium over to Robert Pratt, Avon's executive vice president, to explain exactly what Avon was up against.

Putting it in black and white terms for an audience grown accustomed to willful spending, Pratt said, "Having a positive cash flow means that funds will be available when bills are due. In contrast, when cash flow is negative, you are heading toward bankruptcy." For seven out of the past 10 years, Avon had been operating in the red. The essential rule, said Pratt, is that "sources of cash must exceed uses of cash."

Avon borrowed money to fund its acquisitions. At the same time, it never cut its dividend. It also used cash to repurchase millions of shares of Avon stock.

For the first time, Moody's and Standard & Poor's downgraded Avon's debt rating to speculative, forcing it to pay higher interest rates. "Just how big is the cash-flow challenge we face?" posed Pratt. "It's big!"

In 1990, taking into account proceeds from the business and comparing that to expenditures, Avon was looking at a shortfall of at least $140 million. It would squeak by in 1989 because it pocketed some money from the sale of its last health care business. But after that there was nothing left other than its normal earnings from operations.

The company was able to slightly reduce its debt, but that didn't change the scenario much. In order to achieve its targets, not one item could go awry. Said Pratt, "Operations must deliver every nickel of their cash projections, there can be no increase in interest rates, and there can be no major surprises."

Nevertheless, Avon was vulnerable. It was still the go-go 1980s, after all, and Avon itself became talked about as a likely takeover target. A favorite sport of corporate raiders was to buy up struggling firms, break the company into bits and pieces, and sell each division off. Avon had been bleeding for quite some time, and the sharks were starting to circle.

RALLYING THE TROOPS

Preston swallowed hard and set about the difficult task of telling the members of Avon's worldwide team that things were going to have to change. To this point, limos had been ordered at will and travel and entertainment expenses were routinely above plan. He asked everyone to pay attention to their costs and pitch in to help. It could mean the life or death of the company, he warned.

"Every dollar not spent is a dollar of cash generated. Every dollar saved by sending one person on a trip instead of two, by doubling up in a cab instead of taking a limo, is a dollar that can go toward debt reduction," he instructed his staff.

"I went around the world saying we all had to make sacrifices," Preston recalls. To set an example, Preston tightened his own belt first. Out went the corporate jet he had inherited from Waldron and expansive executive office suite. No longer would he have a private washroom. The executive dining room went, too.

"The thing that used to drive me nuts is that these raiders were going to come in and tear this organization apart," says Preston. "There were three million reps and thousands of employees I felt I had a responsibility to, and I wasn't going to let them down."

If Preston wasn't already committed to keeping the company together, a gesture on the part of Avon's Atlanta division galvanized his resolve. A call came in one Monday from the Atlanta division manager. Three of his employees were requesting a meeting with Preston to make a presentation about cash flow. The group included someone from representative services, the shipping dock, and the assembly station. They were insistent on meeting with Preston in person and offered to pay their own way to New York. Preston was up to his neck in debt problems and had no time for nonessential visits. "What could they possibly want?" he pondered. But he consented and scheduled a meeting anyway.

The day arrived and the three came into his office. They had something they wanted to give him. It was from the Atlanta group's Sunshine Fund. Puzzled, Preston asked what the Sunshine Fund was. Every month, they explained, each Atlanta employee would donate a dollar to the fund to pay for wedding and birthday gifts, or to be used for special occasions or needs that might arise among them. They then proceeded to hand over an oversized check in the amount of $30,475, signed by some 400 Atlanta division employees. It turned out they decided to donate all of the proceeds of the Sunshine Fund to the company in order to help with its cash flow problems.

"You say to yourself, 'Are you gonna let these people down?'" Preston reflects, eyes welling up at the memory of the magnanimous gesture. "No, you are not. That is Avon and it is so worth fighting for." And fight they did.

Throughout the organization, sacrifices were being made, but not quickly enough. And, as feared, the raiders did come. Says Preston, "They thought we were an easy prey." They were wrong.

FENDING OFF THE SUITORS

The first attack came from Avon's nemesis Mary Kay, Inc. Only a few months earlier, an investment banker had approached Avon while it was still on its spending spree to see whether it was interested in taking a look at Mary Kay. Avon management dismissed the idea saying the companies spoke to different markets and Avon representatives wouldn't accept such a merger. If such a transaction were to take place, Avon management insisted, the companies would have to be operated separately.

Mary Kay apparently thought otherwise. Driven by John Rochon, Mary Kay's then chief financial officer, Mary Kay had quietly been acquiring Avon stock. By the time Avon learned of this in December 1988, its competitor already had 600,000 shares in hand.

Rochon had been holding discussions with the Henley Group (a holding company) and investment banker Lazard Freres to make a run at Avon. To try and thwart any attack, Avon began gathering intelligence on Rochon and Richard Rogers, the son of company founder Mary Kay Ash. They were hoping to uncover something that could be used to undermine a merger.

Soon after, Avon learned another group had been formed to pursue Avon. Irwin Jacobs, an investment advisor from Minneapolis, had partnered with Amway Corporation. Together they had acquired about 10 percent or 5.5 million shares of Avon stock. Avon employed a number of means to dissuade an overture from Amway as well. For one, Avon representatives were encouraged to express their disinterest in being a part of Amway. As a result, Amway received thousands of letters from unhappy Avon representatives. A direct-selling company with unhappy representatives is worthless and Amway knew that. Avon also took a more aggressive action. It filed a preemptive lawsuit against Amway charging that Amway violated federal securities laws in acquiring Avon stock. Avon further cited its ongoing business plan as a defense, saying that keeping Avon independent would be the best financial option for its shareholders.

Regardless, on May 10, 1989, Amway initiated a formal bid to buy Avon for $39 a share. Avon's board soundly, and quickly, rejected the overture.

Pulling no punches, in an open letter to Amway, Avon vowed its intent to remain independent. The company pointed to a history of legal problems at Amway and a likely clash of cultures between the two companies as reasons the two should not merge. Amway ultimately gave in and withdrew its offer.

Mary Kay and John Rochon, however, were still lurking. Two weeks after turning Amway away, Avon's Board rejected an advance by Rochon.

By August, Irwin Jacobs, previously of the Jacobs/Amway partnership, resurfaced with a new, higher bid of $41 a share, up from the previous $39. Again, the board threw out the offer.

John Rochon was not to be counted out just yet. In November he was back with a new team, in the form of Chartwell Associates L.P. Avon learned that Chartwell had acquired 6.5 percent of the company's stock. The group behind Chartwell included the Fisher real estate family, Argonaut Partners (headed by John Rochon and Mary Kay), and the Getty Family Trust.

On November 16, 1989, tired of the intrusions, Avon published an open letter in newspapers across the country vowing that it would fight to keep the company independent. That didn't stop Chartwell. The group continued to increase its Avon holdings and, in March of 1990, threatened a proxy fight. By then Chartwell possessed 9.1 percent of Avon common stock.

To avoid what could have turned into a losing battle, Avon agreed to allow two Chartwell candidates onto its board of directors. Appeased for the moment, Chartwell withdrew its proxy fight.

Reflecting back, Preston admits it was a difficult time. "We started to run those meetings by Roberts Rules," he shares. "They would say 'What is this table stuff?' and we'd tell them it means we're not going to talk about it any more."

Once entrenched, it was clear that Chartwell wasn't going to back off its plan to gain control. It bought more stock and demanded four seats on the board. Chartwell also wanted Avon to buy back more of its stock, which would effectively increase Chartwell's ownership percentage.

Avon had paid a price for the temporary truce, and Chartwell became even more aggressive. Disgusted, Preston decreed the company would be up for a proxy fight. "They were trying to get Avon on the cheap," says Preston now. "That was their error. Never underestimate your foe."

In 1990, Avon pulled a switch on Chartwell when it came to voting in directors. It changed its voting slate so as to make it nearly impossible for Chartwell to gain any more than one additional seat on the ten-member board.

Meantime, the Argonaut faction (John Rochon and Mary Kay) claimed to withdraw from the Chartwell group. But Avon had its doubts.

Separately, the two parties (Chartwell and Rochon) could each buy Avon stock and then regroup to own a majority of the company.

Avon possessed a poison pill, formally known as a "shareholder rights plan," that was designed to defend against takeover attempts. If any one shareholder bought more than 20 percent of the stock, all other shares would double and effectively decrease that party's ownership percentage.

Avon wasn't going to wait around to find out what would happen and challenged Argonaut's claim with a lawsuit. By then, the fighting and maneuvering was getting fatiguing for everyone. At the same time, Avon's financial condition had strengthened considerably.

On March 14, 1991, Chartwell finally gave up the fight and sold a majority of its Avon shares. The move significantly reduced the likelihood of a takeover threat. At last, Avon could breathe easy again.

REBOUNDING FROM CHALLENGES

Avon's results in 1990 were stronger than expected and cash flow improved more than anticipated. Sales were up to $3.4 billion from $3 billion in 1988. The company's debt reduction initiatives were ahead of schedule. By 1991, debt had been slashed to $342 million from a high of $1.2 billion in 1988, with sales of almost $3.6 billion.

From that time on, Avon has stuck to its direct-selling model and continues to revere its sales representatives. Granted, there have been numerous out-of-the-box initiatives in the ensuing years, including the development of the beComing retail line. (This product was intended to be an addition to Avon's business, but didn't work out well.) Still, no other initiative has been developed with the intent of replacing Avon's core beauty business model. Through adversity, Avon learned that its original jewel was still the most wonderful— and profitable—part of its operations.

"We lost our way and it was really a terrible time," says Robert Toth, executive vice president for Avon International, who lived through those uncertain days. "The [old] management thought that direct selling was dead and started to diversify, diversify, and diversify. We were headed for real trouble, but we came through. Today we are as strategically focused as we have ever been."

CHAPTER 3

HIRE THE BEST MAN (OR WOMAN) FOR THE JOB

James Preston's white hair is neatly trimmed. When he smiles, his narrow eyes twinkle. Impeccably groomed and friendly faced, he doesn't appear to possess a radical streak.

Yet, it was Preston who orchestrated a forceful challenge to Avon's management status quo starting in the late 1980s when he began pushing for the company to become more female-centric. It can be said Preston boldly set the stage for the new modern era of Avon and the emergence of Andrea Jung as the company's first female CEO. His warm, engaging demeanor almost belies the far-reaching impact of his actions.

There's no doubt that David Hall McConnell was ahead of his time in offering opportunities to women when there were few other attractive options. But for the first 113 years, while the sales force was consistently 99 percent female, Avon had a man at the top running the organization.

Ironically, the revelation that Avon missed the early signs of the women's movement and had to run to catch up pushed management to take notice of the gender of those on its organizational chart.

"Women had a much greater sensitivity to what was going on in the marketplace," says James Preston, who believes men in Avon's organization just were not as aware of what was starting to happen. "When I was made an officer of this company in 1971, there was not one female vice president. There were maybe two or three female directors, in product development and advertising."

Preston credits Patricia Neighbors, who was named one of the company's first female vice presidents two years later, for awakening him to this reality. A former model with a persuasive disposition, Neighbors entreated Preston, then the vice president of sales and marketing, to allow her to make the opening remarks at a meeting he was holding for Avon's regional sales managers. This was in the mid-1970s. Not willing to disclose to Preston what her topic was, she simply asked him to "trust her," as Preston recalls today. "I thought what moxie!" Yet, he relented and she went on.

That daring woman proceeded to go around the room addressing each of the some 20 men and complimenting them on their hair, suits, ties, and other personal appearance details. The men were getting embarrassed and red-faced. She proceeded to explain that, "This is the way 75 [male] district sales managers [who report to the regional managers] start meetings every month with the [female] sales associates. Don't think for a moment that the emotions you just experienced aren't experienced by these women every month."

"I would like to say it was a watershed moment," Preston now reflects, "but all it did was make the men angry."

PUSHING FOR WOMEN

Still, Neighbors did not let up on her mission. She started to push for more women in management and more policies and practices that were favorable to women.

When Preston became CEO in 1988, thanks in no small part to Neighbors, he was already predisposed to breaking down barriers within the company's longstanding male-dominated management scheme.

Preston had benefited plenty from the old boys' network and, as CEO, knew there would be resistance for the changes he hoped to now pioneer at Avon. It was time for women to take on more leadership roles, and he took that message to company meetings and public forums.

"The conventional wisdom of the past held that women and minorities had to change to adapt to the culture of the business or profession to which they belonged," said Preston, speaking at the American Women's Economic Development Meeting in 1988. "But more and more, enlightened businesspeople are coming to understand that it is the culture that must change to accommodate and value diversity in the workplace."

He told the audience that Avon had been making strides over the past four years and now (in 1988) had three women on its board of directors; 13 women in senior management positions (vice president or above); and one group vice president, who directed the U.S. sales force.

That wasn't enough for Preston, though. "My objective was to have at least 50 percent of the management team filled with women and more if necessary if the positions were feminine-market sensitive," he says. "I also felt as if the board had to be at least 50 percent women."

In the early 1990s, Preston started saying publicly and privately that, "In my lifetime, there will be a woman CEO at Avon." It's a surprisingly evolved stance that Preston came to inhabit, particularly given the lackluster attitude he had about Avon before he first came to work for the company in 1964.

Disenchanted with his job at RCA, Preston, a graduate of Northwestern University who had started out working in television, responded to a blind ad in the *Wall Street Journal* seeking someone ambitious with strong communication skills. About a week later, he received a telegram from Avon. He looked at the envelope and asked his wife, "Isn't that the Ding Dong company?" The position held no interest for him and he did not plan to respond—until he picked up a copy of *Fortune* magazine while at the barbershop. It was the Fortune 500 list issue. Avon was among the top "Nifty-Fifty" companies and the subject of an accompanying glowing article.

"I went home and said, 'Where is that telegram?'" Preston says.

THE AVON CULTURE

What immediately struck Preston about Avon was the culture. "There was wonderful warmth and compassion," he recalls. RCA was a very political organization. "I had been with this company that had been so crude and gruff—and that lacked sensitivity and compassion—so I was impacted all the more."

Preston was hired as a trainee at Avon. During his career, he moved throughout various departments at the company including personnel, sales, and operations. "I knew the people, the practices, and the skeletons. This was very helpful to me when I did become CEO," he says.

During his tenure, Preston was driven to articulate the essence of Avon and its management style. There was something different in the air at the company. "It dawned on me that there were certain factors, elements, aspects of Avon's culture that were almost palpable," he recalls today.

Preston captured the core values of Avon in just five words: Trust, Respect, Belief, Humility, and Integrity. Along with these words, the company formulated an explanation for each. These same values continue to guide Avon today:

1. *Trust* means living and working in an environment where communications are open—where people feel free to take risks, give their point of view, and speak the truth as they see it. If you trust people to do the right thing—and they understand the underlying reasoning and philosophy—they won't disappoint you.
2. *Respect* helps to value differences and to appreciate each person for her or his unique qualities. Through respect, you help bring out the full potential of each person.
3. *Belief* is the cornerstone of empowering associates to assume responsibilities and be the very best they can be. If you believe in someone and show it, that person will move mountains to prove you're right.
4. *Humility* simply means you're not always right. You don't have all the answers, and you know it. You're no less human than the people who work for you, and you're not afraid to ask for help.
5. *Integrity* should be the hallmark of every Avon associate. In setting and observing the highest ethical standards and doing the right thing, Avon fulfills a duty of care—not only to its

representatives and customers in the communities it serves, but also to itself and its colleagues.

"While I crafted those words, it wasn't Jim Preston's credo," he notes. "It was what I was exposed to when I joined this company." Those gestures were put into play every day in different ways, Preston explains.

A fundamental truth about Avon's structure is that the sales representatives are independent contractors, and therefore cannot be ordered to do anything. "They have to *want* to do it," Preston observes. As a result, what pervades the organizational management, he says, is a "tinge of humility."

By the nature of the way it operates, Avon is saturated in the concept of trust. Every single order that is placed is sent out on credit. The representative pays for the goods after she receives and delivers them to her customers.

"There are tens of millions of dollars in receivables every day to people we hardly even know," Preston points out. Under his leadership, respect was an honor that should be applied equally. "Not because of a title or position, but because we are all human beings and should be treated with equal respect."

Lynn Emmolo, a former group vice president at Avon, who has also worked at L'Oreal and Victoria's Secret, recalls her first day on the job being taken to lunch by Preston along with three other new Avon associates.

"He [Preston] told us that Avon had a very clearly defined vision and mission. And much of it was really derived from McConnell," says Emmolo. "I never saw that at L'Oreal or The Limited [parent company of Victoria's Secret]. That made a big impression on me."

Supporting Preston's point, Emmolo says that Avon has to continually recruit new people, since there is nearly a 100 percent turnover in direct selling. "You have to be nice in direct selling to recruit people and that permeates the organizational culture," she observes. Without pretense, Emmolo says, "People are just darn nice here."

At a luncheon celebrating an Avon associate's 25th anniversary with the company, the honoree stood up and declared, "What I loved so much about working at this company is when I came to work I never had to leave any part of me at home," according to Preston. "That is one thing I too loved about coming here. I could be the same person with the same beliefs and same style I had at home when I was Jim Preston, husband and father."

THE COMPANY FOR WOMEN

Avon's sales and customer base is 99 percent female. It is therefore hard to argue with the company's slogan that it is truly the company for women. But coming to call it that wasn't an easy sell.

The company decided it was time for Avon to better distinguish itself from the competition. Internally, in both the way it operated and its value system, Avon was different. After putting the turbulent decade of the 1980s behind it, Avon set itself on a firm course and decided it was time to formalize and articulate its new view for the world.

"I looked at Revlon and Lauder and Maybelline and all the relevant competition," Preston reveals. "I felt we needed a vision and a statement that said no other company could put its name on this statement."

The cornerstone, Preston believed, is that Avon should be looked to as a company for women. "There were 99.9 percent female salespeople and 99.99 percent female customers," he observes. "Ain't that a women's company?"

Over the course of 18 months, there was much heated internal debate. Some men felt threatened that if Avon were designated as a company for women it would jeopardize their own jobs.

A global task force gathered for a four-day meeting in June 1992 in Florida. The walls of the conference room were covered with visual material. After months of thinking and crafting and arguing, 18 words casually and subconsciously flowed from Preston's lips. Avon's mission is: "To be the company that best understands and satisfies the product, service, and self-fulfillment needs of women—globally."

As explained later in its 1992 annual report, "We are, uniquely among major corporations, a woman's company. We sell our products to, for, and through women. We understand their needs and preferences better than most. This understanding should guide our basic business and influence our choice of new business opportunities," wrote Preston in a letter to shareholders.

Having secured a general buy-in to the idea, next came the job of redesigning company letterhead, brochures, advertisements, publicity, and so on to reflect the newly defined voice of Avon. Explains Preston, "Everything had to be looked at through the prism of that vision."

A RISING YOUNG TALENT

One day Preston got a call out of the blue from the president of Psychological Associates, a consulting firm in St. Louis, Missouri, that specializes in the testing, training, and coaching of corporate executives and CEOs. The firm had done some work with Avon and recently met with a young woman who was described to Preston as being young, smart, and beautiful. The president of Psychological Associates said this young woman was one of the finest young talents he had ever run into. The woman was interested in doing consulting work, and he wondered whether Preston might want to meet her. The caller further predicted that the talented woman would end up "the CEO of something, sometime," Preston recalls.

Preston agreed to the meeting and in early 1993 a 33-year-old Andrea Jung came to New York for her first visit to Avon headquarters. Preston presented Jung with a challenge: Avon was just getting out of a brief experiment with retail beauty, having been forced to sell off its prestige fragrance brands because of an urgent need for cash. But, should Avon look into retail again? What were the pros and cons in taking the Avon brand into retail?

Preston assumed he'd hear back from Jung in three months or so. However, six weeks later she called in with some of her thoughts. Not only did she have ideas about Avon's probability for success in a retail environment, she also had reasons why it would and wouldn't work. She had looked at cosmetics, skin care, jewelry, packaging, profit margins, and so on, and she had come up with a strategy for each.

"I said 'holy moly!'" says Preston. "I called her back in. She was a little higher priced [than what Avon was paying consultants at the time]. She really gave me an earful."

Jung was offered the chance to execute her plan. "I brought her on and she did it," exclaims Preston. Of all the executives Preston has come across in his lifetime, Jung, he says, possesses great vision and can also plan and execute. He knows many people who are usually good at one or two of these. "Andrea is one of the few people I've met who can do all three."

MOVING UP FAST

Jung graduated from Princeton University magna cum laude with a degree in English literature. Always a disciplined and achievement-oriented young woman, she completed high school in just three years.

Born in Toronto, Jung was raised in Wellesley, Massachusetts, an upscale Boston suburb. Her parents had accomplished careers as well. Her father, a native of Hong Kong, is an architect who taught at Massachusetts Institute of Technology for a while. Her mother, a native of Shanghai, is a chemical engineer, who later pursued an interest in music and became a concert pianist. Her younger brother has pursued a career in computer technology.

As a child, Jung studied Chinese on Saturday mornings and, like her mother, took piano lessons—favoring classical music. Jung planned to go to law school, but got swept up into a training program at Bloomingdale's upon graduation instead. A college recruiter caught her ear and somehow won her over.

Jung started out in the Bloomingdale's stockroom putting Liz Claiborne pants on hangers and placing them on racks. While that's hardly creative stuff, she was intrigued by those aspects of the business that enabled her to delve into the mind-set of the consumer. There was also the challenge of finding and buying the right blend of merchandise, while figuring out how to most optimally price and display it.

There is something compelling about the retail business where a sweater in the right color will fly off shelves, while an unpopular color goes nowhere. Jung fell in love with many aspects of the business and persevered through the tedious learning chores, even while many of her trainee colleagues did not. The constantly changing nature of retail gave her the sense of being in a new job every couple of weeks. But it was the challenge of getting close to the consumer that ultimately reeled Jung in.

From Bloomingdale's, an upscale department store, Jung moved on to even more exclusive retail businesses. At I. Magnin, a San Francisco-based luxury retailer noted for the architectural detail of its stores, she was posed with the challenge of making the chain's elite shops more friendly and inviting, particularly for younger customers. She next moved to Dallas-based Neiman Marcus, where she rose to become executive vice president. Neiman Marcus was in an expansion phase, opening new stores in new markets. It also needed to capture more customers and expose a younger clientele to the affluent Neiman Marcus experience.

When Jung left Neiman Marcus to begin a consulting career and immediately got an assignment with Avon, onlookers were askance. Some felt the transition from an ultra exclusive retail environment to a broad-based mass-market enterprise was questionable, given the great divide between customers each segment targeted.

While there is no hard and fast rule, there is a tendency for department store executives to stick to careers in department stores and for mass-market retailers to stay within that market venue. Suppliers also tailor their businesses to create products for either mass market or department stores. The industries are almost divided along party lines and in industry jargon are referred to as "Mass" or "Class."

In less than a year, Jung parlayed her Avon consulting assignment into an appointment as president of product marketing for the United States. In this role, she was charged with revitalizing Avon's beauty brands, beginning with developing new packaging for its color cosmetics lineup. In 1996, she became involved with Avon's global research and development. A year later, Jung was promoted to president of global marketing, in which she oversaw a relaunch of the Anew skin care brand.

Jung also lobbied for the development of more global brands at Avon, which represented 39 percent of cosmetic, toiletry, and fragrance sales in 1997, up from 22 percent two years earlier. (That number grew to 65 percent in 2004.) Jung was also behind a movement to unify Avon's advertising messages, resulting in the use of one global advertising firm in July 1998. Prior to that, the company used local agencies around the world.

In just a few years, Jung's name was being bandied about as a possible successor to Preston as CEO. Other names being discussed included Susan Kropf, president of Avon North America and long-time veteran of the company, as well as Christina Gold, then executive vice president of global direct selling.

However, when Preston announced his retirement in 1998, the board of directors reached outside the beauty and direct-selling worlds, plucking Charles Perrin, former CEO of Duracell, to succeed him. Perrin was a well-respected member of Avon's board and someone they knew and trusted. It was believed he had the management skills, vision, and global experience necessary to take Avon to the next level.

Avon received a lashing in the press for bypassing its internal slate of female candidates. But the ferment passed and Perrin moved in.

At the same time, Jung was named president and chief operating officer. Though she was still viewed as the eventual heir apparent, at the time some felt she wasn't quite ready for the most senior post at Avon and needed some more operational experience. Her training period could have been a long one, since Perrin was only 52 years old when he took over at Avon.

There was an awkwardness from the start of Perrin's reign. Because of her position and stance, Jung became a messenger to the top office for many and insiders say she earned the respect of her peers during this uncertain period at Avon. As a result, she had their backing for the CEO position when, only 18 months after his appointment, Perrin abruptly resigned.

Perrin's surprise departure came only a few weeks after Avon's stock plummeted 28 percent to $25¹³⁄₁₆ on September 29, 1999, after an announcement from the company that fourth quarter earnings would be lower than expected due to weakness in the Latin America and U.S. markets. Perrin told shareholders he was leaving to work on the Perrin Family Foundation, which helps underprivileged youths and other philanthropies.

Fulfilling Preston's vision, Jung became Avon's first chief executive officer in 1999. The icing came in 2001 when she was elected chairman of the board as well.

WHY AVON?

Jung quickly seized on the challenge of implementing another turnaround plan. In previous years, Avon had survived a disastrous diversification attempt and fought off three sets of raiders. It had been roughed up and desperately needed a new coat of paint.

Jung had considerable experience freshening up businesses and this was another opportunity to do what she thrives on—getting in touch with the consumer. Avon was also a much bigger fish in an increasingly global pond.

Among the advances Jung is credited with is being at the forefront of an industry movement to create mid-tier brands that have come to be known as "masstige." These brands blend the best of a mass and prestige brands, complete with high-quality products and packaging, yet available at an affordable price.

Jung demonstrated her expertise in this area when she oversaw a repositioning of the Anew skin care line and created its priciest skin cream yet—Anew Night Force—which retailed for $20. After that, Procter & Gamble made a bold move with the introduction of its Total Effects anti-age cream sold through mass-market stores for $19.99. Up until then $10 was seen as a comfortable ceiling for drugstores. This was just one of numerous mass market brands that became more daring and that experimented with higher prices, following Jung's lead.

The 2001 launch of Avon's retail brand beComing into some 90 JCPenney stores was the epitome of this masstige brand effort. In this case, it didn't work out. About a year after JCPenney's took on beComing as the centerpiece of its beauty department, the chain did an about face and pulled out of cosmetics altogether. Still, others in the industry must have seen some value in the concept.

The Estée Lauder Companies even broke from its long-held tradition of developing lines for fine department and specialty stores recently by creating American Beauty, Flirt, and Good Skin—three cosmetics and skin care collections with mid-tier prices that are currently being sold at the lower-end department store chain Kohl's. Flirt, a trendy cosmetics brand, is also available at Henri Bendel, an upscale Manhattan emporium. Brands appearing in such diverse retail outlets would have been inconceivable only a few years ago.

Along the way, retailers like Target have used clever advertising and offered innovative and exclusive product selections. Target, for instance, sells Sonia Kashuk Professional Makeup and a fashion line by designer Isaac Mizrahi, making it trendy to shop smart.

Jung, a stylish dresser noted for her signature choker pearls and side swept bangs, always felt there was no need to talk down to the customer, and she demonstrated this on a worldwide basis. Jung introduced Avon's first global scent, Far Away, at $18.50 a bottle, a good 60 percent to 80 percent more than other fragrances offered in Avon's catalog at the time. Interestingly enough, there was no price resistance whatsoever among Avon's customers. The scent reaped sales of $32 million in its first three months, becoming the company's biggest fragrance introduction to that point. Since then prices have inched up even more. Avon's 2004/2005 trilogy fragrances Today, Tomorrow, and Always are priced at $29.50 each.

A STAR CEO

Andrea Jung can be both warm and elusive, which probably adds to her intrigue. She is the first publicly recognized executive figurehead Avon has ever had. In an era of celebrity CEOs, Avon can proudly say it has one, too.

Jung wears celebrity well. One day she is in Washington, DC, being photographed with First Lady Laura Bush for the opening of a new breast cancer health care center that Avon has helped fund. Not long after that she is sitting next to Donald Trump on an episode of *The Apprentice* television program in which Avon sponsors a featured fashion show.

Jung has clout. She is currently chairperson of the Cosmetic Toiletries and Fragrance Association (CTFA), the first woman ever to hold that role. She was single-handedly able to charm Wal-Mart CEO H. Lee Scott into being the keynote speaker at the CTFA convention in Boca Raton, Florida, in the spring of 2004. That's even more impressive given that Avon doesn't even have a business relationship with Wal-Mart, and Wal-Mart's management is notoriously reluctant to speak publicly about its operations. Wal-Mart, of course, is not merely the world's largest retailer. It is the world's biggest company and Scott is a very busy man. In addition to her responsibilities at Avon, Jung sits on the boards of General Electric and Catalyst. She is a trustee of New York Presbyterian Hospital and serves on the international advisory group for Salomon Smith Barney. Photogenic and quotable, the press can't get enough of Jung. There is a fascination with her. She has been featured in cover stories in *Business Week, Fortune, Newsweek, Working Woman, Advertising Age,* and *WWD's Beauty Biz.*

In 2004, Jung was listed in *Forbes* as one of the 100 Most Powerful Women in the world. She has been named one of *Fortune* magazine's 50 Most Powerful Women in Business for six years straight.

Female CEOs are still few and far between. Jung has a natural ability to comfortably transform herself for the occasion. She appears equally at ease in a finely tailored Chanel or Armani suit boldly presenting financial results to a room full of chilly analysts as she does in an elegant gown working the room at the many beauty industry, black tie fund-raisers held each year, where European-style double cheek kissing is de rigueur.

PAYING HER DUES

Make no mistake, Jung has earned this attention. Starting out at Avon, she wasn't meek, but she didn't come in like a firebrand either. She watched and listened, and then thoughtfully laid out her plans. With a temperament more conciliator than dictator, Jung quickly learned to make bold decisions. However, Jung says, she "is not aggressive, but has become more assertive." From day one, Jung knew she had to change and grow in the role and has seen a transformation take place within herself. It has had an emotional effect, especially when she sees how the company's programs impact lives of women around the world. Remembering the story of a woman from Chile who used her Avon earnings to send her child to school in the United States, Jung says, "There is no EPS [earnings per share], no stock price appreciation that can come close to that satisfaction."

One of the most striking changes, she says, is how her affiliation with Avon has made her adopt a more personalized approach to business. That is not to say that Jung likes to open up about her private life. She doesn't. She takes great pains not to mention her two former husbands. Her most recent marriage had been a very public union with Michael Gould, the chairman and chief executive officer of Bloomingdale's.

Now a single mother of a seven-year-old boy and a teenaged girl, Jung speaks about the challenges of balancing work and raising children, something a male CEO would rarely be asked to discuss. "Ten years ago, I never used to talk about it," she reflects. "I was on a team with 15 men executives [while at Neiman Marcus]. If I had to leave, I would say I had to go an outside meeting." Today, Jung says, she is straightforward about her family obligations. "Now I will say, 'I have to go to my daughter's softball game. Bye.'"

Admittedly, it is a balancing act. "There are some days Avon will lose and there are some days that my children will lose," Jung admits. "But it will never be the wrong day. Avon will never lose on the most important day. And my children will never lose for the most important game or the most important concert."

In her position as one of only eight Fortune 500 female CEOs—alongside Anne Mulcahy of Xerox and Meg Whitman of eBay—Jung feels the heat of the spotlight. "There are days when you wish it wouldn't be such a story, because obviously it speaks to the fact that there are not enough women," she shares. "If there were enough women, it wouldn't even hit the radar screen."

JUNG'S VISION

The fact that Avon sales representatives sell beauty products is really just today's conduit for the real mission Jung sees for the company. Starbucks sells coffee and Nike manufactures athletic footwear, but both are really peddling something more significant. For Starbucks, it is socializing and bringing people together. Starbucks just happens to do this through selling coffee. For Nike it is selling the pursuit of dreams.

"I believe the same is true with Avon," Jung says. "We are not in the business of selling lipsticks through a direct-sales channel. We are in the business of changing women's lives."

Avon has a socioeconomic purpose as a company, explains Jung. As a company she sees its role as learning and understanding the needs of women and offering products and services that fulfill those needs.

Avon could easily be looked at as either a cosmetics company or as a direct-selling company, and a large part of the market responds to it that way. Avon has memberships in many organizations, including the Cosmetics Toiletries and Fragrances Association, the Cosmetics Executive Women Group, and the Direct Selling Association.

"I see us having a very unique proposition in that Avon has got a social purpose as well as a commercial purpose to changing women's lives," Jung says.

There has been much conversation in the boardroom lately about the Middle East, Jung adds. Discussions often center on where the beauty market is or what the direct-selling market is like in that region. For Jung, however, there is a third focal point that is far more important. "What are the socioeconomic needs of women? Are the conditions right? Should we go in?" In this broader perspective, says Jung, "Avon's proposition does not have to be limited to selling beauty products. As needs change, Avon can change, too. Hopefully, we can redefine what Avon can be years out and then build a logical plan."

For now, though, Jung doesn't expect women's interest in health and beauty products to wane anytime soon. "My own personal opinion is self-esteem, self-empowerment, and confidence are in all those things when you wrap it up. That's why we went into wellness," she contends. "I say that it is about being economically independent, about being strong, about feeling good about yourself." Jung, who is visibly passionate about the landscape she sees for Avon, adds, "It is about being beautiful in whatever your definition is."

A STRONG NUMBER TWO

In January 2003, *BusinessWeek* magazine named Susan Kropf and Andrea Jung to its list of best managers. Of the 15 superb corporate leaders awarded the honor, they were the only ones cited as a pair. Along with Avon's president and chief executive officer, those mentioned included A. G. Lafley, chairman and CEO of Procter & Gamble; Michael Dell, founder and CEO of Dell Computers; Joe Neubauer, CEO of Aramark; and Lindsay Owen-Jones, CEO of L'Oreal.

This is a testament to how important Kropf, Avon's president and chief operating officer, is to the organization. In many corporate brochures, and even in the company's annual report, Jung and Kropf are photographed together by Jung's own request.

Kropf, a 33-year veteran of the company, is Avon through and through. Having joined the organization right after graduating from St. John's University, it is the only company she has ever worked at. Originally, her intent was to go into education, but after a brief stint in student teaching, she knew it wasn't for her.

Kropf advises young people that it is much more important to find the right company than the right job when pursuing a career. "I'm not saying that the job is not important," explains Kropf, whose slightly husky voice embodies a hint of a New York accent. "But if you find the right company, you can ultimately find the right job within that company. If you are in the wrong company, there is a limit to how happy you are going to be, how successful you are going to be. Companies have personalities like people. It is just serendipity that my personality and this company's personality happened to be a good match."

Starting out as an administrative assistant for $6,280 a year, Kropf is one of those "out of the mailroom" corporate success stories. She is too modest to say that she has really done anything special. The simple fact is that she earnestly applied herself to every new position she was placed in, and when that was mastered she started looking around for what was up next. Assimilating one task after another into her own professional portfolio, Kropf naturally emerged as a potent force within Avon whether she was paying attention to her build up or not.

Along the way, Kropf earned an MBA in finance from New York University. She says she personally never felt herself bumping up against a glass ceiling. "I have had so many opportunities to move into so many different jobs and so many areas of the company," she smiles, recalling her personal labyrinth through Avon. Kropf, who is married, without children, has held senior management positions in nearly every area of the company including marketing, product development, customer service, and manufacturing. She also oversaw operations in the emerging markets for several years.

Kropf's recent trajectory went something like this: She served as vice president of product development from 1990 to 1992. From 1993 to 1994, she was senior vice president of global product management. From 1994 to 1997, she was president of new and emerging markets, followed by president of Avon North America from 1997 to 1999. She was appointed chief operating officer in 1999. Two years later she was named president, while also retaining the COO title.

SUPPORTING FEMALE EXECUTIVES

"There is a disproportionate interest in successful women versus successful men," Kropf observes. "I think it is just because there are so many more successful men today, success being defined as the top one or top two jobs in large companies."

The success among women is particularly apparent among Avon's sales representatives and district sales managers. "To them, this is a company that tells a story that you can be anything and you can achieve anything," Kropf says.

Like just about everyone, Kropf has days that make her wonder why she's doing her job. For her, this questioning may be triggered by another quarterly earnings report, or another set of numbers. But her mission is quickly apparent. "I just go out and spend a couple of days in the field with these women and am like 'Yes!'" exclaims Kropf, who is energized at the thought. "They motivate us. It is supposed to be the other way around. They are really hot stuff."

Now that Avon has achieved a healthy representation of women in its management ranks, it doesn't want to slide back. Today, half of

Avon's board members are women. Of its 17-member senior management team, six are women. Meanwhile, 75 percent of the company's 1,400 district sales managers are women, as are 82 percent of its roughly 80 division managers. In 2003, the company sponsored its first-ever leadership conference for 80 to 100 senior and high-potential women.

Nevertheless, the company does take an even-handed approach when reviewing men and women candidates, Kropf maintains. "We have talent reviews that are gender blind," she says. "But we also have one or two incremental reviews that focus on women only." This is a way for Avon to make sure talented women don't fall through the cracks. Acknowledges Kropf, "We do a few extra things specifically for women."

Janice Teal, group vice president and chief scientific officer at Avon, recalls that when she started at the company 23 years ago, she was one of the only women in the research department. "R&D was very male-oriented. It has changed over the years," says Teal, noting that today the department today is 50–50. "In the old days, you would walk into a conference room and you would be the only woman there. There was just an obviousness about whether you are a man or a woman. Now you walk in and it could be all women or all men, but you don't notice because it is a nonissue."

"We are not necessarily giving women advantages. It is just a nonissue," Teal stresses. "We have reached critical mass. We have women in power at all levels."

CHANGING MANAGEMENT MIX

Jung has brought many new executives into the Avon fold. Some recent examples: Jill Scalamandre, whose background includes Revlon and Prada, is now vice president of global marketing. Gina R. Boswell, from Ford Motor Company, is senior vice president of corporate strategy and business development. Elizabeth A. Smith, who joined Avon on January 1, 2005 from Kraft Foods, is an executive vice president and brand president.

These new recruits stand side by side with Avon executives of more than 20 years in filling out the company's top posts. Along with the newcomers, long time Avon executives include Robert Toth, executive vice president of international; Janice Teal, group vice president and chief scientific officer; Robert J. Corti, executive vice president and chief financial officer; Brian C. Connolly, executive vice president and president of Avon North America; and Kropf herself.

In general, says Kropf, Avon has stepped up its efforts in "people development," or helping internal people move ahead in the company. "I think when you are going through a transformation, the optimum mix is some old and some new. If you have too many new, you run the risk of losing touch with some of the threads that have been in your history, and make you tick, and make the company great," says Kropf. "But if you do too much old, you run the risk of not having enough fresh sets of eyes of what new growth opportunities might be. Andrea and I have spent a lot of time over the last year or two, in particular, recruiting and spending time developing some of our high potential people."

Avon historically has heavily promoted career development, and training programs have been an ongoing hallmark of the company.

Lyn Kirby, now chief executive officer of the Ulta beauty store chain, worked at Avon for 17 years. She remembers being sent to numerous courses and training sessions, including the Kellogg School of Management.

Avon executives have used their management skills to benefit groups outside the company as well. Jung, as noted, is the first woman to serve as chairman of the trade association CTFA. Before her, several other Avon executives took on the role starting with John Ewald (1954–1956), Wayne Hicklin (1971–1973), William Chaney (1976–1979), and James Preston (1988–1990), following in the path created by David Hall McConnell, his son, and a cadre of short-lived CEOs including John Ewald, Russell Rooks, Wayne Hicklin, Fred Fusee, David W. Mitchell, and Hicks Waldron.

CHAPTER 4

EMPOWER YOUR SALES FORCE

Lights flashed overhead and the auditorium pulsed with the beat of the 1970s dance hit *YMCA* as more than 2,000 Avon representatives filed through the rear doors of the Atlantic City Convention Center hall and slid into open seats.

From center stage, Avon's U.S. regional vice president for the northern and southern regions, Maria Peninger, a tall, slender blond, declared, "This is all about you!" Peninger was setting the tone for the "Home for the Holidays" event, one of seven motivational road shows the company will conduct over two months in regions across the country.

Though it was a hot, humid July afternoon, the set inside was decorated with a Christmas tree and two oversized stuffed bears dressed in holiday hats and sweaters, replicas of real products that will be for sale in an upcoming brochure. Like most consumer products businesses, Avon has long planned ahead for the fourth quarter, its biggest sales period.

Only blocks away the resort city's famed casinos and boardwalk beckoned, but the representatives were not distracted. Many had traveled several hours by car or bus to learn about the new products, promotional programs, and sales tools created by Avon's corporate office to help them become more successful. This was an occasion for the women to share stories with one another and to mingle with Avon management, some of whom they asked for autographs and to pose for pictures.

Within moments of Peninger's appearance, the music smoothly segued from energizing disco to patriotic as the recorded voice of Celine Dion filled the room to lead the group in the singing of *God Bless America.* In the background, sweeping visuals of flowering fields, soaring eagles, and open highways streamed across two wall-sized video screens on either side of the stage.

To outsiders, Avon has long been the steady purveyor of both beauty products and a rotating selection of gifts, clothing, and accessories. The name Avon is synonymous with the familiar brochure women flip through during lunch hours, at the bowling alley, or in the privacy of their homes.

But for those inside the Avon family, the company is much more than another commercial enterprise. It is a business guided by a greater purpose: to offer financial empowerment and independence to women. Even those with little or no skills have an opportunity to become self-sufficient and run their own businesses. To keep this powerful generator of not only money, but also self-esteem, running smoothly, everything Avon does is directed at providing an earnings opportunity for the representative. This intention cannot be stressed enough.

DEVELOPING DREAMS AND GOALS

Ask anyone at Avon what the company stands for and the answer is nearly the same every time. "It is a company about dreams and goals," responds Arlene Fitzpatrick, a divisional sales manager based in Newark, Delaware, one of dozens of Avon employees who find the company's culture supportive and nurturing. "There are always going to be good days and bad days. But the saying here is 'A bad day at Avon is better than a good day at any other company.'"

Over the years, Avon has provided the opportunity for many women to step out of low-paying jobs while giving them time to spend with their families. Professional women, too, have taken to selling Avon to retain more control over their lives, raise children, and be their own boss.

Lori Konkowski, 46, of Bell Meade, New Jersey, has a master's degree in education. She has been an Avon representative for 14 years, leaving brochures everywhere she goes—the ShopRite, the library, and the bank. She has built her business through word of mouth and referrals in her community, and has worked it so that she still has time left to spend with her three children. While 14 years doesn't sound that long, Konkowski says the business has changed significantly during that time.

When Konkowski started with Avon, she filled out long paper order forms with a number two pencil. While most were completed as they came in, some customers would wait until the night before the order was due, forcing her to spend hours on the tedious process. Once completed, Konkowski and other representatives in her neighborhood would take their forms to the home of a representative who had been designated as the official drop-off site. From there, the orders would be carried to another home and grouped with even more order forms. The process continued until the orders made their way to Avon's distribution center in Newark, Delaware. For a period, Konkowski even earned an extra $10 for collecting order forms and delivering them to another woman's home in Princeton, New Jersey, about 10 miles away. At that time, her district orders had to be in by noon on Tuesday for a Saturday delivery. Now, much of this is done online. If an order is placed by noon on Thursday, the products can still arrive by Saturday, giving representatives an extra two days of breathing room. "It gives you more time to get more orders," Konkowski adds.

To build her business at the outset, Konkowski didn't knock on doors, but she did leave brochures with notes stuffed in plastic bags on driveways. "That seemed to work best," she says. Years later, Konkowski has a strong customer base and doesn't do that type of outreach often any more.

Avon has also provided 28-year-old Marilina Salgado-Brent of Tampa, Florida, with similar opportunities, including the chance to be a stay-at-home mother. "What motivated me most was my children," says Salgado-Brent, who previously had a $30,000 a year full-time job in the collections department of a financial firm. With Avon, her goal is to build up to the same level of income as before, or more, working part-time on her own terms.

During a rough period, Salgado-Brent almost quit working for Avon and would have were it not for the support of the representative who recruited her. "She has become a personal friend. She is a beautiful person. If it weren't for her, I probably wouldn't still be selling," she says. Because they are independent contractors, Avon has long put few, if any, restrictions on how these women can operate their businesses. As a result, representatives are able to add their own personal approaches and techniques. During one campaign, for instance, Salgado-Brent put a Milky Way candy bar in with every order. One customer was so pleased with the treat, she now orders regularly.

Even before looking to the Avon representative who recruited her for support, Salgado-Brent had a good Avon role model in her grandmother—who, along with her grandfather, raised Salgado-Brent as a young child in their home in New York City.

"My grandmother would store her Avon products in a linen closet upstairs," Salgado-Brent recalls. "I would pull out the bottom drawer and play with all the stuff." Salgado-Brent would watch what her grandmother did and then followed her lead. "I remember playing with samples when I was little, and I used to knock on the doors and say 'Avon calling,' " she reminisces. "Now my four-year-old walks around saying 'Avon calling.' "

While her grandmother went door-to-door in their neighborhood to bring in new business, Salgado-Brent chose another route. She joined the women's auxiliary of the Moose Lodge to network and find new customers. She also sells in nursing homes, as well as to family and friends.

Salgado-Brent's grandmother eventually stopped selling Avon because she started to give too many people products on credit and was losing money. Even though her grandmother's generosity ate into her own profits, Salgado-Brent's grandfather was thrilled to hear that his granddaughter had followed in his wife's footsteps. "He said, 'I am happy for you and I am proud of you,' " she recalls. When he was dying in his hospital bed, she says, "He would still ask me, 'How's Avon?' He told me I gotta go back home and get with it. That you gotta be good and be successful."

Thanks to the company's numerous support systems, many Avon representatives are successful.

During 2003 in the United States alone, Avon representatives have earned $1 billion in sales commissions, broadcasts Brian Connolly, executive vice president and president of Avon North America, during his turn at the podium at the "Home for the Holidays" event.

"It is hard not to have a love affair with the company," says Andrea Jung, the company's CEO, who was first exposed to Avon as a marketing consultant in 1993. "I was intellectually prepared for the strategic challenges and the complexity of the job ahead. I was unprepared for the overwhelming emotional impact it has had on my life as a person, not just as a business."

Jung says across the dozens of markets she visits, be it the Philippines, Argentina, or Russia, "I am continually overwhelmed by what we are actually doing for women and the pride I have in seeing some of these women, and who they have become, because of Avon. They themselves didn't even know when they joined what would become of them."

A new Avon magazine for representatives tells scores of stories about women like Sylvia Tamayo, who moved from Mexico to McAllen, Texas, with her husband and children, nine years ago with hopes of building a better life. She was recruited one afternoon while out for a walk seeking relief from their one bedroom, stifling warm apartment. Last year, Tamayo earned $240,000. The 36-year-old has been able to help her family buy a nice home and recently treated herself to a Cadillac Escalade SUV.

"With hard work and faith in God, your dreams can come true," says Tamayo. "This is what I try to get across to new recruits."

LEARNING FROM THE VETERANS

Some of the most successful and colorful Avon representatives you'll find have been on the job for decades. Florence McCord of Harrisonville, Missouri, for example, has been selling Avon for 58 years. The 95-year-old started out slowly when her son turned six and began going to school. But it became a real job once her husband passed away.

"I would start at 8 A.M. and work until 8 in the evening, but not on Sunday," she shares. "If I hadn't had Avon, I don't know what I would have done."

McCord's business is not as robust these days. A back injury has slowed her down. McCord says there are also new competitors for her business, pointing to a local Wal-Mart store along with an influx of Mary Kay consultants in her area. Still, McCord is a top selling representative, particularly of skin care products. "I have always taken good care of my skin. I don't mean to be bragging on myself, but people will ask me, 'What do you use?' I have always used anything that Avon sold that was good for your skin."

Avon's longest serving representative—with 65 continuous years of service—is WillaMae Heitman of San Diego. She remembers how special it felt to be appointed an Avon lady. "We dressed in dresses. There were no pants. We wore stockings with seams up the back and gloves and hats. We looked very sharp," says the 85-year-old, who continues to sell even today.

Heitman recalls that when she applied for the Avon position, the district manager told her she would have to wear lipstick, even though she was only 19 at the time. "My mother wouldn't allow it," Heitman remembers. The district manager proceeded to call her mother for permission, who ultimately agreed—as long as a light shade was used.

A young widow who lost her husband in World War Two, Heitman was a federal government worker who sold Avon initially as a second job to buy herself a car. There was a black Ford with a V8 engine at the dealership she had her eye on. With $100 down, the monthly payments would be $20. She figured out how many jars of creams, face powders, and soaps she would need to sell to make these payments. "I told him [the car salesman] I can do it," she recalls. "I managed to pay off the car and purchased every one of my automobiles through my Avon earnings free and clear, including my Lexus that I drive today." She has also won numerous Avon sales awards over the years.

Seventy five-year-old Loraine Brown of San Diego, says her family members have been longtime customers of Heitman's. It began with her grandmother, then her mother. Now Brown herself has continued the tradition. "My mother would always let me sit in and watch what she [Heitman] was doing," Brown says. "I was about eight when I started listening in [to the sales conversation]. Willa-Mae was always very patient and she would answer my questions."

Today, the two have developed a personal friendship. "We know each other's families and children," says Brown. "I think that is true of most Avon people. It is not just [about] selling. They get interested in you, the people they are selling to."

Another of Heitman's customer's, 68-year-old Barbara Sabatini, has been using Avon products for 40 years. "The products are just what they claim to be," the San Diego resident explains. "I probably have never used anything else." Before moving to California 20 years ago, Sabatini bought Avon from representatives in her upstate New York hometown. "They have always been so friendly and never pushy," she says. "WillaMae is probably my best friend in San Diego."

A HIGH TOUCH APPROACH

The Avon model remains one of the most personal selling models in existence today. There are many direct sellers but Avon is one of the few where representatives still walk or drive to the homes of customers to take and deliver orders. No direct mail is sent to consumers from the corporate office. Everything is conducted through the individual representative.

Other direct-selling models are built around the at-home party or group selling. Avon's primary approach remains even more intimate than that. Though representatives do offer group demonstrations, it's not the approach for many. "I have never had an [Avon] party," notes Konkowski, who calls customers about special offers or to remind them that an order deadline is drawing near.

For Avon, the brochure is the representative's chief mode of communication and it is never mailed. It is handed out, person to person.

GETTING STARTED

Avon has always taken an egalitarian approach and made it as easy as possible for women to start their own businesses. An initial investment of $15 is all it takes to become a representative. While that fee just went up after holding steady at $10 for years, it remains considerably less than at Mary Kay where the charge is $100 for its Consultant Starter Kit or at Tupperware where the price is $99 for the Taste of Tupperware business packet.

Also, all of Avon's orders are shipped on credit. A representative, even one just starting out, doesn't pay for the goods received until after she delivers them to her customers and makes her collections.

It wasn't quite so easy for founder David McConnell. According to a story told after his death by his long-time secretary, Ann Meany, his first shipment of books was sent to him COD. The enterprising McConnell, only a teenager at the time but already demonstrating salesmanship skills, was able to convince a local banker to lend him the money to pay for this initial supply.

PROVIDING ORGANIZATIONAL SUPPORT

Once you are in, unlike other direct sellers, Avon has a staff management network firmly in place to help representatives get their businesses going.

"There is that force on the ground in the person of the district sales manager that really brings it all together and is one of our competitive strengths," says Angie Rossi, Avon's group vice president of sales and customer care. "There is no parallel position at Mary Kay or BeautiControl or Longaberger," some of the other prominent direct-sales companies.

Avon's structure looks something like this: 1,400 district sales managers report in to 80 divisional sales managers. The divisional managers then report to seven regional sales directors, who report to three regional vice presidents who report to Rossi.

The district sales managers conduct monthly meetings and are readily available to explain new programs or products and make selling suggestions. Nancy Franzese, a district sales manager in New York, insists that Avon is a safe organization to become involved with. "There is no frontloading [of merchandise]. You don't have to spend money. And everybody knows what Avon is. It is not a hard sell."

Franzese says that Avon is an equal opportunity employer when it comes to its staff positions, too. "They hired me at 56 years old," says Franzese, who had run the cosmetics department at the Macy's Herald Square store in Manhattan for 11 years prior to joining Avon. She is now 65 and has no plans to retire. "That is why I love Avon. They don't discriminate." For that and other reasons, the National Association of Female Executives, has consistently ranked Avon as one of the best companies to work for.

Sales representatives also get help through Avon's primary customer service call center in Springdale, Ohio, which fields inquiries from around the county. There are also smaller customer call center operations in Avon's four U.S. distribution centers in Newark, Delaware; Pasadena, California; Morton Grove, Illinois; and Atlanta, Georgia, as well as at its Rye, New York, office where the information technology operation is based. Until a few years ago, representatives had to pay long distance charges for their phone calls to the customer service centers. Now, the centers use 800 numbers.

"Avon gives you the support you need," offers Roni Caruso, 37 of Kittattiny, Pennsylvania. "They are always there for questions and they respond right away. My district manager is very supportive and it is a big family—everybody wants you to succeed."

ENSURING THE ORDER IS RIGHT

Avon takes great pains to see that every representative order is filled accurately. "Because of Avon's unique commitment to our representatives we strive for 100 percent [accuracy]," says Harriet Edelman, chief information officer for Avon. Of course, that is nearly impossible. But it comes close. "We typically hit 97 percent to 98 percent for our piece fill rate," Edelman boasts, noting, "The industry average is 92 percent to 93 percent."

Each order is processed and packaged at the respective distribution center servicing the representative's region. There are no bulk shipments of products sent out for further break downs. Brown cardboard boxes, identified by the representative's name and order number, rumble by on conveyor belts as products are dropped in from overhead dispensers, all controlled by a computer program that reads the order form. In another area, slower selling items are hand picked and placed in the boxes.

Avon wastes no expense on getting those orders safely to its 650,000 U.S. representatives. Once each rep's order is filled, the cardboard boxes are secured with two yellow plastic strips and carted to a tractor trailer backed up to an open bay. From there the trucks move the boxes to local delivery services where the orders are broken out by neighborhood and hand delivered to the representative's door.

"In direct selling, you are shipping little packages to lots of people," notes William Susetka, senior vice president of marketing for Avon, who joined the company after a long career with Clairol. "There is a much higher cost of distribution."

It is a massive operation, with 450,000 to 500,000 orders going out of the four shipping centers every two weeks. The pace is dizzying. It is felt at the Newark, Delaware, site where forklifts and tricycles with baskets whiz by carrying products from point to point. The drivers will wave or smile, but never slow down.

People here are on a mission.

"I was taught immediately that the Avon representative is the focus of everything we do," recalls Rossi, who left a teaching job to join Avon in its Newark distribution center in 1983. "So you better make sure that that box that came into your area was treated with TLC [tender loving care] because somebody's earning opportunity depended on getting it right."

OFFERING EFFECTIVE SALES TOOLS

To pack and ship an order properly, an order first has to be placed. That's why Avon offers its sales representatives a variety of selling tools to help them induce customers to buy. Most of the selling tools offered through Avon come with a modest price tag.

Samples are one of the most popular, and many representatives won't send out an order without one. Typically sold in boxes of 10, prices vary depending on the product. The current cost for a group of 10 Skin-So-Soft lotion samples is $1.99. Ten foundation makeup samples are $2.50. Fragrance samples come a little cheaper at $1. The prices are affected by the cost of goods and packaging technology needed to keep the contents fresh.

There are also Avon brand plastic and paper bags, business cards, and organizers, along with a host of other business paraphernalia to be purchased. Like anything else with Avon, it is up to the representative to do what she wants with her business. She can buy everything or nothing at all if she so chooses.

CREATING THE BROCHURE

There is no more potent instrument to elicit a purchase than Avon's powerful brochure, which is sold to representatives in packs of 10 starting at $5.75. The price decreases as the quantity rises. A stack of 100 goes for $19.

There is occasional grumbling about the costs of the brochure by some representatives who think Avon should distribute those freely. "You have to buy the books every campaign, which is the bad part," complains Simone Powell, a 23-year-old representative in London. "It's bad if you buy the books and then don't get any customers from them."

The brochure is Avon's store and there is nothing remotely accidental in the way it is produced. Every page and every layout is strategically calculated. In the same way a retailer counts sales in dollars per square foot and television shopping networks like QVC tally successes in terms of dollars per minute, Avon quantifies its sales by dollars per page.

Robert Briddon, group vice president of marketing for North America, says the brochure has to possess what he calls the "three E's." It has to be *easy* to understand, *enticing,* and *entertaining.* "You hear of retail therapy," Briddon offers. "People go to the mall as a form of recreation. We want people to get some fun out of shopping the brochure."

And there are lots of people looking at Avon's brochures. With some 17 million brochures going out every two weeks, Avon is the second largest publisher in the United States after *TV Guide.* Worldwide, Avon produces some 800 million brochures a year.

"The brochure generates excitement among the representatives," says Rossi, remarking on the company's constant ability to garner sales orders and then fill them so rapidly. "That brochure and the energy surrounding that brochure is another key ingredient to how we get this done every two weeks."

Briddon says to keep the interest going, the brochure must have new products for each "campaign," the term Avon uses internally for its sales periods. Each campaign is numbered. In markets outside the United States, campaign cycles are three or four weeks.

Like a storefront window, the front page "has to draw your attention" and bring you inside, explains Briddon, picking up a brochure and rifling through the pages in demonstration. "You have one second to have something on the page that is going to make them stop, engage, and interest them. If they keep flipping the pages, they're not buying anything."

Suzanne Grayson, a founder of Grayson & Associates, a beauty industry consulting firm, likens Avon's approach to that of catalogue firms which, she says, use "one of the most sophisticated types of marketing." These firms, she explains, plan and test pages to see what will draw more sales. "To a large degree, Avon is like that."

In the brochure, products are displayed on different pages for different purposes, Briddon points out. "High movers" are placed on the front cover, the middle pages ("because the book naturally opens there"), and on the inside back page. The back cover plays a huge role as a "transaction driver." It contains one feature offered at a low price point—never exceeding $2.99. "The psychology of a transaction driver is that it drives other transactions," Briddon reveals. In other words, customers are uncomfortable buying just one low priced item. "They will think 'I don't want to appear mean, so what else am I going to buy.'"

Before the advent of the compact brochure used today, Avon representatives were issued two 8-inch-by-11-inch catalogs per campaign. They sat down with customers and went over the various product offerings in the catalog in person. This method is known as "fingertip selling," says Alan D. Kennedy, past president of Tupperware and a former Avon executive. The representative held the book and pointed out items to the customer. "The idea was that you [the representative] controlled the interview," says Kennedy.

As WillaMae Heitman, Avon's longest serving representative, recalls, "We flipped the pages and they [the customers] made their selections."

LEARNING CONTINUOUSLY

There are ongoing classes for representatives to enroll in, as well as a plethora of CDs, books, and training tapes to buy. Avon recently announced that starting in 2005, representatives will have access to training materials on the Internet in a program called Online Education. It is another effort designed to support the representatives and will include a virtual instructor.

One of the company's latest educational tools is a CD for new recruits called *Avon Training*. It contains information and suggestions to help them get started.

Another program Avon has been stressing is its Beauty Advisor Training. This is an educational program representatives can enroll in that instructs them on makeup application and makeover tips. In Avon's mind, the more knowledgeable a person is about the products, the better she can service her customers. The course can be taken in person at a training center or through an online option. Only those Avon representatives who have completed the course, which costs $75, are entitled to sell the company's beComing brand, a pricier more upscale product offering that had for a brief time been sold through JCPenney stores.

Avon representatives are constantly drilled on ways to leverage "The Power of Three." This concept encourages representatives to reach out to at least three new people a day to talk to about buying or selling Avon.

Maryann Penn, a sales representative who runs a business with her husband, Ray, says that by practicing the Power of Three, your contacts quickly multiply, and in no time become akin to the "Power of 100." She acknowledges it is not always so easy and that when you hear "no" you must say to yourself, "next."

PROVIDING PRIZES AND INCENTIVES

Motivation and rewards have always been important for salespeople, and Avon representatives are no exception. As early as 1891, the company was awarding top representatives Bibles as gifts. By 1911, the company's top salesperson for the year was presented a Brush Runabout automobile.

Today's top earners receive automobile allowances and can use the money toward the vehicle of their choice, in keeping with Avon's independent approach.

For many, recognition of achievement in itself is gratifying even if there isn't a valuable award attached to it. One of the most endearing symbols of success for Avon representatives is a statue of the first Avon lady, Mrs. Albee. Like the Oscar and the Emmy, a 10-inch-high figure has been created in her likeness and has been awarded to top Avon sales representatives since 1969. Albee statues have even been designed by prestigious gift houses such as Lladro and Hummel. Each year, the figures are in a different Victorian-style dress and have become popular collectors items.

Tara Albee Spender, a distant relation of Albee, knows little of her ancestor's personal history, but is proud of the work she is credited with and of the family association. Inspired, she has begun collecting Albee statues, buying them off eBay as keepsakes for her own baby daughter. "Maybe she will collect them as a hobby one day," Spender says.

There are other collectibles, too, like china teacups and saucers, along with plaques. If a representative increases her sales year over year, she earns Presidents Points, which can be exchanged for a host of gifts ranging from jewelry and house wares to toys and luggage.

Suzanne Bressler of Summerdale, Pennsylvania, has been redeeming her award points for savings bonds. "I now have enough bonds to send two girls to community college for two years. That is about $8,000," says the 50-year-old Bressler, who has been selling Avon for 14 years and spends about 25 hours a week on her business. "That is a nice perk that most people aren't aware of."

What also keeps Avon representatives gunning for more sales is the escalating commission rates they earn as sales reach certain status levels.

To be recognized at Avon as a top sales representative, the entry point is the President's Club for those who sell at least $10,100 worth of merchandise a year. Next is the Honor Society for $20,200. That is followed by the Rose Circle, whose membership tallies sales of at least $38,000. The McConnell Club is for those who hit $66,500. The President's Council honors those accruing sales of $112,000 or more. The pinnacle group is called the Inner Circle for representatives who sell $280,000.   ·

Starting out, representatives earn a 50 percent commission on their first four campaigns. After that the commission rate varies from 20 percent to 50 percent depending on the size of the order. Anything over $1,550 qualifies for a 50 percent commission. But once a person reaches President's Club status, or sales of $10,100 a year, she will earn a minimum 40 percent commission for every campaign the following year. If she reaches the Rose Circle, she'll earn a minimum 45 percent commission.

Avon is also known for sending its top producing sales representatives on fabulous trips to places such as Hawaii, San Francisco, and Alaska. Throughout the year, members of the respective sales achievement groups are also treated to award lunches and dinners.

From the hotels to the dinners to the activities during the trips, "everything is done first class," says Maria Tirotta, from Rockaway, New York, whom you will learn more about later.

The awards programs are international in scope. Swati Sharma, a top distributor in India has been to Amsterdam, Australia, Switzerland, Indonesia, Bali, and Singapore. Natalia Shevchenki from Russia, meanwhile, will be heading off to Prague soon.

PROVIDING WORDS OF ENCOURAGEMENT

"Just as in any sales organization, recognition is important to spur growth and drive behaviors you want to see in your business," says Rossi.

In addition to regional events Avon organizes for representatives, six years ago it sponsored its first national convention in Las Vegas. Now held approximately every two years, events have since been held in New Orleans and Orlando. Each has drawn between 8,000 to 10,000 representatives.

Gail Blanke, vice president of public affairs at Avon until 1997, started at the company as an incentive planner, responsible for planning motivational programs for sales representatives. At a direct selling company like Avon, it is enormously important to keep the sales force encouraged, she says.

"On any given day, the company's fortunes are tied to the attitudes of a couple hundred thousand or so sales representatives who did or did not go out and sell that day," says Blanke, now the president of her own company, Lifedesigns. "There is a complexity and fragility to the business."

"In the end, it is all about her attitude. If she doesn't feel acknowledged and valued, the performance will be affected. That is true about most salespeople, but particularly for women marketing to women," says Blanke. "When it all comes together exactly in the right way, it is magic."

Blanke says she fell in love with the idea of a company "that anybody, regardless of background, education, or prior experience, could become anything she wants to by selling Avon." A woman, she continues, "could reinvent her life. She is only limited by her effort and size of her dream."

Blanke recalls during Avon's trips and at conferences, "usually a gift would be placed in their [the representatives'] rooms that was unexpected. It would be something that was developed only for them. There was never a time in their lives that they felt so appreciated and inspired."

Brian Connolly, executive vice president and Avon's president of North America, wrapped up his presentation in Atlantic City by giving away hundreds of dollars in a high-spirited raffle. Revealing his soft spot for the hundreds of representatives seated before him, Connolly told them, "I want you to know how much I admire and respect each and everyone one of you for who you are, not just [for] the incredible businesses you built. You are truly my inspiration. I'm grateful for you everyday. I want you to know that your management is coming to work everyday, every single day, in an attempt to make your dreams come true."

REFINING THE MODEL

For more than 100 years, the social gratification, personal relationships, individual rewards, and sales commissions Avon offered to women were more than sufficient to keep legions of sales representatives lining up.

But times began to change. Suddenly many of the other direct-selling organizations with which Avon competed for sales representatives shifted their operations into multilevel marketing structures. This sales model offered representatives an opportunity to develop management skills they could use to go out, recruit and train other reps, and then earn commissions on all of the sales those under them brought into the business.

Since its founding, Avon had always been a single-level operation. While there were sporadic programs whereby sales representatives would receive a bonus or an award for a recruit, the primary source of income was strictly commission off of one's own sales. Unless you joined the corporate staff, there were no management opportunities or means to further develop a career.

Watching itself fall behind the times in the direct-selling industry in which it had always led as the 1980s came to a close, Avon management decided that something had to be done. The marketplace was changing, along with the professional needs and desires of women, and Avon knew it had to change, too. Its sales representatives must have the option for something more, the company concluded.

In 1991, John Fleming, a man with years of direct-selling experience at other firms, was brought in as consultant. His mandate was to help devise a program for Avon that would offer women an expanded opportunity for career growth, yet that fit in with the company's culture. In Avon parlance, the program he helped get off the ground is simply referred to today as *Sales Leadership*.

It has monumentally shifted the way Avon operates and recruits its sales force. It is the vehicle the company has turned to in order to carry it through the twenty-first century.

CHAPTER 5

INCENTIVIZE THE TROOPS

Balloons were hung and the music was playing. Anticipation was high, given that flyers had been sent well in advance inviting women to learn more about a new career dimension at Avon during this Monday evening session.

Painfully, John Fleming and his team watched as the clock struck 7, then 7:15, then 7:30. It was already a half hour after this party was supposed to start, yet the meeting rooms remained empty.

Regardless, by 7:45 the show would get going with or without an audience. If nothing else, this was a chance for executives to practice giving the presentation they had worked so hard on. And so it went on many occasions back in 1991 when the company's new management-style program for sales representatives was first introduced. "That is the way it was in the beginning," remembers Fleming, now Avon's vice president for U.S. Sales Leadership. "When anything is new, there is always a degree of skepticism."

Fleming was living out on the West Coast back then, so Avon unveiled its revised career-oriented option first to women in California—beginning in the San Fernando Valley, then Fresno, then Bakersfield, and so on.

Over time, people starting trickling in to the Avon "Opportunity Meetings," as they were called. "We got to the point where we would have meetings of four or five and then they started to grow to 14 or 15," Fleming says.

Finally, there was attendance. But there was still a lot of convincing to do before anyone would give the new Sales Leadership program a try. "I would have a hypothetical income but would have a disclaimer because we had no one who had ever been there," says Fleming recalling the delicacy with which the presentations were handled. "We would show an example of [how someone could make] $100,000 a year in income and people would ask 'How many people do you have that have done this?' I would have to say 'Zero. We are looking for somebody to be the first one.'"

Finally, after several weeks, Avon had a handful of Sales Leadership recruits—Pearl Heilbut from Clovis, California, was among them. Heilbut had already been a top-selling representative and a leading recruiter for Avon. The recruitment program was limited to a one-time financial reward. "It was a one-level program so there was no encouragement to build the department after that," notes Fleming.

Even though Heilbut was intrigued by the vision. It took some thorough explaining and a group meeting that included her attorney-husband before she would sign on.

Soon after, Fleming was able to coax a former colleague out of an early retirement to give Avon's new career-oriented program a whirl. Vondell McKenzie had previously been in charge of party planning at Tupperware and had experience with multilevel marketing programs. Even she wasn't initially interested. "But I looked at the opportunity out of respect for John [Fleming]," says McKenzie, now one of Avon's top 10 earning Sales Leadership representatives. "He showed me an opportunity where I could earn a six-figure income."

Because of her exposure to direct-selling programs, with not just Tupperware, but also jewelry and cleaning products companies, McKenzie said she knew it was possible. "First of all, I understand the multiplication of representatives within a downline can cause growth," she says. "And I had worked with multilevel marketing structures before. You are able to learn something and teach it to other people." The inherent potential she saw in the Avon program was enough to bring her onboard.

The Sales Leadership program got started and slowly percolated in California for more than a year and a half before being expanded into other markets. Even after that, it was a long, time-consuming build. The national rollout didn't come until 1999.

The rules were in place and a handful of representatives had signed on. Yet management support behind the program went from hot to cold. The company was still recuperating from a turbulent period in the 1980s when it had lost direction, accrued a $1 billion-plus debt, and fought off takeover attempts. During the reconstruction period in the 1990s, Avon's North American leadership changed three times in five years. More pressing needs had distracted management.

It wasn't until 1998, when Susan Kropf, now the company's president and chief operating officer, was leading North American operations that the program really started to be taken seriously.

"She decided Sales Leadership could always be an option for the representatives, but it could no longer be an option for the company," recalls Fleming. To be competitive, Avon must offer a multilevel marketing plan, too.

Andrea Jung, who was then Avon's president, notes that throughout the decades, Avon has offered a variety of recruitment and training type programs that provided incentives to representatives. What sprang from her management team, therefore, was not completely new. But it was given renewed emphasis and unwavering support.

"Up until that time, we did not have that kind of forceful sanction for the Sales Leadership program," recalls Fleming. "With many other aspects of the business now running smoothly, it could get the thoughtful attention it needed."

From then on, Sales Leadership began to make its presence felt.

A SERIOUS CAREER OPTION

What Avon offered was an elevated career track. It differed from anything the company had previously devised in its more than 100-year history.

Women were, as always, able to pursue the traditional Avon opportunity whereby they sell and service customers. Now they could also, as expressed by Fleming, "activate a second dimension which is share the opportunity with someone else."

Under the Sales Leadership program, women would continue selling Avon products, but would be financially rewarded for recruiting and training others. These recruits would be known as the Downline.

The Sales Leadership representative would earn bonuses based on the sales of those she recruited and of the recruits of those recruits.

There was also a concern that Avon's independent representatives were developing their own management systems. Throughout the company, several ambitious reps had already been forging their own types of downlines. They would hire helpers—women to help them sell—to whom they paid a percent of their commission on those sales. The benefit to helpers is that they don't have to handle the paperwork or the responsibility of dealing with and signing a contract with the company. They could sell when or if they wanted to.

"If that is allowed to perpetuate, one can consider that the company is moving more to an area of confusion," says Fleming. Sales Leadership offered a formalized approach to business management.

DOING THINGS AVON'S WAY

The company had always provided an earning opportunity for women and encouraged financial independence. For many, however, the social gratification of reaching even modest goals and being associated with a reputable organization was just as rewarding.

Back in the early 1990s, Avon started doing research with its own representatives. They were asked, among other things, how much money they earned through their Avon businesses. The company was surprised to learn that many could not exactly say. Because they aren't receiving a direct paycheck, but rather drawing commissions and then reinvesting in their businesses buying brochures, samples, and other tools, a precise figure was not immediately at hand.

There was no hesitation, however, in ticking off the sales achievement level they had reached, the awards they'd been presented, or the trips they'd been on.

"It is true," says Fleming. "Many people in this industry [direct selling] were in it for the social gratification, and Avon was probably the queen of that."

But the company's goal was expanding. "First and foremost we wanted to start talking about it as a business," says Fleming. The challenge was to create an earning opportunity that would ratchet it up from a chiefly part-time occupation to an endeavor women would consider as a full-time career.

At the same time, any new initiative had to adhere to the principles upon which the company was founded and had always operated. To maintain the company's personal touch was one very important requirement to uphold or, as expressed in a founding principle, "to maintain and cherish the friendly spirit of Avon."

Then-Avon chief executive officer James Preston insisted that some qualifications be built into Avon's program. For one, the Sales Leadership representative had to remain successful in sales. Some other direct-selling companies "don't require the person to be successful in sales, but we do," Fleming maintains. Also in contrast to some other programs, as an Avon Sales Leadership representative rises in the hierarchy and expands downline, her sales requirements increase, rather than decrease. That is, says Fleming, "Because first and foremost, we never want to lose sight that it is about selling and servicing."

To make certain that Avon's program never gets too far a field from its core mission, Avon limited the levels in its multilevel marketing program to three, so that a representative would never be that far removed from her upline Leadership representative. Other firms have downlines that stretch out much further.

DEALING WITH CULTURAL CHALLENGES

The program was intended to expand opportunity at Avon and lure people in who might not otherwise have considered the company for their career path.

"Our biggest challenge was cultural. How do you introduce a career opportunity to people who weren't really here for that?" asks Fleming rhetorically. "We knew we had to become appealing to people outside the company. At the same time, we didn't want to alienate anyone in the company."

The number one objective, of course, was to implement the new program without disrupting Avon's core business. There was a concern as to how to broach the topic within the sales organization. "They loved selling Avon products, and now how do we address this as a business versus the social gratification?" Fleming says.

The top sales leaders shied away from the new program. They had already mastered the existing routine and weren't sure they wanted to do things another way. Meanwhile, a dread was spreading throughout the district managers, who had every reason to believe their jobs would be threatened by this new Sales Leadership model. These representatives were suddenly being encouraged to handle the tasks that had primarily been within the district manager's domain.

Eliminating the district managers "was never in the plan," insists Fleming. "But once that perception got out, that became another hurdle for us to overcome."

What has resulted can be seen as a somewhat awkward management model. The company, however, is more than satisfied with its hybrid system and views the dual approach as the best of both worlds coming together in a smoothly working partnership.

The district manager remains the corporate authority of the company and continues to recruit and train and run educational meetings in her district and do everything she has always done. As a staff member, of course, the manager enjoys the perks of corporate employment, such as health benefits, vacation, and sick time.

Meanwhile, the Leadership representatives engage in primarily the same functions. They don't have the corporate safety net provided by a staff position, but are earning increasing rates of commission and, if successful, can earn much more than district managers.

At least a half-dozen, if not more, district managers have made the jump to the Sales Leadership side of the equation. The district manager ranks have otherwise thinned, down to 1,400 from 1,800, as part of ongoing business transformation efforts.

The district manager's fundamental job of growing the business has become easier because of the Sales Leadership program, claims Fleming. "Every day she wakes up wanting to grow the district. They [Sales Leadership representatives] wake up wanting to grow their personal businesses. So now we have a growth engine that is pretty powerful."

PROGRAM STRUCTURE

Fully understanding the mechanics of Avon's Sales Leadership Program takes some concentration. There are four levels: Unit Leader,

Advanced Unit Leader, Executive Unit Leader, and Senior Executive Unit Leader.

Let's start at the point of entry—Unit Leader. To qualify for *Unit Leader* status, a sales representative must recruit at least five sales representatives. She must also achieve minimum personal sales of $250 per campaign. For her to earn bonuses on the sales of her downline members, the unit as a whole must sell at least $1,200. After those goals are met, the Unit Leader earns a set percentage of the sales of the individual members of her downline. But she only earns bonuses on the sales of representatives who have placed minimum orders of $150. The bonus rate is as follows: 5 percent on sales of $150 to $299, 6 percent on sales of $300 to $599, and 7 percent on sales of $600 or more. These figures are for the first generation, that is the group of representatives that the Unit Leader recruits herself.

If any members of her first generation spawn their own downlines, the Unit Leader earns a 1 percent bonus on the sales of that second generation—assuming the individual representative's order meets the $150 minimum.

Another integral part to Avon's Sales Leadership program is that the Unit Leader must assume an active mentoring role. That said, the rest of the program follows a similar pattern of progression.

The *Advanced Unit Leader* must have 12 recruits. Of those, at least 3 need to be Unit Leaders. The Advanced Unit Leader must deliver minimum personal sales of $300 and the unit must produce $4,000. The bonus rate goes up for the Advanced Unit Leader to 6 percent on $150, 7 percent on $300, and 8 percent on $600. She will earn 2 percent on her group's second generation and 1 percent on the third generation.

The third tier is the *Executive Unit Leader*. The unit must have 20 representatives of whom 7 must be Unit Leaders. The Executive Unit Leader's sales must be $350 and the unit total must reach $17,500 per campaign. The bonus rate now goes up to 8 percent on $150, 10 percent on $315, and 12 percent on $625. In this stage, the bonus on the second generation rises to 3 percent, 4 percent, and 5 percent on sales of $150, $315, and $625, respectively. On the third generation, the Executive Unit Leader draws a bonus of 2 percent.

The highest rank is the *Senior Executive Unit Leader*. Like the Executive Unit Leader, the unit must have 20 recruits. But now it must possess seven Unit Leaders and two Executive Unit Leaders. The Senior Executive Unit Leader must have minimum sales of $400 a campaign, and the unit must gather sales of $40,000 a campaign. The bonus rates are the same as for the Executive Unit Leader. However, on top of that the Senior Executive Unit Leader earns 2 percent on the total unit sales of each first generation Executive Unit Leader in her downline. There is also a $400 car stipend per campaign, or $10,400 per year.

TODAY'S SALES LEADERSHIP PROGRAM

The incentives have been steadily attracting representatives. After trickling in at the start 14 years ago, there are now 41,000 Sales Leadership representatives, up from 31,000 in 2003.

Of those 41,000, 78 have become Senior Executive Unit Leaders. Their average annual bonus is $110,000. The average annual bonus of the top 40 is about $150,000.

Following that group are the Executive Unit Leaders who now draw annual bonuses between $30,000 to $40,000, and then the Advanced Unit Leaders with bonuses in the tens of thousands. On top of that, they earn commissions from their own personal sales.

Compare that to what the upper echelon of Avon sales representatives had earned in the past. A President's Council member with sales of $112,000 would technically draw a 50 percent commission, translating to $56,000. However, that is before deductions for brochures, samples, and other expenses. "At that level, you technically earn 50 percent. This doesn't mean that is what you make. Some people, for example, give the product to relatives at cost," notes Angelo Rossi, group vice president, sales and customer care. "In Leadership now, we really understand the bonuses paid."

Forecasting out over the next five years, the company expects the Sales Leadership base to rise to 70,000, and fully anticipates that the number will grow to 100,000 in the future.

"Leadership opportunity has been a driver in the last four years of extraordinary growth," says Rossi.

RECRUITMENT RESPONSIBILITIES

The Sales Leadership representatives have already taken the lead over district managers in bringing in new recruits to the company. The 41,000 Sales Leadership representatives have been responsible for directly or indirectly recruiting 300,000-plus of the current 650,000 U.S. sales representatives. And the Sales Leadership members are firmly expected to bear the bulk of the recruitment function going forward. Partly, this is based on the sheer mathematics. Again, there are 41,000 Sales Leadership reps and 1,400 district managers.

The Sales Leadership members have been credited with increasing Avon's representative numbers, which had been stagnant in the past decade. New recruits were up 3 percent in 2001, 2002, and 2003. As expected, hand in hand with the boost in representative count, Avon's U.S. sales have risen, too, up 6 percent in 2002 and 3 percent in 2003. In 2004, recruitment efforts suffered a set back in the third quarter with active reps shrinking 1 percent. U.S. sales declined 1 percent as well.

And as previously expressed, the success of a direct-selling operation typically rises or falls along with the number of active sales representatives. Thus, increasing the sales representatives is of utmost importance to expand sales. Each recruit, for all intents and purposes, can be considered a new store opening for Avon.

That's why Avon continues to encourage recruiting through many venues, including speaking to women at PTA meetings, at church functions, and on the soccer field, as well as reaching out, naturally, to family, friends, and customers.

"Of course, the downside of recruiting a good customer is that you lose their sales," says Roseanne Fogarty, a representative from Westbury, New York, with a shrug.

Once they are in the system, you want to keep them there. Turnover of Sales Leadership recruits has been reported to be higher than for other representatives. Fleming says the company has placed significant efforts behind extending the length of stay of its sales representatives.

Avon is not alone in suffering high turnover. It is commonplace in an industry where it is so easy to enter and exit the business. According to a 2003 study by the Direct Selling Association, industry-wide the average annual retention rate was 34.1 percent, the dropout rate was 38.9 percent, and the turnover rate was 64.7 percent. Avon's turnover rate is about 100 percent.

Retention is a serious matter to Avon. "Most people in this business quit before they get started," Fleming admits. "In training sessions, I talk a lot about overcoming fear and overcoming rejection. 'No' is something you have to embrace in this business. Because the next person may say 'yes.'" Besides, says Fleming grinning, "Avon is pretty safe. You are not going to get beat up approaching someone about Avon."

CHANGING THE GAME

Introducing the Sales Leadership dimension was a "game changer" for Avon, according to Jung. It created a platform for women to earn serious six-figure incomes and develop into management roles.

"At the fundamental heart of what we are trying to do as a company is we are trying to change women's lives," she says.

Jung maintains the program has allowed the company to enjoy a competitive advantage as a direct seller, while offering "unbelievable products" and superior processes.

"Yes, they come for the affiliation and love the products," says Jung. "But if they can't make enough money to truly change their lives, then it [Avon] will not deliver on its promise."

Sales Leadership enables Avon to leverage its offerings in a way that opens up more opportunities, says Jung. "It would have been singularly impossible if we had not changed the structure of the earnings compensation. You can sell a lot of lipsticks yourself, but you will not possibly make what these women make."

The women Jung refers to are top earners in the Sales Leadership program, whose annual incomes exceed $100,000. Besides, says Jung, "Avon is them [the representatives]. It is not the company. The upline is their motivation and their inspiration. It is a personal relationship with someone who is a role model."

"Today, Leadership is more of an integral part of Avon more than a separate program," adds Fleming. "It is simply the career dimension. If you come into Avon today you have a choice. If you only want to sell and service customers you can always do that. If you are more interested in a career, whether it be part-time or full time, we have more advanced training and concepts that allow you to do this. The Leadership program is a compensation plan that allows you to earn off the recruits and developmental activity that you engage in. That is really all it is. One day, it may not have that label 'Leadership.' It will just be the career dimension at Avon."

TRAINING AND INCENTIVES

With proof that the Sales Leadership program has spurred an increase in representative count—and, in turn, sales—Avon is putting resources behind both making Sales Leadership more alluring to try and easier to succeed on the job once you sign on.

To push representatives to get serious about the job quicker, there is FastStart, a program that will pay a Sales Leadership representative bonuses of up to $800 if she hits certain recruitment goals within a set time frame.

The Beauty Advisor Training program is also being closely aligned with Sales Leadership because together they are seen as assisting women who want to pursue Avon as a serious career. Fleming oversees both programs.

One major new tool for Sales Leadership representatives is an online, real time computer program called Downline Manager. It is an exhaustive analysis tool that can maintain records on the entire unit. It keeps track of sales of the first, second, and third generation downlines. For a given campaign, it shows how many orders were placed as well as how many reps did not place orders. It keeps tabs on the personal sales of the unit's leader, too. And it alerts the Leader as to how many downline members have reached sales of $150 or more, or if someone is on the verge of missing a sales goal.

There are also social aspects to it. Avon anniversaries are tracked, as well as birthdays. E-mails and electronic cards have even been prepared to send out on the occasion.

Meanwhile, where and how much Avon spends on developmental programs is likely to change in the future. As Sales Leadership continues to grow, the company will pay out more money to representatives in the form of bonuses.

It is highly likely that as the Sales Leadership program evolves, Avon's corporate incentive programs for sales representatives will be modified. To build their businesses, Sales Leadership representatives are already devising their own incentive programs to stimulate and inspire their downlines.

"You will see a reallocation of resources," says Fleming. "We will reevaluate because this entrepreneurial group is willing to share some of the expense of incentives. We are just at the beginning stage of learning how to support this new entrepreneurial representative. We are just beginning to scratch the surface of possibilities."

EXPANDING GLOBALLY

Avon is ready to embark on the growth phase of its Sales Leadership program. Already, versions of the U.S. model have taken root in the United Kingdom, Canada, Ukraine, Germany, and France, while test markets have been established in 16 markets around the globe including Mexico, Brazil, and Puerto Rico. "There will be an explosion of activity soon in Europe and in South America," says Fleming. "We are getting ready to send some U.S. talent to Japan."

Avon is trying to keep the Sales Leadership blueprint as close to the original as possible, although it will be tweaked as necessary to meet cultural needs.

With a compensation program that pays on several levels of performance and an IT program designed to support it, the company does not want to have "118 different systems from around the world," Fleming says.

Still, it will not be implemented worldwide overnight. Like it did in the United States, Avon promises to take a paced approach.

GETTING IN STEP

Avon was almost forced to pursue a multilevel marketing plan in order to stay competitive in the direct-selling industry. Indeed, a seismic shift has occurred in multilevel compensation programs in just the past decade.

In 1990, just 20 percent of the Direct Selling Association's (DSA) members had multilevel payment programs. Today, 80 percent of its member firms do, according to group spokeswoman Amy Robinson. "It is a method of compensation that has become extremely popular as companies have investigated it and seen that it has worked for others," comments Robinson.

Neil Offen, president of the DSA, notes that the term *multilevel marketing program* refers to a compensation system that has been taking over as the premier payment structure among direct selling firms. The term is somewhat of a misnomer, however, for it is not a marketing strategy per se. The movement towards that type of structure reportedly initiated with a handful of firms, including Amway and Shaklee.

The direct-selling model itself has been growing in popularity. In 1992, there were 5.5 million people acting as sales representatives for direct-selling firms in the United States, compared to 13.3 million today, says Offen. Worldwide, the ranks have reached 49.5 million. Avon is the largest direct-selling company in the world, and has been for decades.

The Avon Sales Leadership program is described by Offen as a "hybrid" model, in that its sales representatives earn money on their own sales as well as from recruits, but within a restricted number of levels. It's a method he considers to be, "The best of both worlds."

Because of the rise of companies shifting to multilevel marketing compensation structures, the DSA has been working with its members to add an addendum to its Code of Ethics that would call for companies to disclose what a sales representative is likely to earn within a given system. The point, says Offen, is to prevent companies from making unrealistic earnings claims. Offen thinks it could take up to three years for the DSA to finalize and adopt such guidelines.

The DSA's educational programs have also become geared to addressing the issues of companies with multilevel plans. It's such a high priority, to ensure that members not operating under that type of system still get their issues addressed, the DSA has formed the Party Plan Council, as well as the High Ticket Council (for companies selling high priced items like vacuum cleaners).

The whole multilevel structure continues to evolve. The next phase in multilevel marketing now blossoming is a program called "cross border sponsoring." A handful of companies enable sales representatives to recruit and earn commission on representatives in other countries in which the company operates.

Perhaps along with its entrenched culture there was a hesitancy to change the structure at Avon due to the periodic public distrust of multilevel systems. Lisa Wilber of Weare, New Hampshire, is one of the company's top Sales Leadership representatives. She readily admits that she contemplated the program for a year before deciding to try it, largely because she was dubious about its legitimacy.

There have been negative associations with fraudulent pyramid schemes in the past, where people at the bottom rung of an extended network are left holding merchandise and losing money. Avon's sales representatives have full control over their orders, only submitting orders for products that they want. Additionally, as previously noted, the company has always had a money-back guarantee so everything can be returned.

The DSA introduced its Code of Ethics in 1968 to guide the practice of direct selling. This Code, provided to all members, has since been expanded and modified. In 2003, the DSA, in conjunction with the World Federation of Direct Selling Associations, kicked off a multiyear "reputation building, image-enhancing program," Offen says.

The direct-selling industry, Offen adds, has suffered from too many negative perceptions. First it was "high-pressure sale types," followed by "pyramid schemes operating in the guise of direct-selling companies." The reality, he says, is "we empower, recognize, nurture, and show respect for our sales people."

Avon, he notes, "has been the most progressive ethical leader in the industry. Others have been right up there with them, but no one has been ahead."

Jung maintains that Avon hasn't suffered any taint from scandals in other parts of the industry. "Multilevel done in a controlled way is a very powerful growth engine," she observes.

CHAPTER 6

CONSTANTLY INNOVATE

The beauty industry is notorious for its love affair with products. There is hardly a cosmetics firm in existence that does not unveil something at least every spring and fall, even if it is only a new pallet of lipstick shades to match the season's fashions.

In this milieu, Avon has a business model unto itself that puts an even greater emphasis on new products than a typical beauty store department. Before delving into Avon's aggressive approach, let's first take a look at how the competition operates.

Beauty brands found in drugstores and discount stores like Wal-Mart—a group that Avon competes with on price—tend to present their most important skin care and cosmetics items in the spring, which is considered to be any time from January through June. Retailers do what they call major "resets" in the early part of the year. They rearrange the store's beauty department to allow new products in, push poor sellers out, and add new touches to freshen the ambience.

For the fragrance segment, however, the most important new scents emerge in the fall. This provides the best opportunity to capture year-end holiday sales, the most brisk selling period for the gift-oriented cosmetics category.

That is not to suggest that new products don't flow in all year long. They do. The previous guidelines simply reflect basic industry practices. If it is an important item—something that the manufacturer has spent heavily on to promote and advertise—it will get in the store at any time of the year. New items are also frequently introduced in countertop sets and on other temporary floor stands to make store departments attractive to customers.

Beauty companies, of course, want their new products to sell well. But, nearly as important, they hope each new item serves as a lure to entice shoppers to its display. In the process, it exposes them to the brand's full merchandise assortment. For instance, Cover Girl's new foundation may draw you to that section, but once you have a bottle of the makeup in hand, the company hopes you'll pick up a Cover Girl mascara or lipstick, too.

MOVING AT A WHIRLWIND PACE

Because Avon issues a new brochure in the United States every two weeks, and in international markets every three or four weeks, product development at the company is done at a much more intense pace. Traditional retailers reset their departments a couple of times a year and can lean on several manufacturers to deliver new products and novelty to keep interest high. Avon, on the other hand, is essentially resetting its beauty department 26 times a year, and only has itself to count on.

The scientific arm of Avon's product development machine has been centered at the same Suffern, New York, site since 1895, beginning with a makeshift lab. The process is like a spinning top that may wind down at times but never slows enough to tip. Avon invents at least 1,000 new beauty products every year. It is an astounding number that far outpaces the productivity at any other beauty company.

If a newly hired scientist at Avon's research and development staff lasts a year, Janice Teal, group vice president and chief scientific officer, knows she's found someone likely to stick around for a while. The perennially cheerful Teal, who has been with Avon for 23 years, thrives on the constant motion, yet recognizes the pace is not for everyone.

"I look for high-energy people with a positive, enthusiastic outlook," says Teal. "You have to be someone who can have lots of balls in the air and not get rattled when one is ready to hit the floor. You need to be able to pick it up and keep going." Given those required credentials, Teal notes, "Turnover the first year [in research and development] is on the high side." After that, it slows down.

A typical department store cosmetics brand may contain some 800 items. A drugstore line such as L'Oreal Paris—which offers cosmetics, skin care, and hair care—totals about 950 core items. To come out with 1,000 items would be akin to reinventing those entire lines every year.

At any given time, Avon might have several thousand items available for purchase, notes company spokesman Victor Beaudet. The portfolio has expanded considerably in the past 50 or so years. In 1959, for example, Avon's line contained a mere 259 items. Given the wide variety of scents, shades, and sizes the company offers, having a constant flow of new products has always been important. In 1959, the competitive landscape was far different. Many of the mass-market brands that Avon contends with today, such as Cover Girl, Mary Kay, and even the Bath & Body Works chain, were not yet in existence.

To make sure it is always providing its representatives the best earnings opportunity possible by offering new items in the brochure, and to keep its model operating successfully, Avon's new product introduction rate is at least double its average competitor.

"Our percent of 'newness' exceeds most packaged goods companies," says William Susetka, Avon's senior vice president of marketing. "On average, the competition's newness [or number of new items introduced] a year is 15 percent. Avon's is 40 percent."

"Nobody [other than Avon] introduces 1,000 products a year," confirms Allan Mottus, a long-time beauty industry consultant and publisher of *The Informationist*. Some of Avon's introductions may be as simple as a new lipstick shade. This still requires a reformulation, along with new packaging and marketing. A holiday collection of sexy reds cannot be promoted in the same fashion as a pallet of spring pinks.

"Many products at Avon are novelty products, and that is the tradition of the company, where it runs a lot of products on a seasonal basis," says Mottus. "That is how the reps sell." For instance, Avon's cologne decanters designed for men and shaped like horse heads and cars have been extremely popular over the years as gifts. Many are now collectibles, Mottus points out. Avon collectors guides abound, such as *Bud Hastin's Avon Collectors' Encyclopedia: The Official Guide for Avon Bottles and CPC Collectors,* now in its 17th edition.

Robert Briddon, Avon's group vice president of marketing for North America, says Avon has two descriptions for its introductions. There are "limited life" products that will be presented in two or three campaigns, and "regular life" products that are available for six months or more. "So we plan, purchase, and manage accordingly," he says. "Avon tries to avoid having a customer say, 'I've seen that already. I've got that.' You don't want them to send the representative away." Thus, the mix is constantly changing.

Of course, "the problem to having newness," Briddon continues, "is you have to take things out. It inevitably leaves people saying, 'Why don't you bring this thing back? It's my favorite fragrance.'" If the company gets a lot of those requests, it will restore products that may have been replaced along the way.

LAUNCHING A PRODUCT

Along with the 1,000 new beauty products that are birthed in Avon's laboratories, Avon introduces another 800 items annually in other product areas such as toys, videos, clothing, gifts, jewelry, and home decorations that are sourced through outside suppliers and licensing deals. During campaign 21 in 2004, Avon offered a whole array of Christmas tree ornaments for $4.99 and $5.99 each, along with a tabletop display of a holiday village scene complete with a working train for $29.99. There was also a ramie/cotton blend knit sweater for $39.99 and a three-piece corduroy travel bag set for $24.99.

Still, cosmetics, toiletries, and fragrances have been the heart of Avon's business from the start and today account for more than two-thirds of the company's sales. These will remain primary areas of emphasis going forward. Avon has also been developing its Avon Wellness business, a product line of vitamins, nutritionals, and exercise equipment, to foster the connection between beauty and health.

A few years ago, Avon relaxed its commitment to the beauty market, allowing fashions, novelty gifts, and even accessories like luggage to squeeze onto the pages of its brochures. These categories, the company found, helped elevate the excitement of the brochure by surprising customers with new and different items every time.

However, the company has started paying more attention again to its bread-and-butter operation. Beauty has been put back on the front burner, and the heat is being turned up. Avon anticipates that by the end of 2005, its Cosmetics, Fragrances, and Toiletries (CFT) segment will contribute 70 percent of its sales, up from 62 percent in 2001. Besides, note Avon executives, beauty products offer higher profit margins than its non-CFT categories.

"A focus on beauty continues to make a lot of sense. The beauty consumer is a more loyal consumer," Susetka observes.

A broad selection of products, however, can help increase the amount of a customer's order by triggering an impulse purchase of, say, a cute holiday decoration or pretty earrings. So while beauty is being treated as the destination category that draws customers to Avon, the company will continue to offer other products as well. The company takes pains to make sure that the novelty gifts and other items it offers are unique to Avon and cannot be purchased anywhere else.

"You want to build loyal customers who are going to come every campaign, to buy a product like Anew, and then always have something exciting and different for them as well," Susetka says.

In 2004, Avon's four beauty segments—skin care, color cosmetics, fragrance, and personal care including bath, body, and hair care—each accounted for about 25 percent of the company's $5.2 billion in worldwide CTF sales. This translates to more than $1 billion-plus per category.

Among Avon's key brands are Anew skin care, Avon Color, Skin-So-Soft, AdvanceTechniques hair care, and Avon Wellness. It is also slowly developing the mark beauty line for young women as a way to lure a new consumer base to Avon. The brand was launched in August 2003.

Avon's business model forces it to come up with one new product after another, notes Lyn Kirby, a former product development and marketing executive at Avon and now chief executive officer of the Ulta beauty store chain.

"The department store brands, or mass brands, don't run two-week campaigns. That requirement at Avon called for this level of newsworthiness," remarks Kirby, recalling her 17 years at the company. "We were in the market [with a new brochure] every two weeks," she says, emphasizing the frequency. "In those books, there needed to be something newsworthy."

Kirby has watched other brands start to follow Avon's pattern in recent years, including Lancome and Estée Lauder. Both have hastened their new product development functions, she observes. "I think Avon led that strategy and the rest of the industry has started to catch up. Avon always knew the power of that."

The company has long been proud of its ability to continuously refresh its product lineup. In the company's 1988 Annual Report, management boasted that Avon, "has by far the most comprehensive and versatile product development capability in the beauty industry. At any given time, the company has more new products on the market or in development than the rest of the U.S. [beauty] industry combined."

CEO Andrea Jung says Avon spends about $50 million on research and development annually. That is separate from the $100 million set aside for a new state-of-the-art research and development facility that replaced the existing labs in Suffern in the spring of 2005.

A CULTURE OF INNOVATION

From the start, Avon used its own labs and chemists to devise and refine its formulations. The company also enters into numerous alliances with outside firms to provide a rough technology or to perform product testing. And, like other perfume marketers, it partners with fragrance houses such as Quest International, Firmenich, IFF (International Flavors and Fragrances), and others to develop scents to match Avon's marketing briefs.

Neil Wasser, vice president of sales at Quest, says his company helps Avon develop its global scents by using Quest's "global creative resources and knowledge to make the fragrance appealing to different cultures and demographics. Avon's target is much broader and diverse than many other marketers." Because of Avon's unique selling cycle, notes Wasser, "turnaround is quicker than most companies." Avon, he adds, "has dynamic energy since there is pressure to launch new products for each new campaign throughout different countries."

Yet, just like in the beginning with David McConnell, who concocted fragrances in his own kitchen, the company's product development function remains very much in-house and hands on. "At the end of the day, we will take the product and do the execution," says Teal.

"The culture is about innovation. We want to have unique products," says Teal. "What makes a product a win in home direct sales is when it looks unique in the brochure. The product result has to have a 'wow' factor once you try it. The lipstick has to provide that moisturizing feel, or the skin cream has to provide noticeable results."

Home direct selling, adds Teal, "is a lot about word of mouth. If the representative gets excited, they tell everybody."

Whether in the U.S. or international markets, Avon customers encompass a wide range of women. The company's product range, therefore, is developed to meet the needs of those who want to dab on one light moisturizer and go, as well as those who want to layer their skin with various products. "Some ladies want a whole library of colors to match all their dresses, and some only want one red lipstick," Teal observes.

Products come in a broad price range, so there is something affordable for everyone. In a recent brochure, one specially priced lipstick was $1.69, and it was sandwiched between advanced treatment skin creams selling for $32.

INSIDE THE PROCESS

To complete so many new products a year, Avon has finely honed the process into a matrix-like system where members from several departments work simultaneously on various aspects of the same project.

"We have come out with a lot of new products for a long time," says Teal matter-of-factly. "Our innovation is faster than at any other company, because we have to keep raising the bar. The customer is not going to buy the new product if is not better than the old product. If you come out with a product that erases wrinkles, then what do you do next?"

At Avon, the process starts with a product idea that is expressed on a document referred to as the "marketing profile." It enters research and development (R&D) on Avon's computer system, where it can be simultaneously tracked by all parties involved in the development process.

In the beauty industry, new products ideas are generated in a variety of ways. But often it is kicked off in the marketing department. It is the marketing staff's job to watch cultural and industry trends and keep track of what consumers are looking for in beauty products. The marketing department engages in consumer research studies to try to unearth some insight into what consumers may find appealing or think is lacking in the market. The company's scientists are then asked to come up with a product to match this need. Inventive scientists also toil on their own. When they feel they have struck on something worthwhile, the concept is presented to the marketing team.

When a cosmetics company has completed a new product, frequently marketers promote their latest innovation by saying it "fills a need gap."

Some companies have a distinct product development staff in addition to the marketers and scientists. These people are artistic and creative types with a flair for and knowledge of the beauty market. At Avon, this function is folded within marketing.

Whether it is someone from marketing or product development, part of the job is to go out and scour every corner of society to find where new ideas are emerging. Anything can lead to a new beauty concept, be it a nightclub fashion trend that needs a matching nail color or a popular food ingredient that can be used as a star scent for a new lip gloss. Lately, the fragrance industry has jumped on society's obsession with celebrities and blanketed the market with namesake fragrances including those by Celine Dion, Jennifer Lopez, Beyonce Knowles, Britney Spears, Antonio Banderas, and P. Diddy (Sean Puffy Combs), just to name a few.

At Avon, Teal's department is responsible for connecting all the dots on the science side of the project. Her staff is divided into four teams: the skin care team, the color cosmetics team, the hair care team, and the bath and body products team. Each team is its own matrix operation where members are linked in an interwoven communication system. "That is the whole organizational trick," Teal shares.

On a typical skin care project like Anew Retroactive, there are chemists from product development who work with and are knowledgeable about skin care formulas. Additionally, there is a representative who works with developing new technologies, "because you want to add innovation—so people who are involved in blue-sky thinking are on the team," notes Teal, referring to imaginative members of the staff who are on the lookout for the next big idea. A scientist may be knowledgeable about a new ingredient, but it's up to a skin care specialist or a lip color specialist to determine whether there is an applicable use for an item in that product category.

Nearly all products are scented, so someone from the creative fragrance department is also on board. To ensure that the final formula is housed in a package that will keep it fresh and safe during shipping, someone from package testing is also on the team.

Next there's a product safety specialist who tests for the safety and efficacy of the product. "We also might have someone from consumer science to test and make sure that consumers like it," Teal explains. Even if the product is tested and found safe, it's worthless if consumers don't like the scent or the texture.

The scientific team matrix balloons out from there into an even larger one that draws in specialists from various other departments based at the corporate headquarters in New York. Depending on the project, it could include marketing, advertising, public relations, brochure design, and any other input that is needed to create, plan, and market the product.

Marketing determines how the product should be positioned and priced. Advertising determines what, if any, vehicles should be used to tell the world about it—be it newspapers, magazines, TV, or the Internet. The public relations team is responsible for drumming up media interest in the new product. In the image-oriented, emotional business of beauty, getting a mention in consumer magazine is highly important. A single article can set sales of an item soaring.

To keep the process on track, a schedule is developed around expectations for the new product. "There is a standard schedule, but then we will modify it," Teal says. "Again, it goes right on the computer [tracking system] so that everyone knows when they have to do what, and that this is the strategy of what we are going to do. We are pretty good at developing these schedules."

The marketing profile contains all of the information pertaining to the product, including its cost parameters, when it is going to be tested, and what kind of package it's going to go into. "All of the information is really there at this point and now it goes into execution," Teal notes.

Of course, Teal admits, "Execution is obviously not without its challenges." Everything has to be timed to meet deadlines that also take into account when the product needs to be photographed for the brochure. If it's not ready in time, a composite version will be dummied up, possibly using Lucite rather than the glass bottle, to stand in for the real object.

"Because we do this so much, we have highly skilled people in all of these functions," Teal says. "They sit around a table and each person knows what they have to do to deliver that product and by what time. Everybody executes with very little supervision because of the talent level we have."

Vendors who work with Avon frequently will have direct computer links to the company. This way Avon can send over CAD drawings and other working models for the project. What helps keep Avon's processes running so efficiently, says Teal, "is having access to these modern tools. To have somebody hand drawing these things, like in the old days, just doesn't make sense."

While it is all about innovation, there are cost constraints for Avon. "At the same time, we do sell more at value pricing," Teal adds. "So when we develop a product, we have to make sure that we are going to meet the cost objective of that product and sell it at the right price."

The hurdle is harder for Avon than for most other companies, Teal contends, "because we can't just throw any ingredient in there. We may have to look for alternative ingredients that might do the same thing but cost a little bit less."

Teal believes one of Avon's greatest accomplishments is its ability to execute efficiently. In addition, she says, the company is strong on the creative side. "We are great at looking at a technology and quickly applying that technology into a consumer-relevant product," she insists.

Lynn Emmolo, a former senior marketing executive at Avon who has also worked at L'Oreal and Victoria's Secret Beauty, says Avon doesn't necessarily spend a lot more on R&D than others. But the company, she says, "is smarter with it."

Because of the matrix structure, there is a series of bridges that link people in the organization involved with formulating to those studying new technologies, Teal says. "We all have these [new product] concepts and we need homes for the technology," she points out. "We quickly find a home for it, and away we go."

PREPARING THE GLOBAL MENU

Supporting the Suffern facility are six satellite research and development labs. One is in Europe, two are in Asia, another two are in Latin America, and the sixth is in Japan.

It wasn't so long ago that Avon's international markets were a loosely connected patchwork. Product development, for the most part, was very regionalized. That was true for other global competitors, too.

Over the past decade or so, there has been a broad scale globalization effort. About 10 years ago, "things were much more local," Teal says. "Even the global competitors were much more local. So the regional marketing groups were always comparing themselves to the local products, not to the global products."

That has all changed. Now Avon's strategies come through its Global Marketing Council. The Council is comprised of representatives from each of Avon's four regions: Asia, Europe, Latin America, and North America. Then there are the heads of product development, global advertising, and market research. Teal represents the research and development arm.

"The Council makes sure the marketing and strategy is right," Susetka says. The Council meets four to five times per year and holds several hours of conference calls each month. Additionally, two global marketing workshops are held each year for the purpose of doing competitive product reviews.

From a new product standpoint, "This is the most efficient [system] I have ever seen," says Susetka, who has been in consumer product marketing for at least 25 years. "The system includes the delivery of the product without being late, adhering to all timetables, and ensuring that we deliver on time, which is crucial."

Forecasting sales projections in all local markets and having plans with the supply chain team is another critical element, he says. The guidebook for Avon these days calls for global products with a smaller number of local products. If Avon's global products menu can't meet the needs of customers in a certain region, "then we will do a local formula," says Teal.

Of Avon's beauty product mix, 65 percent are global brands. Hitting about 80 percent is the current target. Twenty years ago when the company introduced new products they were typically introduced to foreign markets a year later, if at all. Now notes Teal, "we try to marry everyone's needs in one formula." If Latin America and Europe both want an SPF 30, but Europe also wants vitamin E in the product, the development team will try to put the vitamin E in from the start. "We meet both their needs in one formula," she says.

The big exception is for Japan where the product line is distinctly different. Japan is a huge skin care market where women favor a several-step cleansing and treatment regimen. They also like to display skin care products in their bathrooms, so the packaging for Avon's line is created to be decorative. Japanese women want a different result from their hair care products, as well.

"They like a lot more oily feeling, so as to get the beautiful shine with their dark hair," says Teal. "And they don't like a lot of fragrance." For skin care products, they favor light essences to heavy creams, "so products must be in different formulations."

Throughout its long history, Avon has enjoyed huge sales with many products, even though what really made them special wasn't discovered until far down the line. The company is now trying to get ahead of the game by recognizing these attributes well in advance.

The organization has also been refocused on building what Susetka calls "mega-brands." The goal is to have 10 brands of at least $200 million each, with at least five of them possessing sales of at least $500 million annually. At present, Avon has four brands over $200 million mark and two others over $500 million (Avon Color and Anew), and that number is expected to increase over the next year.

To drive this kind of growth, Avon is heavily investing in some products it internally identifies as "super hits." Retroactive, a block-buster product within the Anew franchise, is one such item. It is not unusual for beauty companies to designate products as centerpieces or stars of their new lineup for the year. Those products will receive a bulk of the company's advertising support, the most in-store promotional materials, and a greater public relations outreach campaign. For instance, Procter & Gamble's launch of Olay Total Effects anti-age skin care in 2000 got blockbuster treatment, as did L'Oreal's True Match foundation in 2004. Both were backed by multimillion-dollar promotional and advertising campaigns.

Jung notes that, in the past, Avon "would do product development and then every several years something would be a block-buster." Yet, as Jung admits, it would only be recognized as a blockbuster in hindsight.

The company's perspective has changed dramatically. Under Jung there is a mandate to have a breakthrough product every two years, "that will exceed the benchmark of anybody else in the industry—mass or prestige," she says, referring to brand groups sold in the industry's two distinct beauty retail channels—drugstores (mass) and department stores (prestige).

"Now our goal is to fund it, fuel it, and make it as a target," declares Jung.

Jung gave Teal a dictum to design a skin care blockbuster in 2000. With that kind of zeal behind it, Retroactive was born. It has become one of the world's best-selling anti-aging creams.

To fuel this approach, and to continue such innovations, Avon has invested in a new R&D center, and will continue partnerships with university scientific communities doing "whatever it takes to lead," in Jung's words.

Avon's most noticeable triumphs have come from its skin care labs, but there are now expectations from other segments, particularly color cosmetics. "I believe there is a great opportunity for us to do this and to continue it in other categories," Jung says. "It is very critical for Avon to have blockbuster products."

One reason is that it speaks to the company's goal of helping women around the world by devising powerful technologies and making the products accessible. For instance, Anew, Jung points out, "is affordable to women in the outskirts and villages of China and Eastern Russia, and in the Amazon in Brazil." Customers are getting breakthrough technology at prices much lower than products sold at department or specialty stores.

MAKING HISTORIC BREAKTHROUGHS

Avon has been the force behind many dominant beauty products in the past 100 years. But there is no contention that in the past 20 years some of the company's biggest technological breakthroughs and historic market firsts have come through its skin care division.

One of the first major innovations that put Avon's skin care department on the industry's radar screen came in 1985 when it stabilized the pure form of vitamin A and was one of the first out with a retinol product. The product was BioAdvance, a two-phase system that users had to mix together. It was "very potent," says Teal. BioAdvance was part of a new approach to an aging market with Avon devising "Visible Improvement Products" that also included the VIP line for the face, Moisture Therapy for the hands and body, and Sunseekers for tanning.

A year and a half after its introduction, BioAdvance remained a top seller for Avon. The company hailed the line as being on the "leading edge of beauty recovery products."

BioAdvance kicked off Avon's forceful march into the anti-aging skin care market. Soon after, the company heralded another breakthrough. In 1987, a product called Collagen Booster that possessed a 5 percent concentration of stabilized vitamin C made it to market. It was the first use of vitamin C as a key anti-aging ingredient, "beyond its use as an antioxidant at low levels," Teal adds. It was a patented process. If not stabilized, vitamin C turns brown. This, according to Teal, was an issue Avon's competition had to contend with if it tried to follow Avon's lead, because of Avon's patent on the formula. Vitamin C products are said to fight free radicals (environmental elements that cause damage and aging), leaving skin firmer and more radiant.

But it was a product breakthrough five years later that catapulted Avon's reputation as a skin care innovator and helped set off the explosive growth of what was then a fledgling anti-age skin care market.

Avon was at the forefront of the alpha hydroxy acid (AHA) anti-aging skin care phenomenon with the launch of Anew Perfecting Complex for Face in February 1992. This was the first mass-market product to reach consumers offering the AHA ingredient, a compound found in grapes and citrus fruits. AHA is an exfoliant that is lauded for smoothing and retexturing skin.

"It really put the industry on its edge," says Lynn Emmolo, a former group vice president of marketing at Avon who left to join Victoria's Secret Beauty. "It was a success because it really worked. There's been nothing quite like it since then."

The Anew introduction helped trigger a movement that swept through the prestige and mass retail markets within months. Drugstore skin care brands got into the act with a form of an alpha or beta hydroxy acid, including Procter & Gamble's Olay, L'Oreal's Plenitude, and Chesebrough-Pond's Ponds. There was also Neoteric's Alpha Hydrox brand. In department stores, Clinique, Estée Lauder, and Elizabeth Arden, among others, all quickly got on board. "The fruit acid story has added a huge layer to our business," said Linda Petersen, at the time the cosmetics buyer for Marshall Field's department stores.

In retrospect, Avon probably didn't capitalize on the Anew event as much as it could have. Emmolo remembers that internally Anew was viewed as a product, rather than a brand or concept that could be leveraged. Although there were a couple of items added to the franchise, it wasn't until 1997 that Anew was finally expanded into a fuller skin care line complete with cleansers, toners, and moisturizers incorporating other advanced technologies.

During this time, Avon had branched out in another direction. In 1996, the company patented a new molecule using vitamin C.

AVC10 was invented by a team led by Dmitri Ptchelintsev, a research scientist in Avon's skin care lab in Suffern. Avon first used AVC10 in its Anew Night Force Vertical Lifting Complex. "The molecule is exclusive to Avon, and was subject to several patents exclusive to Avon," says Ptchelintsev. "It continues to be available only through Avon. You feel like a trailblazer."

Even before that, in the early 1980s, Avon had begun to put UVA/UVB protection in its facial moisturizers, most times not even putting notice on the package. This was before the issue of sun protection became popularized.

"We were really the first to understand [the benefits] of adding UVA/UVB protection," Teal recalls. "We added it to our daily moisturizers. It was something good for her [the Avon consumer]. At the time, she didn't know she wanted it. But we wanted to protect her even though she maybe didn't appreciate it at that point. Sometimes we gave her a few extra things she didn't even know she needed."

Anita Roddick's The Body Shop has gained the most recognition worldwide for its ban on animal testing, which began in 1990. However, Avon sneaked in a little before that—in 1989. Avon has even received an award for its efforts in this area from the animal rights group, People for the Ethical Treatment of Animals (PETA).

Teal says it's sometimes frustrating for folks at Avon to hear beauty editors comment about a new product or methodology that another company has come out with, especially since it's often something that Avon came out with first. Because of the minimal external advertising put forth by the company, the industry often doesn't hear about these innovations. Upon reading such articles, "I want to say, 'Hey, we did that!'" says Teal, who by nature is modest and a team player.

A SKIN CARE POWERHOUSE

It may have missed a beat the year or two following the Anew blockbuster, but Avon has since made up the difference. Without a doubt, the company has become a skin care powerhouse. In the United States, Anew is the second best-selling skin care brand after Procter

& Gamble's Olay, and a best-selling skin care brand worldwide in dollar sales, Avon executives claim.

Since 1997, Anew has been expanded to include items with distinct positioning such as Luminosity, a skin lightening cream that is patterned after skin whiteners popular in Asian markets. Retroactive followed and was the company's first cream to treat skin at the cellular level.

Then came Ultimate, designed to firm, brighten, and smooth skin. At the time, it was Avon's priciest item yet at $30. Cellu-Sculpt, a skin-firming body cream, has turned into another homerun.

The rise of cosmetic surgery and dermatological facial treatments like chemical peels and Botox injections has pushed many beauty companies into the sphere of becoming dermatologists. Avon is no exception.

In the fall of 2003, under the Anew umbrella, Avon introduced Anew Clinical starting with one product—Line and Wrinkle Cor rector. This formula was intended to plump up wrinkles and fill in lines. Then came Two-Step Facial Peel. Now there is Anew Clinical Deep Crease, an item said to relax facial lines while filling in deep creases.

The sassy advertising tagline reads: "So before you go to your doctor, call your Avon Lady instead."

CREATING COLOR COSMETICS

In September 2004, Avon introduced its latest incarnation of the Avon Color line, its core makeup brand. The packaging was converted from straight-lined blue and white components to a metallic cosmic blue shade in curvy packaging—offering a rounder, sensual feel.

With its intention to infuse cosmetics with more technology, a key launch is My Lip Miracle, a lipstick promising a host of benefits such as long wear, moisturization, shine, and rich color. Avon's group vice president of global marketing, Jill Scalamandre, says the lipstick is "intuitive," in that it provides what women want in a lipstick. The previous year, Avon introduced Beyond Color, a lipstick with retinol to treat lips.

A decade ago, Avon was one of the first beauty firms out with a long-wearing lipstick. Perfect Wear Lipcolor came out in 1994, placing it in consumers' hands the same year Revlon's famous ColorStay hit stores. ColorStay is still regarded as the industry classic.

Avon Color was introduced as a standalone brand in 1988. It was designed to take the guesswork out of buying cosmetics by dividing shades into four color groups: warm, cool, ultra warm, and ultra cool.

While Revlon is revered as the cosmetics industry color authority, Avon has gained a reputation for the breadth of its shade ranges. As early as 1966, the company noted in marketing materials that there was a continuous need to create new shades of makeup products to complement the latest styles and colors in fashion. In its 1974 annual report, Avon boasted that one-third of all lipsticks sold in the United States were made by the company. Its market domination in color has since diminished as more competitors have ambled into the industry, but it still remains a formidable lipstick distributor.

Throughout its history, there have been products designed to meet special needs or specific consumer desires of the period. For the gentle-skinned, there was the Delicate Beauty and Pure Care lines, both catering to sensitive skin. Ultra Sheer makeup products, introduced in 1966, came in time for the mod look of dark eyes and a little blush. They served up a pallet of products to create an "unmade-up look" that gave one's skin a "soft lustrous finish." One product that came and went was Fluff Foundation, an aerosol foam makeup collection.

Paying attention to the growing ethnic market, Avon launched a line of products for Black women that included makeup, skin care, and hair care in 1975. Since then, many general market brands have integrated such product lines and the extended shade ranges into their core brands.

Tapping into the environmental awareness of the 1970s, Envira was born. This makeup line claimed to protect skin against environmental effects and featured subtle shades. It was followed up with Fresh Look, a light natural makeup.

As previously noted, novelty items have always been popular at Avon. Pop-top—a mechanized, lever-operated lipstick—became one of Avon's best-selling color items ever in 1972. Avon also periodically develops specialty lines such as the 1987 Fifth Avenue Collection offering fragrances, makeup, and jewelry.

SMELLING GOOD

From its first moments, Avon sought to offer the finest products on the market. The company's executives regularly traveled to Grasse, France, the world's center of fragrance development due to its rolling fields of lavender and roses, to purchase fragranced pomades to use in making Avon's perfumes.

William Scheele, Avon's former secretary and general sales manager, wrote in 1916 that he would travel by train to the region, so that "we have the true flower base which makes our floral odors so true to natural flowers and so lasting."

Avon has held firm to its founding principles ever since. While the company has developed in many other areas, it has remained one of the most prolific fragrance marketers in the world.

A short list of Avon scents for teens includes Sweet Honesty, Wishing, Pretty Peach, and Zany. And there has been Miss Lollypop, Her Prettiness, and Sunny Sky for little girls.

For men there has been Trazarro, Excalibur, Bravo, Wild Country, Clint, Everest, Black Leather, Black Suede, Paradigm, Perceive for Men, R.P.M, Mesmerize, HisSTORY, Peak Zone, and Imperfect. Along with the decanter selections, there has also been a Stein Series of scents sold in beer steins.

For women, the list is endless. The roster has included Here's My Heart, Breathless, Night Magic, Bright Night, Elegante, To a Wild Rose, Nearness, Forever Spring, White Rose, Cotillion, Topaze, Persian Wood, Somewhere, Occur!, Unforgettable, Roses Roses, The Sonnet, Somewhere, Brocade. Then there was Charisma, Elusive, Timeless, Unspoken, Candid, Ariane, Tempo, Tasha, Toccaro, Imari, Far Away, Rare Gold, Rare Pearl, Millennia,

Women of Earth, Little Black Dress, Treselle, Dreamlife, and Incandessence.

Contrast Avon's abbreviated list with Chanel, also considered an industry fragrance powerhouse. Chanel has introduced a total of 10 women's scents since 1921, the year it brought Chanel No. 5 into the world.

Avon has also experimented with fragrance technology. Cologne Silk was described to offer the scent of a cologne with the appearance of a lotion. There has been Avon Mood Creations, an electronic environmental (for the home) product, plus fragrance pencils. In 1999, Perceive, a radiant oriental scent, featured synthesized human pheromone and was intended to awaken a women's inner spirit.

In between there have been celebrity scents beginning with Billy Dee Williams' Undeniable, which produced a smash hit for Avon. Inner wear designer Josie Natori delivered two scents for Avon with Natori and Josie.

Outside the box, there was Uninhibited by Cher and Deneuve by Catherine Deneuve. Both were sold exclusively at retail locations during the 1980s when Avon briefly operated a prestige retail fragrance business. Within that business were fragrances from French designer Louis Feraud. By far, the most successful of Avon's retail scents was the Giorgio Beverly Hills line, a business the company owned briefly. In 1989, Giorgio Red was the best-selling department store scent in the United States.

Avon continues to drive its fragrance business with a major launch every fourth quarter. In 2004, it was with Today, the first of a trilogy—Today, Tomorrow, and Always—that would be rolled out over six months. The company's holiday single scent launches have exceeded global sales of $50 million each season for at least the past four years. It is a strategy Avon plans to repeat going forward.

THE MANY FACES OF SKIN-SO-SOFT

If Avon has a beauty product with a cult-like following, it is Skin-So-Soft. First introduced in 1962 as a bath oil, it has expanded to be one of Avon's megabrands. During a rebirth of the brand in the late

1980s, sales skyrocketed 50 percent, leading Skin-So-Soft to become the company's single most popular product in 1988.

Tales of unusual uses for Skin-So-Soft abound. On their own, consumers discovered that Skin-So-Soft was ideal at repelling insects. The oiliness that made bugs literally slide off smooth skin, and its citronella scent, is a natural bug repellent.

"Few are the sportsmen that have not had a bottle of Avon's Skin-So-Soft bath oil in the tackle box to keep those pesky bugs and mosquitoes away," writes Jim Binns in *Bass Fishing and Fly Fishing* magazine. "It's a familiar sight in most all of the south Texas, Louisiana, and Mississippi bait shops, and the distinctive yet pleasant smell of the product is quite common to both saltwater and [fresh water] fisherman."

Linda Wells, editor of the consumer beauty magazine *Allure*, recalls being a guest at an outdoor black tie wedding in East Hampton, New York, when the mosquitoes started to descend around dusk. "The waiters brought out bottles of Skin-So-Soft on silver trays," she says. Along with Wells and her husband, other New York society guests included comedienne Joan Rivers. "Joan poured it all over," Wells laughs.

On at least one occasion, Skin-So-Soft was used as an emergency propellant for a private airplane that had run out of fuel, though Avon does not promote that use.

The company may have inadvertently pioneered the bug repellent sector of the sunscreen market when it launched Skin-So-Soft Moisturizing Suncare in 1994. To build on the success of this new product, it introduced a formal set of products to address insects under the Skin-So-Soft Bug Guard name in 1997.

"We marketed it as a three-in-one product—a moisturizer, a sun protection item, and a bug repellent," says Joe Bierman, Avon's vice president of U.S. and global fragrance and personal care at the time. "We did more research after the first couple of years and found out that 90 percent of our consumers used our product for bug repellency."

To keep it fresh 42 years after its introduction, Avon once again repackaged its Skin-So-Soft bath collection giving it a fresh twist with pastel colors and a new logo in 2005.

BUILDING THE PERSONAL CARE CATEGORY

Starting with toothpowders, Avon has always offered personal hygiene products alongside its fragrances and cosmetics. From the very beginning, the company was credited with presenting toiletries and cosmetics directly to women in their homes and awakening the public to an interest in better grooming.

In addition to Skin-So-Soft, another major brand is Naturals, a bath and body care line featuring natural ingredients and Advance Techniques hair care. There is also the Tranquil Moments aromatherapy line. When launched, "We actually did EKG testing and found that it relaxed your brainwaves," Teal says. Rounding out its personal hygiene lineup is Foot Works and the new Planet Spa collection. And Avon Life vitamins was a forerunner to Avon Wellness.

The company has also introduced a number of "fun" products in the personal care area, such as Randy Pandy (first introduced in 1972), a floating soap dish and soap for kids, and licensed characters including the members of the Peanuts gang and Barbie.

BRANCHING BEYOND COSMETICS

Avon has learned that sometimes it is worth taking the chance on something completely different. In 1971, that belief led the company to become a top jewelry seller overnight with items priced at $5 to $10 making up a majority of the business. By 1974, Avon was the nation's largest distributor of costume jewelry, with sales up 45 percent over 1973. By 1975, jewelry represented 7 percent of Avon's sales. By 1977, jewelry represented 16 percent of sales and the company started testing jewelry in international markets. In 1979, with sales of $400 million, Avon became the largest distributor of costume jewelry in the world, according to the company.

Avon's meteoric rise has been blamed for the downfall of Sarah Coventry, which filed for bankruptcy in 1981 after 30 years in the party plan business. The trade name has since been acquired and the company has resurfaced recently on the Home Shopping Network. Meanwhile, Avon's jewelry sales continue to thrive. The company declines to say, but industry sources indicate Avon's jewelry sales are at least $750 million annually. It is part of Avon's $1.3 billion "Beauty Plus" product group that also includes accessories and apparel.

Other categories Avon has sampled and stayed with in just the past 20 years include casual clothing and lingerie—now called Avon Style. It also ventured into video sales in 1989 with an aerobics video by TV personality Mary Hart that sold 400,000 copies. That same year it also added sleepwear and toys.

As in fragrances, the company calls upon some well-known names at times for its clothing products. Diane Von Furstenberg designed a casual wear line for Avon called The Color Authority. "The idea is to create a small wardrobe of great items, that are very adaptable," Von Furstenberg told *Women's Wear Daily*. In addition, actress Delta Burke designed a plus-size resort wear line in 1999.

A NEW PHASE IN R&D

Avon may draw sales in several categories other than beauty, but beauty is what makes the company's pulse race. It even refers to its nonbeauty businesses as Beyond Beauty and Beauty Plus. In 2005, the company said it will scale back its Beyond Beauty offerings, a segment that includes gifts and home décor, to refocus on its core strengths.

In Suffern, New York, where Avon's beauty creation takes place, construction completed in 2005 will replace existing facilities with a new modern complex on the company's 11-acre business campus.

The three-story structure, made with tinted glass, will encompass 225,000 square feet. Computerized systems and the use of advanced technology have always been a hallmark of Avon. As early as 1968, the company was reported to be installing in its U.S. manufacturing labs "new computers for the complete production, planning, and scheduling so necessary in our business."

The new facility will enable Teal "to put more chemists on the bench," she says. "We were out of lab space."

Avon, she says, has been investing all along in the latest technology, so the systems are already up to speed. What the new facility will provide is a more creative environment. "It is really about space," says Teal. "Our whole model is based off a matrix and people sharing and interacting. We wanted to build a whole facility to encourage that."

A lot of thought went into laying out the building. Each lab is deliberately situated in a way to best facilitate collaboration. The design strategically includes easily accessible stairs so that a person can quickly get to the floor above and below to encourage personal interaction.

There are conference rooms without tables. Instead, there are chairs that roll with flip-top arms, "so that people can just casually sit and talk. It is meant to be creative," says Teal. One such area is called the "Think Tank."

Additionally, there are attractive coffee bars to encourage mingling. "Rather than getting a cup of coffee and going back to your desk," says Teal, team members can interact with each other. She adds that a person from skin care might bump into a person from the color group and exchange some information through an informal conversation. "There is that synergy from bumping into someone who you wouldn't have talked to otherwise," Teal says.

"Most people in R&D know each other. It is pretty friendly. Just the fact that these people will be interacting with other departments will add a lot of synergy to our group," Teal continues. "We think that already exists. But I do think that this will make a big difference."

Avon has long been proud of its accomplishments. Yet, no matter what its achievement, the feeling remains that it's never quite enough. Expressed in its 1969 Annual Report, management said, "We maintain a healthy dissatisfaction with what we did yesterday, so that we can do it even better tomorrow." That tone has not changed much over the years. Susan Kropf, the company's president and chief operating officer, says that while the management team is "by nature optimistic," there is a "glass half empty kind of mentality." Says Kropf. "We always think about what more we could have done, or how we could have done it better."

CHAPTER 7

KEEP UP WITH THE TIMES

New York Jets star quarterback Chad Pennington walked unnoticed into a studio at the Chelsea Piers sports and entertainment complex in Manhattan, accompanied by three middle-aged men, all business associates. It was a gray Wednesday morning in April and, with the vagaries of New York City traffic, the group had been slightly delayed on the drive in from Long Island.

The well-mannered Tennessean, hungry after the longer than expected trip, prepared a breakfast plate from a small buffet set up in the corner of the room. He was joined by two newspaper reporters, who sat at a table anxiously waiting to find out why the football star was now working for Avon—a company known for catering to women.

The 27-year-old put his fork down and allowed his food to get cold. Men's grooming and appearance is very important to many of his teammates, particularly off the field, Pennington told the inquisitive journalists. "Some of the football players are really into fashion," he said. "But being a professional, you have to look nice and present yourself well. It will affect how people look at you and interact with you. And, as athletes, we are asked to do a lot of corporate appearances."

For those reasons, along with endorsements from his wife and mother that Avon was a reputable company to represent, Pennington had agreed to pose and be featured on the cover of Avon's first-ever men's brochure. It is simply called M: The Men's Catalog.

Avon has learned many business lessons over the years, and one is that if you want to hold onto your customers, you must keep up with the times. Reaching out directly to men was something Avon knew it had to do.

WIDENING THE AUDIENCE

Avon has paid close attention to staying on top of changing markets ever since it nearly lost its way in the 1970s. "I felt that Avon had been slow to react to changes in the marketplace, in society," says James Preston, who became CEO in 1988. "Most important, I believe we had totally missed the early significance of the women's movement which started in the late 60s and early 70s. One of the reasons we missed that is that we were a male dominated company. When I was made an officer in 1971, there was not one female vice president in this company." That, of course, has drastically changed and Avon's management ranks are now rife with women.

Avon also keeps its antennae up to quickly detect and take advantage of marketplace shifts. Before it unleashed M's kickoff issue in the fall of 2004, Avon was already starting to miss out on sales in the burgeoning U.S. men's grooming market. While men's shaving, hair, and cologne products have readily been available through Avon catalogs for many years, its selection lacked the specialty facial skin care and anti-aging products that had been cropping up in the American retail market over the previous year and a half.

In conjunction with the M brochure, Avon introduced the Pro-Extreme skin care collection, designed to combat the signs of aging, along with the Pro Sport Daily Performance brand, offering a roster of masculine facial care and body products.

Donald Tirotta, a former banking executive who runs an Avon business with his wife, Maria, in East Rockaway, New York, says he had started to buy skin care products for men made by Nivea at his local pharmacy. "I hate to admit it, but I was going to other people's stores," he says. He has since tried the Avon ProExtreme line and likes it. Now he says, "I buy that."

M: The Men's Catalog has been designed as a quarterly publication. Each issue is tied to a theme popular with men. The first was linked with sports. Eight million copies are set to be printed for each edition. Avon hopes to get the brochures into guys' hands through its female customers, who are expected to pass the books on to the men in their lives. There is no plan to recruit an all-male salesforce. Avon is, after all, the company for women.

In the past, the men Avon is now specifically targeting had been filching product samples from wives and girlfriends. Now they're hoarding stockpiles of products made just for them.

Nivea, Neutrogena, King of Shaves, Gillette, and Zirh are among the host of new lines for men that have been making their presence felt in recent years. Even the classic Old Spice has expanded into a scented body care line for men that is packaged in bold red plastic bottles that look like oil cans. French designer Jean Paul Gaultier took a leap ahead in bringing to market a cosmetics collection with mascara and base makeup for men that is sold in upscale department stores.

There has been so much product activity that *Women's Wear Daily* now has a reporter dedicated to covering the men's grooming market and *Men's Health* magazine added a grooming column. The CVS Pharmacy chain even has a four-foot wide shelf section that carries just men's facial skin care items.

Avon isn't the only company that thinks men want to shop for themselves. Fairchild Publications just introduced *Vitals* and Conde Nast has *Cargo*, both shopping magazines for men.

The industry has been taking notice, too. "Avon has really started to bring in a younger customer and a male customer in a more aggressive way," observes Wendy Liebmann, president of WSL Strategic Retail "The whole thing around the men's category is they [Avon] are recognizing that they can't depend on their traditional sales associates to generate the kind of new business that they might need."

Indeed, the booming market for men's body care items is only one of several emerging sectors that Avon has begun to cultivate both in the United States and around the world.

In addition to strengthening its voice in the men's market, over the past three years the company has initiated programs in the United States to engage younger women, Hispanic women, and the health conscious. This latter group is the target of a line of health and nutritional products marketed through a new business called

Avon Wellness. The company has not only changed directions in the area of product development, it has also taken new paths with its selling model over the years as more women have moved out of the home and into the workforce. And it has an incredible global effort as well, which we'll explore in greater detail in Chapter 8.

TARGETING A YOUNGER AUDIENCE

Miss Mississippi, Jalin Wood, a cheerful brunette with plans for a career in health care, is one of the top-selling U.S. representatives for Avon's new mark brand. (The company spells out the name "mark" using all lowercase letters.) The 23-year-old beauty pageant winner, an enterprising and warm-hearted young woman, started selling Avon's new youth-oriented mark collection to help cover her college tuition expenses. She is just the sort of person Avon has been angling to gain the attention of.

The number of Avon sales representatives has rebounded and grown in the past few years, thanks mainly to its Sales Leadership Program, which has become an effective recruiting machine. There has still been a falloff among younger women. The average age of a typical Avon representative today is 42. The company is anxious to bring more women like Wood and her younger cohorts into the fold.

Wood, a champion horse trainer and honors graduate, also happens to be the daughter of an Avon representative. "When I went to college, I made a commitment to pay my way through school," says Wood, who proudly wore mark jewelry during her televised appearances on the Miss America Pageant in Atlantic City. "One of my first jobs was to help my mom sell Avon. I would enter all of our orders online. When I saw and heard about mark, I immediately saw dollar signs."

So inspired is Wood with the opportunities presented to her as a mark representative, she has taken to signing her autographs, "Make Your mark." It is both an encouraging message to her fans to strive for their own achievements, and a nod to the Avon brand she loves to wear and sell.

David Hall McConnell, originally a bookseller from Southwest Oswego, New York, founded the California Perfume Company in 1886, which was later renamed Avon Products, Inc. Lauded for being ahead of his time because he recruited women as sales agents, he is also credited with advancing the door-to-door selling system in the United States.

Persis F. E. Albee, from Winchester, New Hampshire, is recognized for being the world's first official Avon lady. She was appreciatively nicknamed "the mother of the California Perfume Company" by McConnell. A Sunday school teacher, she traveled by both train and horse and carriage, delivering products and signing up new sales representatives. In her honor, Avon still awards statuettes dubbed "Albees" to its sales leaders. This photo is circa 1890.

The first permanent laboratory for the California Perfume Company was built in Suffern, New York, in 1897. The three-story wooden building measured 3,000 square feet. It was strategically located on the Erie train line.

Long before automation, everything in the factory was done by hand. This scene inside a California Perfume Company laboratory shows workers building products on the facial cream filling production line.

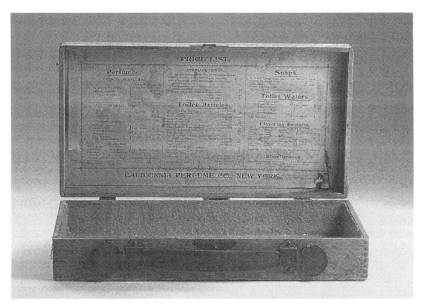

This early California Perfume Company selling kit was used to carry product samples. An itemized list of available items and the respective prices is affixed to the inside cover of the wooden box.

Along with a selection of perfumes, the California Perfume Company collection blossomed to include talc, shampoo cream, toothpowders, and cleansers. By 1906 the product line counted 117 items, including such pantry essentials as olive oil, baking powder, and food coloring.

These are early examples of the Avon brand rouge and lipstick. The package incorporates the first Avon logo that featured a sketch of Anne Hathaway's cottage. Cosmetics under the Avon brand name were first introduced in 1929.

This skin care collection from the 1940s shows Avon's second logo, which was used from 1936 to 1953. Since the debut of the Avon brand, the company has had about one dozen different logos. This particular "Facial Set" was sold between 1938 and 1940.

Claudette Colbert was one of several actresses to appear in Avon advertisements in the 1940s and 1950s. She is shown here meeting with an Avon representative in a lipstick advertisement from April 1948. This campaign appeared in national magazines such as *Good Housekeeping,* *Woman's Day,* and *Cosmopolitan.*

This "Avon Calling" print advertisement commemorated the company's seventy-fifth anniversary in 1961. The company's signature "Ding Dong Avon Calling" advertising campaign ran through 1967, making it the longest running series in television history. The company continued to incorporate the highly successful "Avon Calling" slogan and doorbell chime in its advertisements for several years thereafter.

Skin-So-Soft, Avon's 40-plus-year-old bath oil, has long been a best-selling product for the company. This advertisement from 1967 is a good example of how Avon uses promotional pricing as a marketing strategy.

Cologne decanters are among Avon's most popular collectibles and have been designed in a range of themes, including beer steins and animals. Shown here is a collection based on car models from the 1950s, including a 1956 Ford Thunderbird (center) and 1958 Edsel convertible (right).

Current Avon chairman and chief executive officer Andrea Jung with Ben Gallina, senior vice president of Avon's Asia-Pacific region, take part in a ribbon cutting ceremony for a new boutique in China. Avon has been operating retail sites in China since a government ban on direct selling took place in 1998. The ban could be lifted shortly and Avon is already preparing to re-establish a sales representative network there. More than 70 percent of Avon's sales today occur outside of the United States.

Avon's way of doing business has not changed much in all these years. Its selling model remains highly personal—and woman to woman—whether in the home at the kitchen table (as depicted in this picture), at the workplace, or on the soccer field.

Salma Hayek, Avon's new global spokesperson, was chosen for both her beauty and her commitment to women's issues. She is also partnering with Avon to educate women about domestic violence. Hayek is seen here in an advertisement for My Lip Miracle, a new Avon lipstick. This is one in a series of "Let's Talk" ads. "Let's Talk," launched in 1999, is Avon's first globally synchronized advertising campaign.

In an effort to keep its products fresh, Avon recently revamped its Avon Color cosmetics brand with new packaging. Products from lipstick to eyeliner sport a cosmic blue shade using components that give items a softer, sleeker feel. Avon Color is the company's largest brand. Amazingly, an Avon lipstick is sold somewhere in the world every three seconds.

Avon's trendy mark brand offers a constellation of 300 products—from cosmetics, bath and body, and fragrance to funky costume jewelry. Like Avon's other brands, it is continuously infused with new products to keep customers from losing interest in the brochure.

NOT JUST FOR TEENS

Mark is not just another fun youth brand composed of light fruity scents and glitter gels. There had been a run of those throughout the late 1990s, when literally dozens of cosmetics brands emerged on the scene to capitalize on what was expected to become a booming teen category. Population data determined that teenagers were on the rise and their spending power was enormous. Beauty marketers, always on the lookout for the next hot trend, got swept up in the excitement of opening up what was believed to be an untapped consumer segment.

It started in mall-based junior specialty stores like Claire's, Hot Topic, and Limited Too, where handbag and hair accessories makers such as Townley broadened their product lines to include lip glosses, nail polish, and scented glitter gels in round plastic containers called glitter pots. It was a staple of every teen girl's cosmetics line, and the products came in multiple colors.

Sassaby, a West Coast maker of cosmetics bags and hair accessories, got into the act, too, with the introduction of Jane Cosmetics. Its creators took the concept a step further, offering a more complete cosmetics line with gentle formulas that were easy to apply and not too heavily pigmented so that girls just learning to use cosmetics would never look overly made up.

Still, most of the teen brands consisted of simple color products with basic formulas. The roster of players grew to where there were almost too many to count. In addition to the hoards of upstart manufacturers that introduced brands with names like Fun Cosmetics and X-tatic, nearly every retailer imaginable—including Macy's, Wal-Mart, CVS, and even Toys 'R' Us—offered their own exclusive youth brands. Of course, powerful general market brands were not to be left out. Revlon introduced StreetWear and Maybelline offered up the Cosmic Edge collection. Avon joined the party with Color Trend and a fragrance to match called Scent Trend.

But just as quickly as it had exploded, the teen market deflated. What marketers learned was that many of these lines intended for teenagers were really finding a customer in much younger girls—8 to 12—cutely dubbed the "tweens." That is, they are between girls and teens. Teenage girls aspire to be older and were more interested in lines such as Cover Girl and Clinique, depending on where they shopped.

What also made it difficult to succeed is that most of the teen lines had focused on trendy glitter and lip and nail color products. They found it difficult to secure a following and get customers to buy repeatedly. The items and quality of the brands were comparable, with little real difference among them. What became the bestseller of the day was the item with the newest, most clever package. And the current hot product lost its luster and favor with young, fickle consumers just as fast.

Glitters and lip glosses were being packaged in every kind of cute container imaginable—from ladybugs to finger rings, key chains to cell phone cases. Nail polish bottles looked like lollipops and came in animal shapes. It became an exhausting process for the manufacturers involved. The competition was excruciating and several companies filed for bankruptcy. A few short years after it all began, the teen market imploded. Avon's teen Color Trend brand disappeared as well. A handful of brands have survived, including Jane Cosmetics and Caboodles Cosmetics, but each has lost millions in sales in a short period. In both cases, new owners are presently lobbying to convince retailers there is still a demand for these products.

Just as the teen craze was winding down, Avon started drawing up plans for mark. This was the company's solution to the puzzle of how to reengage young women and spark sales among teenagers.

As Avon learned long ago, it's important to stay aware and be ready to alter your direction at a moment's notice, depending on where the marketplace (not to mention consumer taste) is going.

When the new mark business was first announced to the public in August 2001, Avon heralded that it was developing a new line for teens. Upon realizing the teen industry had become nothing more than glitter dust, Avon hastily retreated on the teen designation and a year later referred to its new venture, set to debut in 2003, as a beauty brand for "young women ages 16 to 24," taking the target market range up a couple of years.

Avon became so insistent that mark not be construed as a teen brand that the company denied interviews to reporters who were writing stories about cosmetics for teenagers. It wanted to keep its fresh, new brand at a healthy distance from any connection with the scores of failed attempts that preceded it. Without fanfare, it quietly renamed the division housing mark from "Teen Business" to "Avon Future."

SPEAKING LIKE YOUR CUSTOMERS

In an industry where genuine progress has been made in formula technology, and where most brands deliver solid quality and safe products, image—coupled with price—becomes a key factor in what moves a woman to buy. Women will reach for a brand because of how the association with it makes her feel. Cover Girl promotes a clean, fresh natural look, while Revlon implies glamour and sexiness. Meanwhile, to wear MAC is to be hip.

Much discussion is made about packaging design and even on the weightiness of a lipstick tube because of the inherent quality a heavier package implies. Beauty is unquestionably an image-oriented business.

Mark is being used to establish Avon's image with 20-year-olds. There has been grave concern that the existing business model and incentive programs at Avon are not sufficiently alluring to this age group. After all, winning an Alaskan cruise with a group of 50-year-olds is not a great incentive to pull in the college crowd to join its ranks of representatives.

Avon is not the only mature beauty company that has tweaked its message to grab the attention of younger ears. Not long ago, Procter & Gamble inconspicuously dropped the Oil from its Oil of

Olay brand name because, to young women, a skin care brand associated with oil was a turnoff. This was a quiet, but deliberate, marketing move.

Meanwhile, both Chanel and Ralph Lauren added scents specifically targeting younger shoppers. Chanel unveiled Chance and supported it with advertisements featuring a young model. Ralph Lauren introduced Ralph in bright blue packaging to catch the attention of youthful eyes. There again, the concept is to draw them in and, along the way, introduce consumers to the brand's other merchandise, which they hopefully will progress into.

THE BEGINNINGS OF MARK

Avon's chairman and chief executive officer, Andrea Jung, resolute about keeping the company vibrant and appealing to the next generation, wanted to inaugurate a program that similarly would draw the attention of a younger generation. While Avon had been modernizing its image overall, to really pull young people in, Jung felt it was necessary to take a bolder and more sweeping approach. There would have to be a separate and distinct program, she concluded—a venture that this up and coming group could claim as its own.

"There is another whole generation of women who need to be introduced to Avon in a very different way," Jung said. "There is a lasting and sustaining model here. But each management [team] that goes through has to be able to reinvent. When it is not reinvented, we have found that the business model suffers."

Jung is taking a patient approach with the company's new baby. Originally forecast to reap sales of $100 million in 2004, mark's actual numbers rang up closer to $47 million. Plans to roll it out globally have been pushed back until 2006 for now until the formula is perfected in the United States. Nevertheless, Avon executives maintain they are pleased with the progress of mark and continue to guide it with a steady hand. Mark hasn't turned a profit yet, but company executives say it will likely break even in 2005.

Jung admits it is frustrating dealing with the financial community at times when it comes to talking about developing operations like mark. "Mark is a strategy, not for 2005, but for 2050," she insists. "That is a really important thing. When we talk to Wall Street, they want to know what is the profit going to be in 2005. That is not it [the point]." Jung adds that, as CEO, her job is to make quarterly numbers while guarding the future "and nurturing those things that will take us there."

All along, Jung has stressed that mark is part of a long-term strategy, designed to keep Avon on the forefront and feeling youthful for many years to come. Her primary goal is to assure this younger demographic that Avon has options for them as well.

"We want young women to know that instead of working in the cafeteria Monday, Wednesday, and Friday, they can get 10 people together every two weeks," Jung says. "They each just have to buy three products and you will make more money. You can pay your phone bill, you can have time to date."

College campuses had once been a stronghold for Avon. It pained Jung that the company lost its footing in that influential demographic. To get a fresh perspective on how to reconnect, she reached outside of Avon's once insular management team. In 2001, Jung tapped Deborah Fine, a former publisher of both *Glamour* and *Bride's* magazines, to pilot the project. Fine had personal and professional links to cultural trendsetters, the media, and the fashion world. She had been named by *USA Today* as one of the "Top Ten Women" in publishing.

Fine's mandate called for creating more than another flavored lipstick line or fruity scent—items highly popular with teenagers, but that engender little brand loyalty.

"The fundamental rationale behind this business was to create an opportunity for the next generation of Avon," says Fine, who oversaw the mark business from 2001 until March 2005.

Fine, a rapid-fire talker who quips she can type even faster than she speaks (100 words per minute), saw her mandate as a once-in-a-lifetime assignment. "How often are you given the opportunity to recreate a company for the next generation—to change each and every thing?" she asks. "Everything [for mark] was created from scratch, from the magalog to the products." The magalog, a cross between a magazine and a catalog, is mark's answer to the Avon brochure. In addition to showcasing products, it provides makeup tips and newsy items. It is distributed every four weeks. Reps earn a 40 percent commission on mark beauty items and 25 percent on everything else.

As the cosmetics industry learned too well, "You don't need another lip gloss for the sake of a lip gloss," Fine maintains. It is, "a lip gloss with an earnings opportunity." Fine's job was to create not only a fun cosmetics line, but to construct a new style direct-selling business that would appeal to young women and meld perfectly with today's modern lifestyles.

To get started on building mark, Fine assembled a hybrid team—composed of members that came 50 percent from inside Avon and 50 percent externally—to blend the best of the old ideas with fresh new thinking. Over late nights of pizza and diet drinks, Fine and her team brainstormed and determined that the core of mark would be about "Social Beauty." It is about being social and beautiful. What emerged was a platform built around the concepts of friends, opportunity, beauty, inspiration, and fun.

LAUNCHING THE BRAND

Mark representatives now sell the brand in as many diverse ways as women themselves are diverse. One representative, for instance, hosted a party in her family's home for a group of 30 girls from her sister's high school. Some sell in their college dorms, while others rely on a network of family and friends.

Avon hopes young women will be drawn to mark as an alternative job option that offers them freedom and a better earnings opportunity. The company declares that mark offers unlimited sales and commission potential, and thus is a better alternative to traditional teen jobs like babysitting, fast-food burger flipping, sweater folding, and dog walking.

What also makes the mark model different from Avon's core offering is the brand's multiple strategic partnerships. There have been tie-ins with Ford Motors for sweepstakes to win a Ford Focus. Another deal with Loews Cineplex Entertainment allowed magalogs of mark products to be placed in movie theater lobbies. Nextel Communications, meanwhile, offers mark reps discounted cell phone plans and New Line Cinemas provides content for the mark web site (which is dubbed "meetmark"). Mark also has its own sales incentive programs, including trips to Caribbean beaches for the rep and a friend.

Like Avon's core business, which is closely associated with the breast cancer cause, mark wanted a charitable affiliation of its own that would resonate with young women. It decided to link up with the American Legacy Foundation and its anti-smoking campaign.

With the expectation that nearly 100 percent of young women are Internet connected, the web site meetmark.com is considered the brand's "command central." But because only 70 percent of Avon representatives order online, the company maintains numerous ways to communicate with them.

To really drive home that mark is a serious entrepreneurial venture, Avon has created a customized program with the online University of Phoenix, offering young women up to 12 credits for business training to gain the knowledge they need on how to better run their own enterprise. Seventy percent of the universities in the United States accept these credits, according to the company.

Some potential mark reps are being converted to Avon representatives even faster than anticipated. The reason: Mark representatives can only sell mark. Avon representatives, on the other hand, can sell mark and the entire core Avon line. Plus, unlike their older counterparts, mark reps have to pay for goods ahead of time. They don't have the luxury of being billed later, which is another reason some make the switch. But the mark reps have promotional programs that appeal exclusively to younger women, making it a toss up for some in deciding which route to take.

One 24-year-old beauty editor tried her hand at selling mark with a party at her New York City apartment and then wrote about the experience. "Mark isn't a hard sell in theory. The products are designed well, the colors are current," wrote Bryn Kenny in *BeautyBiz* magazine. "They even smell good and you can stock your vanity table [with everything from blush to nail polish] for less than $50."

But probably the hardest part of the evening, Kenny concluded, is, "You're not only required to take money from your friends, you're also required to treat them in a businesslike manner, which means no favors and no exceptions." That part became sticky when two of Kenny's friends asked to pay her later. Still, it should be noted that making customers ante up before they receive their purchases is business as usual for most direct-selling enterprises—including Tupperware and The Pampered Chef.

In its short life, mark has received worthy recognition from numerous magazines and business associations for its products, packaging, and even marketing strategies. A product group Avon calls "Hook Ups"—consisting of lip glosses, eye shadows, and blushes that snap together so you can make up your own set—have proven particularly popular.

Linda Wells, editor-in-chief of *Allure* magazine, is exuberant when speaking of mark, which she says, "gives a sense of fun and a sense of youth to Avon with a trendiness and a vitality that really adds to the dimension of Avon's image." The Avon core brand, she says, "is more earnest and good and mark is fun and sparky and lively. It is great, particularly for women under 35 who enjoy the fun of makeup and not using it to cover up problems."

A HEALTHY BUSINESS

By keeping its eye on the ball, Avon was able to track the movements of another emerging consumer area. A majority of women were developing a growing interest in monitoring and controlling their own health. They not only wanted to live longer, they wanted to lead better and more active lives. That prompted Avon to launch one of its most successful new enterprises in decades—Avon Wellness.

What started out in 2001 with a new line of vitamins and nutritionals, formulated in a deal with pharmaceutical maker Hoffman-LaRoche, Avon Wellness has turned into a multimillion dollar business that the company's president and chief operating officer Susan Kropf now believes is just getting started. "Wellness can be unbelievable," Kropf predicts. "It can be a $1 billion business for us."

The distinct Avon Wellness catalog bears the tagline "Beauty Starts from Within." Along with vitamins and supplements, the collection contains low-carb snack bars and drinks from Slimwell, plus tea-infused mints in tins with inspirational messages such as "Be a Dreamer." There is exercise equipment from Bally Total Fitness, such as its $24.99 Ped-O-Bike, along with other tools to relax and revive. There are also products promising relief from colds and muscle aches.

Beauty, health, and wellness have become interlinked. Women are very concerned about both the ingredients in the foods they eat and the products they put on their skin. A Roper Starch study in 2000 found that 80 percent of all women regard maintaining an attractive physical appearance as essential to feeling good.

These merging interests moved the General Merchandise Distributors Council (GMDC), a trade group that supports the interests of nonfood manufacturers supplying supermarkets and other retailers, to begin studying the whole health, beauty, and wellness markets. Since 2001, the group has completed at least four studies that address aspects of this subject matter.

In 2002, GMDC wrote that whole health is no longer a fringe interest, "but a way of life for a consumer segment that reads labels and makes conscious decisions to purchase." The group recognized that there was a "growing awareness of consumers that a self-reliant approach to health can prevent serious illness and vastly improve quality of life."

As part of the 2002 study, GMDC surveyed 600 women, of whom 77 percent said they were taking more personal control over their health compared to a year ago. GMDC advised its members to "expand the scope of women's health to include personal care, beauty care, and other categories that women directly link to their overall sense of wellness."

Avon's program was already well underway by the time this study came out. With beauty and health going hand in hand, beauty companies like Avon have begun offering more products to address those tie-ins.

There are now scores of products that provide additional health benefits, such as moisturizing lipsticks that prevent lips from chapping, foundations equipped with SPF protection, and vitamins for skin health. Sally Hansen, best known for its nail polishes and nail treatments, expanded into a full cosmetics line called Sally Hansen

Healing Beauty. This line offers a range of products with formulas that provide healthy additions, such as its Beyond Perfect nail polish containing protein and French lavender to renew and strengthen nails.

Avon research shows that women are concerned with inner health as well as outer beauty. Other consumer companies have also entered the vitamin and nutritional segment. Procter & Gamble, for example, introduced Olay vitamins specifically targeted as skin care enhancements.

KEEPING ELECTRONIC TABS

Avon isn't just concerned about which items its customers use. It also wants to know how they spend their day so the company can adjust and refine its programs and products accordingly. At present, some 75 percent of all women in the United States work out of the home. That's why, out of necessity, the famous door-to-door sales method, Avon's primary marketing approach for decades, has been modified over the years to recognize this shift in society.

For many years, the company divided the United States into territories, with each representative presiding over an assigned area. By 1977, Avon was developing what it called Advance Call Back brochures to leave on doorknobs for women who were not at home. These materials included fragrance and makeup samples and customer flyers.

The territory restrictions have long been lifted, though the company continues to recognize it must find new ways to speak to working women. Back in 1986, it rolled out a workplace selling program to aid representatives in building their businesses in arenas outside of private homes. As society continues to evolve, Avon has been keen on tapping into the use of the Internet to reach busy women with promotional and other related messages at convenient times. Already it has begun supplying representatives with timely e-mail product reminders that can be sent to potential customers and include the representative's name and contact information. These messages also allow for personalization.

One such e-mail card for holiday sales shows a picture of the "Snowman Surprise," a stuffed snowman that plays Jingle Bells when you touch his foot while a little festive character pops out of his top hat. He can be yours for just $14.99. The message reads: "Need gift ideas? Contact your Avon Representative and get over 500 products for under $10! We've got gifts for men, women, and children—beauty gift sets, jewelry, fashion, gadgets, toys, and electronics."

Targeted e-mail marketing is just one of the many ways Avon has become more technologically advanced over the years. We'll take a closer look at the many ways the company has used technology to grow its business around the world in Chapter 9.

REACHING THE LATIN POPULATION

The rising population of the Hispanic market in the United States has been well publicized, and consumer products companies from all corners have been devising special programs to gain the attention of this already lucrative and expanding consumer market.

The U.S. Hispanic demographic shot up from 9 percent of the population in 1990 to 13 percent in 2000, according to U.S. Census data. By 2050, analysts predict the Hispanic population will represent 24 percent of the U.S. population. Avon recognized the blossoming Hispanic demographic in the United States early. By 1988, it was already testing marketing programs to target Hispanic consumers, including the company's first Spanish-language television commercial.

Avon's selling model has always worked well in the social Hispanic culture where there is an admiration for the extended family. The company has been putting more efforts behind meeting the needs and wants of this burgeoning demographic.

In 2002, Avon expanded its attention to the Latina market with the introduction of *Eres Tu,* a brochure speaking directly to Latin women—not just in the Spanish language, but with products specially selected to appeal to their unique beauty needs and lifestyle. Avon already offered a Spanish language version of its core brochure.

To jump start the *Eres Tu* effort, Avon introduced Untamed for her and Iron for him, scents intended to reflect preferences in the market. Latina women use more fragrance overall than the general population, so Avon has been churning out more scents to please these special interest customers.

In addition to devising tactics to target niche and developing populations within the United States, Avon has been creating specialized programs to build its appeal in international markets.

For starters, the company publishes its brochure in as many as 40 languages, says Robert Toth, Avon's executive vice president of international. Products are developed to take regional needs into account and they are priced to fall in line with market and economical conditions of the country.

To really make Avon a snug fit with any given culture, the company hires and trains local talent to run the businesses. "Our experience is not to smother them in expatriates," says Toth. "We will not have more than one expatriate per country."

It's a strategy that has paid off, and international sales—and the roster of independent representatives—now exceed those in Avon's own home country of America by a healthy and ever-growing margin.

CHAPTER 8

SPEAK IN EVERY LANGUAGE

Few exemplify Avon's international strategy better than 57-year-old Agustina Alvarez Diaz. Born in Morelos, Mexico, she has been selling Avon products for some 32 years. Now separated from her husband, Alvarez Diaz is the sole earner for her household and managed to raise two children over the years thanks to her Avon earnings. The company, she says, has changed her life. "Avon has allowed me to grow professionally and to develop myself as a person," she shares.

Before starting with Avon at the suggestion of a friend, Alvarez Diaz worked briefly in a bakery and then as a nanny. She looks back fondly on that time of her life, adding that watching the children was a "beautiful experience." But it is Avon that offered her what she classifies as her "first job opportunity." Alvarez Diaz is a top salesperson in her zone of 1,200 representatives and has won numerous prizes over the years including two refrigerators, televisions, crockery, and grocery coupons worth 55,000 pesos, or about $5,000. While she still delivers many orders on foot in her neighborhood, her 22-year-old son now drives her by car or motorcycle to visit more distant customers.

This year Alvarez Diaz hopes to sell $86,800 worth of products, which would qualify her to win 100,000 pesos, or about $9,000.

BRANCHING OUT

Latin America is one of the first regions Avon entered when it began pushing outside of the United States and Canada in 1954. It started operations in Puerto Rico on April 28 of that year, and added Venezuela exactly four months later. Even early on, Latin America proved to be a receptive market.

"The results thus far in these countries have been extremely encouraging—sufficiently so to justify the serious consideration now being given to extending the Avon operation into certain other Latin American countries," the company wrote at the time.

Global expansion continued steadily from there with a move into Cuba in 1955, although the country's communist government stepped in during 1961 and halted Avon's operations, as it did with many foreign businesses at the time.

In 1958, Mexico was brought into the fold and has become one of Avon's largest international markets. Latin America was followed by Brazil, the United Kingdom, Belgium, Australia, and West Germany.

Like any fledgling operation, there were special issues to work out. In 1959, Avon noted that new operations in "West Germany, Brazil, and England were costly," and the international division posted a loss for the year. Those countries, however, proved worth holding onto. Today Brazil and England, like Mexico, are among Avon's healthiest markets.

After a handful of losses in the early days, Avon's international business gradually strengthened. By 1963, global operations were growing nicely and contributing smartly to the company's profitability. In 1965, Hays Clark was named Avon's first president of international operations. The company declared, "We are convinced that the foreign area offers unlimited opportunities for Avon." That year international sales grew 46 percent, to $69.8 million, with an earnings increase of 137 percent, to $8 million.

Encouraged by these results, Avon soon after rolled into Spain, Italy, Ireland, Japan, France, Argentina, Sweden, The Netherlands, Belgium, Hong Kong, Paraguay, Malaysia, Chile, New Zealand, Thailand, the Ivory Coast, and the Philippines.

James Preston, former Avon chairman and CEO, credits Clark, "for opening up a lot of early markets for Avon." Looking back,

Preston says, some of those early investments have paid off grandly. "We paid $7.8 million for manufacturing and [to buy] a direct-marketing company to break into the Philippines," he says. "Now it [the Philippines market] kicks off $40 million in profits every year."

In 1979, Avon's international sales exceeded $1 billion for the first time and inched closer and closer to matching sales in the United States, perennially Avon's largest market. Meanwhile, Avon continued to spread. By 1980, El Salvador, Uruguay, Senegal, and Liberia were added to the mix. Those countries were followed by Honduras, Saudi Arabia, Peru, Portugal, Taiwan, and Nigeria.

The company learned early on that, "in the foreign as well as the domestic area, success depends to a large degree upon Avon's ability to offer the consumer superior products at reasonable prices."

Over the decade of the 1980s, international sales continued to creep up, but had not yet matched the United States, which was moving forward on a parallel growth course of its own. Nevertheless, more markets were added, including Indonesia and, in connection with a joint venture with the Guangzhou Cosmetics Factory, China came online in 1990. That was a risky time to enter China. It came on the heels of the Tianamen Square massacre in June of 1989, and many U.S. investors were holding off while watching for improvements in human rights conditions.

At the time, Preston said he considered the views of those opposing new American investment in China before approving the venture. "I decided that this was a commercial endeavor—not a political endeavor," Preston said. "The venture will not benefit the government of China; it will benefit the women of China and Avon's shareholders."

By 1990, the scale had begun to tip and sales internationally pushed past those in the United States—ringing in at $1.9 billion and representing 55 percent of Avon's $3.5 billion tally for the year. Avon has kept accumulating overseas markets ever since.

SPEAKING TO ALL WOMEN

Mexico's Alvarez Diaz sounds very much like her fellow successful representatives in the United States when speaking of her experience with Avon. "I would recommend never letting a day go by without working to get more customers," she advises. "The key is not to lose hope or faith, and to keep giving out brochures in order to increase sales."

Her colleague, Hortensia Orozco Romero, a representative for seven years, is encouraged by Avon's nurturing culture and philanthropic efforts. The 46-year-old Orozco Romero was diagnosed with uterine cancer and was able to transcend her depression through the support of her Avon friends. "I was able to continue selling and move on," she says. "I had the opportunity to live despite suffering this disease."

In developing countries such as Mexico, Avon's sales model remains closer to its origins. Women still go door to door to hunt for new customers. Alvarez Diaz, like many enterprising women in the United States, has also engaged other women to work for her as "helpers." These representatives help her pass out brochures to family members at their places of work. (As noted in Chapter 5, Avon hopes to replace these individual systems as the Sales Leadership program is eventually rolled out worldwide.)

Says Orozco Romero, "I always keep a positive attitude at each visit and I win people's trust in order to gain more customers. I show them the catalogues and the advantages of using Avon."

Avon has been insistent that its message of beauty, earnings, independence, and empowerment be a multi-tiered and flexible platform that women around the world can embrace—and one that translates across cultural divides.

Brenda Cardy, of Milton Keynes, England, has been selling Avon for more than 30 years. Today the 67-year-old sells to some 300 customers. She has consistently been a highly ranked sales person in her district and reaped the benefits. "The company rewards top sellers with summer holidays and I went to Cyprus, Madeira, and Tenerife," says Cardy. "I was treated like a queen, like a film star."

Cardy says she has never missed a customer order. When an Avon lady first came knocking on her door in 1971, she was a young housewife and in the process of washing the floor. "She [the Avon representative] was a vision of loveliness and so glamorous," Cardy recounts. "She wore a big Astrakhan coat, tightly belted, with long boots and a big Cassock-style hat that came down over her eyes. Avon was to me something impossibly glamorous and rare. I was completely bowled over that she had picked me to represent the company."

While the selling of beauty products is a relatively genteel act for the most part, there have been some rugged stories associated with Avon ladies around the world. "In Iceland, Avon ladies traverse huge icy wastes with their products on their backs, and after the Turkish earthquake in 1991, one woman single-handedly rebuilt her family's fortunes by sending off for her first package of Avon products on credit and building up a thriving business selling lipsticks from tent to tent," according to a report in the *Observer* magazine.

In Brazil, women paddle canoes through the piranha-infested waters of the Amazon River to find customers who only make it into town about twice a year. Although Avon was not in favor of the project, there was once a plan to make a movie about them that would have starred Bette Midler, Goldie Hawn, and Diane Keaton. Though these plans fell apart, the true-life version plays on.

WHATEVER IT TAKES

Brazilian representatives working in areas where homes are shanties on stilts tell stories of customers who want to barter for lipstick. "Women want to give me chickens, manioc flour—but what am I going to do with a chicken?" said one 52-year-old representative in the Amazon River Basin. In areas where there are no doorbells to ring, women clap their hands and shout out their arrival to customers from their boats.

A few years ago, Setta Rodriguez of Pantel, Brazil, was one of six Avon ladies in her town of 3,000—a village so small it only had a total of 10 cars. "Even hard-to-reach people with scant incomes can still become willing customers," says Rodriguez. "They don't have enough money to go to the city to buy things. It's hard. They only go to the city once every six months. And, so here I am." Rodriguez says she is willing to negotiate and barter for goods. Once she exchanged a dozen eggs for a roll-on deodorant and 20 pounds of flour for a cologne.

In 2003, Avon conducted a global study of women focusing on topics such as appearance, self-esteem, and aging. Through the responses of the 21,000 women polled in 24 countries, the survey uncovered many common threads. "Regardless of where you live or what your age, the majority of women worldwide report that how they look is important to defining who they are," said Debbie Esser, Avon's vice president global marketing research.

Avon found that 85 percent of the women polled use fragrance. Most said they want a scent that makes them "feel more confident, happier, or more feminine." Worldwide, women owned, on average, four scents and wore two on a regular basis. An astounding 75 percent of the respondents said they viewed beauty products as a "necessity, not a luxury."

H. Lawrence Clark (the son of Hays Clark, Avon's first president of international) remembers conversations with his father, who is now in ill health, about Avon's impact in other parts of the world.

"I think he was very pleased," says Clark, a great-grandson of founder David McConnell. "He was in international for years and would talk about other parts of the world where they were taking on this direct selling philosophy and empowering women. He would talk about how the different cultures, whether it was Japan or [Europe], would embrace that marketing strategy."

The younger Clark also has recollections of conversations between his father and his grandfather, W. Van Alan Clark, who worked as a chemist at Avon and retired from its board in 1961.

From a business standpoint, recalls Clark, "My grandfather would say that no matter whether there was a recession or war or whatever, women are always going to want to look their best. He would say that the cosmetics industry is going to come out alright, no matter what was going on in the world."

His omniscient grandfather wasn't far off. The beauty industry has been lauded by investors for its ability to remain strong during periods of financial and cultural turmoil. Indeed, it has earned a well-deserved reputation as a recession-proof business. The theory is that in tough economic times, families may forego big-ticket items like a new car or beach vacation. But women will always find enough loose change for the small indulgence of a lipstick or eye shadow.

A GLOBAL FUTURE

Leveraging the universal appeal of beauty products, Avon has begun to bank on its ability to take the Avon model into new markets, while more fully developing existing ones around the globe in order to build its business. Since first surpassing the United States in 1990, foreign sales have continued to gain ground. By 2000, international businesses accounted for about 66 percent of Avon's $5.63 billion in sales. At present, international accounts for almost 70 percent of Avon's $7.7 billion annual sales and a similar percentage of overall profits. Avon now operates in 143 markets in some 50 countries with 4.9 million representatives worldwide (of those, 650,000 are in the United States).

The United States is a mature market for Avon, particularly since competition for beauty products has become fierce. It is therefore challenging for Avon to significantly expand its business on its home turf by securing more market share. In the fall of 2004, the company posted its first U.S. sales decline in five years due, in part, to a decline in the sales of toys, gifts, and color cosmetics. A relaunch of the Avon color line is expected to pick that back up in 2005 and beyond.

Still, Avon's escalating sales outside the United States fully support the notion that international is where the company's potential expansion lies. Some of Avon's most prized developing markets at present include Central-Eastern Europe, where sales reached $1 billion a full year ahead of schedule. Within that region, sales in Russia have been skyrocketing and the market there is on its way to becoming a $400 million business. The company's sales there have climbed quickly from just $22 million in 1999.

Avon entered Russia in 1991 and has just completed construction on a new $40 million manufacturing plant to support the region. The 250,000-square-foot facility is said to have the capacity to produce 185 million units of cosmetics, creams, lotions, deodorants, and fragrances per year. The market potential in Russia is enticing. According to the Perfumery and Cosmetics Association of Russia, the Russian perfumery and cosmetics market in the country reached $3.5 billion in 2000. A projection by Euromonitor International, another data firm, is even more compelling. It predicts the Russian cosmetics and toiletries market could grow to between $15 billion and $18 billion annually within 20 years.

China, blanketed with some 6,000 Avon boutiques because door-to-door selling is currently illegal, now delivers sales of more than $200 million annually. This retail operation is being used to lay the groundwork and build Avon's brand message, pending the return of direct selling to China. After a several year ban, the government is expected to permit door-to-door companies again in 2005. China, boasting a population of 1.2 billion, is a behemoth that could eventually produce sales of $1 billion for Avon.

Then, there is Turkey, another developing market for Avon that is currently yielding sales of nearly $100 million, a 50 percent increase over the previous year. Turkey is not only a jewel in itself, but more importantly is eyed as Avon's golden gateway to the Middle East.

To keep sales rolling in its robust markets, Avon has allocated an additional $30 million toward advertising and other strategic marketing initiatives. This money is being used to sustain growth in Russia, China, Brazil, and the United Kingdom.

DIVIDING THE GLOBE

Over the years, Avon has reconfigured its organizational structure and currently divides its markets into four groups:

1. *North America* includes the United States, Canada, and Puerto Rico.
2. *Latin America* includes Mexico, plus Central and South America.
3. *Europe, Middle East, and Africa* contains European countries along with Turkey, South Africa, and the Middle East.
4. *Asia Pacific* includes Asian countries, as well as the Philippines and New Zealand.

North America is Avon's soft spot for the moment. Sales in that region have been dipping of late, although a projected falloff in earnings here will be more than compensated for by robust returns in

Avon's other three international units, according to the company. Until 2004, Avon's sales in North America had been on a steady climb, with an increase of 5 percent in 2000, 6 percent in 2001, 6 percent in 2002, and 3 percent in 2003. The United States represents about 90 percent of all sales in Avon's North America division. Asia Pacific, meantime, had sales of $1 billion in it most recent full year, with volume continuing to climb at a rate of 15 percent annually.

The company recently reorganized its field operations in Malaysia and has seen an upswing in sales in the Philippines after transitioning to an increased number of sales campaigns every year. That region alone contains some 13 different countries. Avon entered Vietnam in April 2004 where the cosmetics market has just come alive after being ignored by the industry. Vietnamese women, who generally have little disposable income, previously bought inexpensive cosmetics brought in from China. With major brands scarce, Korean companies made the first inroads in Vietnam and have since been followed by others including Avon and Oriflame, a Swedish direct-selling beauty firm. Vietnam has a population of 80 million and Avon expects to have 10,000 representatives there soon.

"So far, brand loyalty in Vietnam is still not very developed," says Sylvia Mu, research manager in the Singapore office of Euromonitor. "That gives international companies opportunities to build their brand."

For Avon this means winning over the cosmetics business of Vietnamese women, and showing why its products are better than Oriflame's or anybody else's. At this point, it really could be anybody's game.

Throughout the Asia Pacific region, Avon says it has "aggressive" expansion plans that will include bolstering market share in existing regions, while continually evaluating new markets to enter.

Latin America is a powerhouse region for the company. In its most recent full year, Avon posted net sales close to $1.9 billion there. Sales have been growing at the rate of 13 percent annually with an operating margin of 24 percent, the highest of Avon's four regions.

Mexico, with sales of close to $700 million, and Brazil, with sales of nearly $500 million, are Avon's second and third largest individual markets. In Brazil, Avon now has a million representatives. There are more Avon ladies in Brazil than the total number of men and women in that country's army and navy.

The Avon direct-selling model is said to work well in both a strong and weak economy, which is particularly valuable in markets such as Brazil, where the economy's strength has shown wide fluctuations. "Brazil's crises have drawn more and more women to direct selling to supplement their income," says Joao Carlos Basilio, president of a Brazilian cosmetics industry association. "That has created a market."

Adds Saulo Nunes, Avon's vice president for sales in Brazil, "If the economy is strong, we sell because consumers are inclined to buy. When the economy is weak, sales remain brisk because we attract more representatives to get consumers to buy."

The brand claims a dominant share in all of the countries that make up Avon's Latin America business, according to company executives. "In beauty overall, including fragrance and skin care, it ranges from 20 [percent] to mid-40 [percent] market share throughout Latin America," says Susan Kropf, Avon's president and chief operating officer.

Kropf says she is pleased to see that Avon is retaining a stronghold in Mexico, where there has recently been an infiltration of "big box" or large format discount-type stores like Wal-Mart. Despite this, direct selling has gained share in the beauty market, according to Kropf. "Particularly in cultures that are very social and very family oriented, you really can't keep up with [demand for cosmetics products] with peg boards and blister packs."

Europe is blossoming for Avon. As noted earlier, the Eastern-Central Europe region posted sales of $1 billion in 2004, giving healthy padding for the division. In less than four years, Avon's sales in all of Europe have more than doubled.

Andrea Jung, Avon's chairman and CEO, says Europe is a "Latin America in the making for us," and China, because of its vastness, "is not a market, but a multiple market. There are so many provinces to tap into." Jung, who speaks fluent Mandarin Chinese, has visited the country to help pave the way for Avon's expansion.

GRASSROOTS MODEL

Avon has found its grassroots door-to-door business model to be particularly amenable for breaking into underdeveloped markets. It can quickly go in and set up shop in areas where traditional brands find difficulty because retail enterprises are so loosely established. With little infrastructure necessary, Avon has entered such regions as Poland in 1992 and Vietnam in 2004 with relative ease. It has devised a strategic system for analyzing what markets to go in to by using metrics such as the gross domestic product (GDP) growth rate, inflation, and literacy rates in women ages 15 to 59.

Once it settles on a new market, "because of our model and because of the low fixed investment required, we can establish a profitable business in a very short period of time," declares Robert Toth, executive vice president of international for Avon. "We can get profitable in a new country within year two of operation, which is really fast. Usually there is an investment period of three to five years."

Avon, he says, has a "lot of benchmarks" that it uses to project growth rates for the top and bottom line. If a new market isn't immediately performing as anticipated, says Toth, "we would go in and make the necessary model changes." If the company doesn't see growth happening within five years, it would possibly exit. But that hasn't happened lately. "There haven't been any markets where it just hasn't worked," Toth insists. While Avon already has a large global footprint, company officials believe it is only the beginning. "There is an awful lot of white space," he says.

Looking ahead, some of those areas Avon may want to fill in include countries in northern Africa—such as Egypt and Algeria—and throughout Central Asia, including Karakhstan, Uzbekistan, and other parts of the Middle East. As Jung told analysts at a meeting in late 2004, "It is still the early days in terms of what this company has in it."

When it opened in the Ukraine, some 14,000 women showed up to attend Avon's informational open meeting. India, where Avon has already launched operations, also presents "a big opportunity," says Jung. "You have to believe that in emerging markets there will be a sea change of women's readiness to be independent in the next 10 years," she says. "Avon can play a big role in helping them." As a Fortune 500 company, Jung adds, "we have a unique way, beyond government or other supported initiatives, to help women do that."

ENTERING A NEW MARKET

Before Toth was named executive vice president of international in January 2004, he lived in Poland (from 1993 to 1997), starting up Avon's business there. Avon was not well known in Poland when Toth first began strategizing how to bring the brand and business into that country. Poland became a foothold that Avon has since leveraged to expand into Central and Eastern European markets. "I am very proud of the franchise we have built in a short period of time," Toth says.

Toth amazes over how the opportunity Avon offered through the sales of its products had such a strong impact, even beyond the earning potential. "I found even more powerful forces at work, [notably] that this was helping women feel better about themselves in small ways, including the self-esteem of learning new skills in terms of selling products and training for building a business," says Toth. "It had a cascading effect on their families, their work, and into the community and society that they lived in."

Toth says that when Avon entered Poland, the country's culture was primed for a system like Avon's. Under communism, quality consumer goods were hard to find and women, he explains, developed their own networks to find good products where they could—and then would—tell each other about them.

"We naturally tapped into that natural network that existed back then between women," says Toth. At that time, he notes that Poland was less economically developed and Warsaw was vastly different. "Today, it looks like a western European capital."

Once Avon decides to enter a market and go forward with the investment, the first thing it does is borrow the blueprint for its existing business model for that region. For instance, when it entered Vietnam, it applied the plan used for Asia Pacific countries and tailored it to the idiosyncrasies of that specific region.

A market entry team is appointed with company representatives from sales, marketing, the supply chain, and any other disciplines necessary. That team works in conjunction with a designated country manager who develops the strategy and business plan. As previously mentioned, the country manager then hires local residents and trains them.

"We really have been committed and pride ourselves to develop local talent," says Toth. "Although we leverage global brands, we sell our products on the ground." The point is for Avon to fit into the local framework.

From there, to build awareness of the presence of Avon, the company holds something called an "Open Day" at locations around the country. This is a public relations event where women are invited to come and learn about the Avon opportunity.

Avon does some advertising, but only on a limited basis. At the moment of entry, the marketing effort is not "advertising heavy," Toth notes. The most important goal at the start is to build a representative network. "It is really through recommendations and word of mouth that we build our channel."

Avon differs from other direct-selling competitors that come to these countries and heavily advertise at the outset. "When Oriflame enters, they will heavily advertise to build brand awareness," observes Toth, who proudly claims, "We have been more successful than Oriflame."

It is after the representative count gets to the point where the ratio is at least one per 1,000 population (or 40,000 in a market of 40 million) that Avon will institute a standard advertising plan. "We really want to spend these dollars wisely. We want to make sure that we cover the country, and that there is a rep near the potential customer," Toth says. (By comparison, in the United States, where Avon currently has 650,000 representatives and a population of roughly 290 million, the representative count per 1,000 is about 2.2.)

THE PAST

As recently as 10 years ago, Avon's international business could best be viewed as a loose confederation of individual local operations.

Each country had a business plan and sales goals to attain. If these goals were met, the country's representatives were generally left alone to continue on in their own way.

"The joke used to be that, if you wanted to find the most creative [market], look the most miles away from the corporate office in New York," chuckles Kropf. There was a general feeling by the leaders of the local markets around the world that "I know better than them [in New York]. So I will keep my head down and send my money."

In the late 1990s, management started to assess how things were operating and suddenly became conscious that "this was not just about a holding company." Avon had a greater mission than simply meeting its numbers. It was decided that Avon would evolve from being a company of many local markets to a world-class unified enterprise.

"We were enthusiastic," says Kropf. "but when I look back at some of the presentations I made to our management team on the subject in the late 1990s, we were so naïve about how you could change behaviors and change thinking."

For years, there were dozens of local general managers running their own businesses, says Kropf "Then suddenly we said, 'We are here for you.'" It is a "gigantic change. You can't just make it in one step," says Kropf. "I didn't know that then, but I know that now."

"We have had a big geographic footprint for quite some time now," Kropf assesses. "But we weren't really global in terms of leveraging our global infrastructure and leveraging the opportunities."

Avon initially began the process of getting to this point by clustering its international businesses. It then further streamlined through regionalization. While there will always be market differences, eventually Avon wants its entire global organization to beat with one healthy pulse. In fact, Toth's promotion in early 2004 to the newly created position of executive vice president of international was another move to strengthen this integration program. In this post, the 25-year Avon veteran is responsible for overseeing the Latin America region, in addition to his previous responsibilities for Avon's markets in Europe, Asia, the Middle East, and Africa. At the same time, John Owen, who joined Avon in 1980, was appointed senior vice president of Europe, the Middle East, and Africa, reporting to Toth.

Previously, the company had not been taking advantage of the integration opportunities available to an organization with the scale and a global scope as large as Avon's, says Kropf. Now that it has embarked on that mission, she maintains. "This is a big, big, huge, huge change."

CENTERS OF EXCELLENCE

To help develop regions around the world, Avon has begun to create what it calls "Centers of Excellence." These centers serve as the primary source for marketing and other administrative support for a given region. For instance, in Warsaw, Poland, a center serves the needs of 17 countries in Central and Eastern Europe. It is there that brochures are developed for all of those markets. The brochures differ from country to country because of the language differences and varying product prices.

William Susetka, Avon's senior vice president of marketing, explains that a skin care product from the Anew line carries premium pricing compared to a standard mass market brand wherever it is sold, yet remains a value when compared to what's sold in department stores. Still, though that same image and positioning strategy is applied globally, the actual price will vary due to local market conditions. What might be priced for $30 in the United States may carry a $15 price tag in Brazil, for example. "The strategy is going to be the same, but depending on local competition, the price will [vary]," says Susetka.

The content of each brochure can differ anywhere from 10 percent to 20 percent, primarily due to the many gift categories outside of beauty and the handful of products unique to that market. "Each culture has different gift giving occasions," Toth points out.

Robert Briddon, group vice president of marketing for North America, previously oversaw operations in the United Kingdom. He remarks that cultural sensitivities vary from country to country. That can impact, for instance, what goes on a brochure cover or what special items might be carried. "What I struggle with in the U.S. brochure, having come from Europe, is how provocative and sensual, or how much flesh can I show," he says. "I'm often told, 'Bob, you are going too far,'" especially since residents of the United Kingdom are more tolerant of sexually suggestive images.

One time, Briddon bucked his more conservative U.S. team and opted to put thong underwear for women in the brochure. The item sold six times more than projected. "If I had listened to my research or to what my representatives were saying, I never would have done a thong in the brochure," he notes.

Rather than operating a duplicating marketing center in each country, having a central source has freed up financial resources that are now being applied to buy more advertising and invest in other areas. "That has fueled our growth," says Toth.

For a company that produces more than 100 different versions of its brochure, in nearly as many languages, centralizing operations appears wise.

SUPPLY CHAIN

Centralizing its operations applies to the supply chain functions as well. "In the old world we would have done everything individually. We are now moving cross border and becoming cross functional," says Toth.

Already the company has established a regional supply chain and marketing operation for Europe. It is now moving to mimic those models, first in Latin America, and then in its Asia Pacific region.

The supply chain process can be broken down into four basic functions: planning (estimating demand), sourcing, manufacturing, and delivery (distribution). Essentially, Avon is moving from a country-by-country system to a regionalized system. For instance, Avon had about eight manufacturing plants in Europe 10 years ago. Today, it has whittled down those sites into three. "We leverage across the region and benefit from those economies of scale," Toth says. Manufacturing, notes Toth, "is highly complex. Each product [package] has to be in its own language."

In the sourcing of ingredients, the company has scaled back by well over 50 percent to under 100 individual suppliers, says Toth. By using fewer suppliers, Avon gives its existing business partners more volume. In return, Avon gets a better price.

As part of this effort, Avon now requires its suppliers to also run a globally diversified business. "That has been a challenge for some of them," says Kropf. But she points out that the way global enterprises like Avon operate is changing. "I know that we are not the only company that is asking for that kind of thing."

CHAPTER 9

EMBRACE TECHNOLOGY

If it weren't for technology, Avon's global expansion plans would be difficult, at best, to realize.

While fragranced lotions, skin softening creams, lipsticks, and nail polishes in a rainbow of matching colors are the face of the company that everyone knows, pulling the strings behind this visible beauty business is a brainy core that keeps the production lines humming and delivery trucks moving to the right homes with the correct orders. It is in an unseen control center and technology hub that Avon conceptualizes the mechanics behind its Internet activities, while forecasting the sales of every single product in each country market using algorithms and trend statistics.

In the past few years, the advent of the Internet and the introduction of increasingly sophisticated computer software programs has impacted Avon's day-to-day business greatly. Taking advantage of technological innovations to improve its backroom functions has become just as important to the company as coming up with sophisticated marketing programs and product breakthroughs.

Avon's operation is massive and far-flung. It is also incredibly complex. Many of the concepts that keep its levers moving in perfect synchronization emanate from departments overseen by Harriet Edelman, the company's chief information officer and senior vice president of business transformation.

151

Edelman, a 25-year Avon veteran, brings a depth of vision to the job. But she's not a techie and hasn't written a single line of code in her professional capacity. Before being anointed to this extremely important, but not headline-grabbing post, Edelman was transferred across numerous departments throughout the company. Starting out in marketing, she moved through customer service, supply chain operations, and ran the field sales organization in the Northeast division of the United States. Five years ago, she moved into information technology. Several years ago, she also did a six-month turn as an Avon sales representative in order to fully understand the selling process.

"In the management of IT, I did have my own learning curve," she now says. "But as a big customer of IT [while holding other positions in the company], I was able to make the move over." Her past business-related roles have helped her, she says, "understand the threads between the different business processes to see where the different leverage points might be."

Today, Edelman oversees the running of the information technology solutions that maneuver Avon. She is also responsible for keeping the daily infrastructure on track. That includes necessary, but unglamorous, things like making sure the lighting throughout the corporate offices is right and stays turned on, and that assembly lines roll smoothly. In other words, she looks over all the individual bells and whistles that set the rhythm of the company around the world. Edelman has a bachelor's degree in music and an MBA in marketing. She displays one of the largest privately-held collections of Albee statuettes in the company in her office.

Avon's global information center is based in Rye, New York. In this and other offices around the world, Avon has 1,400 IT associates. It is in Rye that Avon runs all the data systems for North and South America, as well some business applications used by every one of its markets. There are also smaller data centers in Europe and in Asia. Global telecommunications is also based in Rye. These professionals support the company's 100 network locations, providing security and any other needs. Avon, notes Edelman matter-of-factly, "has a large number of IT professionals developing the business and keeping the systems running 24/7."

"People see us as a very one-on-one company," Edelman observes. "They don't necessarily associate us with a high level of science and technology. They just see us a very approachable and warm business."

SHIPPING ORDERS

As noted, each Avon representative's order is picked, packed, and delivered directly to their home. That, according to Edelman, translates into between 70 million and 80 million individual orders going out each year worldwide. To do this, not only does Avon organize its salesforce into about 1,400 districts in the United States, but this same type of blueprint is also applied around the world. This enables Avon to create computerized delivery systems and build its transportation network around clusters of sales representatives.

The mapping of those transportation systems is something that falls under Edelman's domain. From the time shipments leave a distribution center in the United States, it may take up to two days to arrive at the most remote location. In a country like Brazil, it could take up to six or seven days to reach a distant representative. Regardless of the location, orders are individualized and shipments are created one by one.

In the company's early days, orders were sent to headquarters on Chambers Street in Manhattan, where the sales and shipping department was found on the third floor until 1909. Then, like today, each order was processed the day it came in. Bins of products sent in from the company's manufacturing site in Suffern, New York, were arranged around the room in the same sequence that items appeared on the order forms. The orders were hand picked and packed in wooden boxes, and then sent to the homes of each sales associate by freight, because it was less expensive than parcel post. There was no elevator in the building and boxes were hoisted up on pulleys and passed through windows. "It was an inflexible rule that every order must be shipped the day it was received," Ann Meany, founder David McConnell's secretary wrote in her memoir.

Today, computer technology has turned it into an automated process. Each order is assigned an account number once received at the respective distribution center. A white sticker encoded with necessary information—such as the representative's address, billing information, and each item to be included in the order—is applied to a box. A computer program guides the box as it traverses the product areas that are set up throughout the center to collect items. Scanners read the sticker and the appropriate products are then dropped onto a conveyor belt from automatic dispensers. These products are then gathered together and ultimately released into the box.

For slower moving products, Avon has created nook-like areas where workers hand place items in boxes as they pass by. A red light comes on over a bin with the item that is to be included. This, too, is triggered by the information on that sticker.

This type of system is used throughout Avon's distribution centers in North and South America, Latin America, and Western and Eastern Europe, although China and a few other markets in Asia have a different type of operation, according to Edelman. That is because in a few places like China and Malaysia, where direct selling isn't viable, Avon operates retail boutiques instead.

FORECASTING SALES

To make sure every representative's order can be fulfilled when it comes in, Avon puts an incredible emphasis on forecasting sales. To get an accurate idea of the quantity each Avon distribution center will need for any product for a given brochure, Avon stores all relative historical sales data for all items, and combines this with trend information (for instance, the fact that green is a hot fashion color right now). The company then draws on this information to try and predict future purchase rates.

There are estimating departments stocked with statisticians who make predictions for every country, Edelman adds. "They are constantly looking at demand against price points," she says. "And when you have a new product they are looking for a reference product."

For example, if there is a new Naturals shower gel—a popular line that already has eight or nine scents—the company will probably be able to calculate the velocity at which the new one is likely to sell.

The formulas used to arrive at these estimates have become more complex as advanced computer programs to aid in the process have been developed. The sales projection takes into account not only price, but also the all-important question of where the item is going to be positioned in the brochure.

"An item on the front cover or in the first 10 pages is going to [sell] a lot differently than the same item positioned farther back. It all has to do with the nature of the way we shop, and how we read magazines," Edelman says. "It is the upfront [merchandise] that gets the promotion, the pricing, and a little bit of the sizzle in the stores."

The estimating department produces sales projections for each product for every campaign. "That is how we forecast the business," comments Edelman. Based on these calculations, supplies are sent to each of Avon's respective distribution centers around the world. As a vertically integrated company, Avon produces most of its products itself with the help of its suppliers. Notable exceptions are products such as apparel and jewelry, both of which the company now sources from outside vendors after closing its own jewelry plant in Puerto Rico.

Avon operates on a "just-in-time" inventory flow process. Shipments come in to distribution centers just as it is time to set up the floor to fill orders for the latest brochure. Distribution center floors in the United States turn over merchandise every two weeks. In other locations around the world, it varies depending on the respective campaign cycles. Avon calls this process "the changeover." Products come in for the new campaign no sooner than a week before and could arrive as late as the morning of the start of the opening of the new store.

There is an "ecosystem around the creation of the store," says Edelman. "The company is synchronized around this store turning."

An item may be sold in one campaign at full price and in the next at half price, which could boost sales four times. As a result, the number of picking stations for that item on the floor could be quadrupled.

Of course, forecasts are not always perfect. Within the first days of a campaign, it will become apparent whether real orders are matching what Avon expected. If not, the company is immediately prepared to tweak its system. It will add or subtract supplies as necessary and reconfigure the pattern of the floor with the correct amount of picking stations for that item. "The supply chain has the capability to be flexible once we do get our trends in to respond to something that has upside to it, or something that has disappointed us," says Edelman. "The supply chain is attuned to understand that our model has a lot of volatility in it, and has [built in] manufacturing or tooling to be able to respond to that."

The staff management on the floor is constantly reacting to information coming down about how demand is going to flow into their location that day. Compared to other companies, Edelman assesses, "I can't say that we have more demand volatility than anybody else, but we do have a more punishing standard on the fill rate."

Not long after Edelman was named to the CIO post in early 2000, the company formed a dedicated "demand-planning" organization that is completely separate from marketing. The goal was to improve forecasting accuracy by 30 percent so that sales would be predicted within 10 percent accuracy.

It is of utmost importance to Avon to try and fill every order completely, every time. The company's intensive forecasting mechanism is crucial, says Edelman, "Due to our commitment to our representative. Without the product, she doesn't get paid." Representatives will complain about "shorts," or items missing from an order, because it is an inconvenience that necessitates a second delivery to the customer when the item does come in.

Edelman points to physical retail stores like Target, where a customer may come in and find that an item on display yesterday has been sold out. "You are not [necessarily] going to know that because they have placed something else in that space," Edelman points out. "So the disappointment rate is managed more because you didn't know what you were missing," unless you saw it in an advertisement or had a coupon for it.

The Avon brochure, however, remains unchanged once printed, and that space can't be filled until the next catalog comes out—even if the item is no longer in stock. That's why the company is so committed to its store (the brochure). "It becomes a different act for us to manage if all of a sudden we don't have something that is right there on the page," says Edelman. "There is an impact to the representative's earnings, and there is an impact to the relationship of the representative to her customer because she is the one who has to deliver the news that their product is not in."

In Avon's Newark, Delaware, distribution center, new $1 million robotic cranes move boxes into 10-story high storage racks. A computer program dictates where the boxes are to go based on barcodes. The company recently spent $5 million at this location to upgrade its conveyor system. It is a fully automated operation, creating a paperless warehouse.

Throughout the process are random checkpoints where boxes are weighed to ensure they contain all of the requisite products. If an order is large and has more than one box, the system takes the boxes to different points to be filled, then automatically rejoins them later in the process.

LIFE BEFORE ARTIFICIAL INTELLIGENCE

Before Avon's distribution processes were so computer-controlled and systemized, people like Thomas M. Ford, a manager of purchasing contracts at the Suffern manufacturing facility until his retirement in 1980, shouldered some of that forecasting responsibility. Ford also had to make sure the assembly lines were moving properly. "I used to go out on the line and time items to monitor the productivity level," says Ford, who still lives in Suffern.

Ford remembers that, given Avon's emphasis on inventory control, it was a sin to be short on an item. "You had to have supplies in, but don't be over supplied," he shares. "We had to try to run a close ship." Ford had tight relationships with Avon suppliers and knew he must be in a position to call suppliers when goods were needed immediately and Avon was running short. Because the company is bigger than its competitors, Ford says suppliers responded quickly to Avon's calls for help. Fortunately, he adds, "The company is much more sophisticated now than it was then."

One Christmas season, he recalls, "Sales were so great and the law wouldn't allow for more overtime, so managers went to work on the [production] line." It wasn't felt to be a hardship. Indeed, says Ford, "We had an awful lot of fun."

Ford says he would travel to the company's headquarters in Manhattan once a month for inventory control meetings. Then, as now, there were 26 campaigns a year in the United States and we would "find out what would be on special and make adjustments for it." It was largely a manual process.

The product schedules were out six to eight weeks ahead of time. "Every now and then you'd get a lemon or a miscalculation and you'd be left with 50,000 finished goods," says Ford, looking back with good humor on the mishaps. "That didn't happen very often."

Still, even with the use of high-tech computer calculating programs, Avon can make a mistake every now and then. In 1999, while testing software provided by an outside vendor to improve forecasting accuracy, the process went awry for one featured item during the holiday season. Avon's supply of Pokemon watches fell far short of the number ordered. Pokemon was a hot character at the time and that trend information had not properly been taken into account. Avon has since tried several other programs as well, and sometimes even combines software to see how programs work in conjunction with each other.

These programs not only try to predict at what rate a product will sell at a certain price and position in the book, but also calculate the expected impact of an adjacent product. For example, Avon recently introduced a new lip gloss flavor to its Tasty Treats Lip Juice line—Mocha China. On the page next to it was an existing flavor called Chocolate Mint. The programs apply a formula that attempts to predict how much cannibalization of the Chocolate Mint flavor will take place because buyers will opt for Mocha China instead.

A PARALLEL SYSTEM

Avon's system to meet the demands of the campaign cycle has been in effect since the company's founding. Only in the past 10 years, though, has it been forced to add a new dimension to its already fast-turning fulfillment operation.

Avon has had to grapple with new customers that buy products through Avon.com, which handles a small number of sales transactions (representing less than two percent of its U.S. business), or by calling in to the company directly. Those orders are from customers who want their products immediately. These new channels forced Avon to create an off-cycle system to meet the needs of those wanting "something tomorrow," and not a few days later when the representative gets it, says Edelman. Avon now has the ability in a number of countries to ship something out sooner through home delivery services such as UPS. These expedited orders can be placed either directly by customers or through a sales representative. "That is our cognizance of the competitive nature of replenishment these days, and that people want it now," Edelman says. For decades before this, she says, "We had had this [one] cycle that runs very efficiently."

These more immediate orders do not "represent a huge piece of the business, but are large enough to build a new process for," Edelman adds. Along with the United States, the United Kingdom and Japan are leading markets for customers using this type of service.

DOING BUSINESS ONLINE

In 1996, Avon was credited as the first beauty company to go live with an e-commerce site. It was a small operation that evolved out of an information site created to raise awareness about Avon's breast cancer campaign a year earlier. Avon tapped an Internet consultant group to expand the scope of the site, turning it into an e-commerce operation that was primarily an online presentation of the brochure.

Despite its early lead in jumping into what trend reporters called the "new economy," it was a very small-scale operation. Along the way, Avon.com was reworked and relaunched in 2000. It is now a complex site with a selling platform, along with expansive sections presenting product news and company information. But when it came to incorporating the Internet for internal business purposes, Avon lagged behind many of its counterparts.

Dottie Heilbut, a leadership representative from southern Utah who has been selling Avon for 13 years, says, "I remember those little order books they used to give us, and that it would always take a while to fill out the bubbles on a purchase order. I look back and I think we had to wait quite a while for Avon, [to catch up with everyone else]."

Heilbut says the company is now up to speed. "They had to go through a lot to get us [representatives] online." Now, she and many of her colleagues around the world can do just about everything electronically.

While Edelman acknowledges that Avon wasn't the quickest to get its online programs going, it now operates both Avon.com, the company's business to consumer site, and YourAvon.com, a business-to-business site for its U.S. representatives.

It took a few years for Avon's Internet strategy to settle out. For a while, it operated three web sites—MyAvon.com, YourAvon.com, and Avon.com. It was a somewhat chaotic approach. A freshened version of all three sites was launched at the same time in the fall of 2000. MyAvon.com, developed as a company site for representatives, managers, and Avon employees has since been abandoned.

From 1997 to 2000, Avon went through three chief information officers, while investigating and pursuing a wide array of software programs. The company nearly had a "corporate nervous breakdown" in the process, Edelman acknowledged.

DEALING WITH FALSE RUMORS

While Avon was in the throes of figuring out its Internet strategy, there was industry speculation it was considering the idea of going full force into an Internet-based selling model. That would mean abolishing Avon's force of sales representatives. Consultants were brought in to evaluate a range of possibilities, so it was said. One thought purportedly supporting the move was that the company could save the average 40 percent commission sales representatives earned.

Like so many other beauty companies in the late 1990s, Avon was reviewing many options, including acquiring a women's content-oriented web site like ivillage, or even becoming a women-centric Internet service provider.

Had Avon gone forward with a direct-to-consumer selling strategy, cutting out the representative, it would have had to retool its entire distribution model. Plus, the old system of sending orders to representatives who broke them down further into bags for customers would become much more expensive.

Edelman shakes her head at the reminder of such reports and insists they were all false. "There has always been intrigue with our model. A lot of people haven't always understood it," she says. "Others were speculating about us. Would this become the evolutionary stage? But we were never there. We never said that [we would eliminate the sales reps]. Absolutely never."

GETTING IT RIGHT

Edelman says there was a lot of external cultural pressure regarding the Internet businesses. "There was so much hubris with it. If you weren't talking about it, you were so last century," says Edelman. "So for us and many companies that said we want to figure out how this aligns with our strategy and aligns with our channel before we spend a ton of money, it was an interesting time."

In the few short years since, things have changed rapidly. A tour guide at its Newark, Delaware, facility tells visitors that Avon is "making strides in moving from a paper company to an online company." In the past three years, the number of Avon representatives using the company's online ordering system in the United States has skyrocketed—from about 20 percent in 2001 to 70 percent at present. The two other methods by which representatives can place orders include the old 48-page forms that require the use of a number two pencil or black ballpoint pen, and the automated FastTalk system, a 24-hour telephone service.

Things have progressed more quickly than imagined. "Five years ago, we would have been happy to have 10 percent of our people faxing in their orders," says Angie Rossi, group vice president of U.S. sales and customer care. "Now we have almost 70 percent ordering online. And we continue to look to enhance our electronic capacity so more folks can order online." Rossi noted that 80 percent of new U.S. representatives order online. "Do we ever think we'll get to 100 percent? We'd love to see the day. But we don't want to exclude any representatives who aren't as computer savvy. So there will always be an opportunity for them to order by paper."

Since the handling of online orders is still relatively new, Avon's processes are still being developed. It has been steadily improving its methods. For starters, online orders are grouped in sets of 24, partially because in the distribution centers there are carts for 24 bins to correspond with each order. As recently as a few months ago, if one of the 24 orders had an error or problem, the entire bunch would be held up until that one issue was resolved. Avon has since found a way to streamline the process that enables it to remove the bad apple and keep the rest of the bunch moving through the system.

AVON.COM

The approach for Avon.com is the same now as it was a number of years ago, Edelman stresses. "We want it to be a business that is compatible and not competing with our representatives. That is very important."

If someone does have a sales representative, but just wants to buy a quick mascara and receive it the next day, the representative will get a reduced commission on that sale if placed directly by the customer online. "We are not trying to compete with her on that site," Edelman insists.

The hope is to increase overall sales and the company's exposure. "It has been very successful in building some brand recognition, moving some key brands like Anew, and dealing with the access issue," Edelman says. The company has also discovered that promotional techniques on the Web are different than on paper. "We've learned some things online that we can migrate back to the rest of our store." The web site, Edeleman notes, is also very beauty oriented. "So it is very image enhancing, versus the core store which is very diverse." Adds Edelman, "We have been able to boost sales of some of our key beauty brands, and at the same time be respectful of our core channel."

Internationally, the company currently operates sites in 40 to 45 markets offering one or more of the following functions: representative ordering, public relations for public brand exposure, and online sites for field management to convey information such as sales reports and sales performances to zone and division sales managers. These sites have all been based off a common Internet model. The novel approach has proven to be successful and very affordable for Avon.

Each country can customize its site in its own language and pick and choose the modules they desire. "If you went onto Argentina's site and then onto the U.K. or Taiwan site," says Edelman, "you would see the same look and feel. The same colors are there and the basic structure is the same. The language is different and content is managed locally. But it provides a common look and feel to the corporation." It is similar to the way the brochures are created around the world—using common art provided by the global marketing department.

Moving the Internet development in this direction had less to do with technology and more to do with having the multiple markets agree that having a common global brand image on the Web was a good thing. "They harmonized their requirements with each other and all signed on to a common core," Edelman says.

Getting representatives around the world online is a market-by-market initiative, the success of which will depend solely on the development of each individual region, Edelman acknowledges. "The country, the telecom infrastructure, the affordability of PCs, the bandwidth," all of these factors will somewhat dictate the pace at which Avon's Internet programs expand, she says. "Outside the United States, there are models that may never exactly be affordable in the remotest of towns. Representatives may go to a cyber café or a zone manager's hub and get the business done, so we will watch this as we go."

YOURAVON.COM

Through YourAvon.com, Avon representatives can place their orders online. This presents a tremendous savings opportunity for the company. It's estimated the cost of processing an online order is 30 cents, compared to $1.50 for the paper forms.

With Avon's system, representatives only have to use their numeric keyboard, not the letters, to order online. In addition to providing a means for representatives to order products, the YourAvon.com site provides information and is the portal for the Downline Manager and Beauty Advisor online training programs. It is through YourAvon.com that the company also sends representatives numerous information updates via e-mail with the Avon Enews newsletter.

The use of YourAvon.com is only beginning, as far as Edelman is concerned. "We have just started to scratch the surface in terms of how to transform the business between us and the representative," says Edelman. Other offerings on the site include "Webinars," which are training sessions on a range of topics such as information on the company's award programs and instructions on how to order online. The site also just added a "Selling Tools" page that provides information on topics from "fragrance wheels to ring-sizers" in one location.

Avon has recently launched a pilot program that will enable representatives to process product returns 100 percent online, Edelman emphasizes. "It dramatically cuts down the time it takes her to do it, and for the first time enables her to see where her package is on the way back to us. It provides accuracy and visibility to her and to us."

Representatives have complained that Avon's return process is cumbersome, more so lately because product identification numbers were being changed from brochure to brochure making it tougher to keep proper track. Further technology enhancements will presumably prevent such potential problems from occurring in the future.

EQUIPPING THE E-REPRESENTATIVE

Beyond offering representatives access to YourAvon.com and enabling them to submit orders online, Avon encourages them to become more Internet involved through its e-representative program. It costs $7.50 per campaign, or $195 a year, to join. Membership enables representatives to create their own personalized Web pages that are linked to the Avon.com site. There is an icon on the Avon.com homepage that connects customers to a registered e-representative in their area when clicked. E-representatives also receive additional benefits that general representatives do not, such as online brochures, which can be forwarded to customers.

When first launched in September of 2000, 16,000 representatives signed up for the program. The numbers have grown, but still represent only a small percentage of Avon's 650,000 U.S. sales representatives. The program enables reps to create and send customer invoices, make payments to Avon, and manage other aspects of the business online. Periodically, there are other special features, such as the use of e-cards in both English and Spanish that can be sent to customers with personalized messages. E-representatives also have access to Professional Motivations, an online program that presents inspirational messages and speeches by authors like Marcia Wieder, who talks on the topic of integrity, and Jim Rohn, who addresses confidence.

Dottie Heilbut, an e-representative in Utah, says she takes her laptop computer with her wherever she goes now and plays Avon's programs as recruiting tools for potential new representatives. Heilbut's mother, Pearl Heilbut, who was introduced in Chapter 5, was one of the first sales representatives to sign on to the Leadership program. Dottie Heilbut employs the computer extensively in her work with Avon.

"When I go to sign someone up, I take my laptop. It allows me to do more effective training," says 33-year-old Heilbut. "I can show a video of the *Rich and Famous of Avon*. I go to the part where my mother, my aunt, my brother, and I are featured. And I go through the basics of selling Avon really fast."

By using the computer and playing Avon's training programs that are available on DVD, says Heilbut, "I can go faster and give them more information faster." She says she always goes in with a pitch for the Leadership program. "I don't sign up anybody without signing them up for the Leadership program. I go in for the kill."

Heilbut says her family has become an Avon family. Her mother, 73-year-old Pearl, has run an Avon business for more than 20 years. Her aunt and two brothers are also Avon representatives. Another sister doesn't sell but sends potential customers and recruits her way.

Heilbut says her mother is in ill health and now she feels even more compelled to do well with her Avon business, which she recently resumed after slacking off for three years off. When her mother was recently hospitalized, says Heilbut, "All these Avon representatives and district managers called and came by. I wasn't living up to what she is.

"It just motivated me. It is no longer a need for the money. I want to let my mother know how she has influenced me," says Heilbut, who has upped her own goals to reach the next Leadership level and attain the sales needed to win the next Avon trip. Even though her mother recently underwent open heart surgery and was terrified by the prospect, just before being wheeled into the operating room, she couldn't help but try to recruit the two nurses who had just prepared her. Tells Heilbut, "She asked those girls if they wanted to make some extra money."

MARRYING HIGH TOUCH WITH HIGH TECH

Heilbut is a second-generation Avon representative and reflects the direction Avon's chief executive officer sees the company headed by perfectly melding personal relationships with business technology.

"The Avon representative Internet business is a significant underpinning to the transformation of the company," says Andrea Jung. "My vision is that we are going to marry high touch and high tech in a combination that is unique and that only Avon can do. We have the unique ability to marry the human relationship with the technology tools that can enhance that relationship, not disintermediate it or take away from it." Through the use of the Internet, Jung says, "representatives will know more about their customers, have greater access to the company, and their customers can e-mail an order, so you don't have to wait and call."

A GLOBAL SOFTWARE TOOL

While Avon wants to see representatives make better use of the Internet to build and track their businesses, the company wants to better monitor its own operations. Therefore, along with its efforts to globalize the product line, advertising, marketing functions, and supply chain, Avon wants to be able to track everything that is happening around the globe.

To do this, the company is installing an Enterprise Resource Planning program. It is part of the company's Business Transformation initiative that you'll learn more about in Chapter 12. This is a supply chain tool, developed by J.D. Edwards (now part of Oracle Systems), that will enable Avon to manage its business in an integrated manner, says Susan Kropf, president and chief operating officer. Essentially, the software will link Avon's facilities and provide immediate access to information inventory and sales data on a global basis. "If you are sitting in Indonesia, you can see how many caps we have of our new Today fragrance in the United States," Kropf illustrates.

Peer companies, such as Procter & Gamble and Gillette, already have implemented similar types of instruments in their operations. Through the use of this program, Avon expects to be able to illicit more savings from its system, better allocate resources, and have immediate information at its fingertips on how products are selling in different markets.

Before, if Kropf wanted to know how many jars of Anew Retroactive sold last month, the data would have to be gathered and compiled from each region. Once this system is in place, a click of a mouse should retrieve the answer in seconds. "This will provide Avon immediate access to top line and bottom line data," says Kropf. "This is going to be part of our next generation transformation. It is a big enabler."

The program is not inexpensive. It will cost Avon about $200 million when complete. Implementation of the program begins in 2005 in Europe because that is where Avon's global supply chain is most established and centralized. It should be fully adopted worldwide within three to four years. Over the long haul, it can affect Avon's decision making on manufacturing, suppliers, and everything else. For instance, it might be determined that Mexico is a low-cost supplier with high-quality labor, prompting Avon to center all of its lipstick manufacturing in that country, especially since lipsticks are small, light, and inexpensive to ship. Says Kropf, "There are just a lot of things you can do when you have access to this kind of information," including the development of more effective communications for your customers.

CHAPTER 10

CONNECT WITH YOUR CUSTOMERS

A woman wearing a sleeveless, narrow waist dress and long white gloves daintily presses the doorbell outside the front entrance of a suburban home. A rich two-tone chime responds. Ding dong. The door opens. She enters and pirouettes around the living room, her dress radiantly flowing.

In a rear area of the house, two women are seated at a table looking over a collection of beauty items. She moves toward them with her arms outstretched. In the background, a jingle plays, "Avon calling at your door, bringing cosmetics and much more." It is circa 1954. Little does Avon know, but this television commercial was about to launch what would become one of the most memorable advertising campaigns of all time. The "Ding Dong Avon Calling" series ran through 1967, making it one of the longest running advertising campaigns in television history.

For more than 50 years, Avon has been linked with the sound of a doorbell and its signature "Avon Calling" advertising slogan. Even though it hasn't used either of those symbols for nearly two decades, the association has remained one of the most deeply ingrained brand identities of the past century.

A succession of TV spots that ran through the 1970s carried on the famous ding dong sound and variations on the Avon Calling signature phrase, such as "Avon Is Christmas Calling Now." Some commercials, like one of Avon's first spots to target African American consumers, show an Avon representative walking down the street as the famous doorbell is heard. There is no door to open anywhere in sight. But by that time, there was no explanation needed.

The theme was also carried through in-print advertisements. As one magazine ad from the 1950s explains, "Avon Calling means selecting cosmetics and fragrances at home, with the help of your Avon Representative." Avon Calling was incorporated in dozens of different ways over many years. As a half-page display in a 1970 *Reader's Digest* aptly summarized, "It All Starts With the Doorbell."

The Avon Calling theme rang throughout Avon's international markets as well. Not long ago, an enthusiastic Avon lady in England suffered a mishap thanks to the legendary doorbell slogan. "I was trying to balance a large parcel of shampoo in the front basket [of my bicycle] when some of the young local boys began shouting 'Ding Dong, Avon Calling' at me, all in good faith, mind you," says 67-year-old Brenda Cardy of Milton Keynes, Britain's fastest growing city. "I turned round to wave at them and went straight into the curb."

Britain is one of Avon's most developed markets, with about seven Avon ladies per thousand population. In a recent independent survey, 96 percent of the public there immediately identified with Avon by the ding dong sound alone.

Despite this strong association, Avon corporate executives have been trying hard to distance the company from this dated symbolism of the doorbell. With fewer women home during the day, most Avon representatives do not wait for doors to open anymore. If they do visit homes, typically they simply leave a brochure behind.

The public does not appear nearly as ready to let go of the past. Newspaper and magazine headlines continue to incorporate novel twists with ding dong and Avon Calling. To wit, in just the past two years, headlines have appeared touting: "Real Life: Avon Calling," "Avon Is Calling Lots of New Reps," "Avon Calling: On Woman CEO," and the tad negative, "Ding Dong: Avon Stalling."

Doctors no longer make house calls and milkmen have gone by the way of the convenience store. Yet, there is still the possibility of having an Avon lady come by to chit chat about pleasant things like lipstick. People may just be hanging on to the comfort of that.

GETTING THE WORD OUT

Avon is unique among direct-selling beauty firms for its use of advertising in the United States. Because of the nature of the business model, most direct sellers don't advertise at all. Among its peer group of Mary Kay, BeautiControl, Nu Skin, and Amway, Avon is the only company that consistently advertises in print or broadcast media outlets.

Direct sellers typically view their sales force as their most potent vehicle to reach the consumer, and thus apply most of their promotional money toward incentive programs to inspire and motivate representatives. Additionally, some companies, like Amway, that operate a multilevel marketing payment structure stretching out for many levels, also need to allocate more funding toward commission payments.

While Avon does buy advertising, it spends far less than other mass market beauty brands such as Cover Girl and Maybelline, which are sold in retail stores. Instead, Avon allocates a good portion of its promotional budget toward representative incentive programs.

While Avon had always run advertisements in regional editions of magazines, it wasn't until 1936 that the company broadened its approach with its first national campaign in *Good Housekeeping*. At the time, Avon outlined four objectives it expected its advertising program to fulfill. The ads would serve to provide a nationwide calling card for all Avon representatives. The advertisements would act as a showcase for Avon products. They would be designed to promote the prestige of the Avon brand and Avon products. And, last, the advertisements would serve to create and maintain continuous consumer desire for Avon products and services.

The goals remain similar today.

BEYOND THE DOORBELL

It has always been of primary importance for Avon's advertising to highlight the advantages of the company's personal relationship selling model. In a 1972 print ad, the company wasn't above taking a poke at traditional retailers with: "To My Avon Lady, I'm Emily, not 'Who's Next.' It's a nice feeling."

Then in 1976, Avon struck upon what would become another memorable chord with consumers with a catchy jingle that ended, "With Avon, You Never Looked So Good." The ad was so successful in the United States, it was translated for international markets. The company also signed Sunny Griffin, a former supermodel and noted beauty expert, to advise on product development and appear in advertisements.

There have been periods when Avon ceased to advertise entirely, a luxury it can do without given that it is able to rely primarily on one-to-one communication between sales representatives and their customers.

At the end of the 1990s, a movement emerged among beauty companies to emphasize the connection between inner and outer beauty. Thinking evolved to where people realized that beauty was not a reflection of external appearance alone. Many companies got on the bandwagon, and that included both the prestige and mass-market brands. Women began demanding to see models and lifestyles that they could relate to.

Avon was a forerunner in endorsing the concept that beauty is more than skin deep when, in 1993, it introduced its "Women Are Beautiful" theme. Beyond simply selecting the right color lipstick, the campaign examined the lives and relationships of women. Soon after Avon began to turn the messages to itself. In 1996, the company came out with the "Just Another Avon Lady" series, inaugurated to update the public's perception of its sales representatives. That was followed in 1997 with "Dare to Change Your Mind About Avon," featuring portraits of real Avon users.

At the time, Andrea Jung, then president of global marketing, said the company began working on its image after consumer research found that nonusers "perceived the brand as old fashioned and dated." Jung said, "This is a deliberate plan to turn up the volume." The ads emphasized the company's money-back guarantee and were designed to get more nonusers to try Avon again.

By 1998, the company was tired of apologizing for what it felt had become a stale public perception of Avon. Gears shifted with "Claim Your Beauty" a campaign that once more forcefully embraced the individuality and diversity of women. The spots pictured women in a variety of situations—from sporting events to formal evening affairs.

In 1999, Jung led the creation of Avon's first global advertising campaign. The effort superceded the collection of individual local agencies previously used by Avon to develop unique ads for various markets around the world.

Out of that came the "Let's Talk" series that is still running. In its second year, Avon signed tennis pros Serena and Venus Williams to be a part of the campaign and to help introduce its Wellness collection. This was a major step for Avon, and a sign that Jung was serious about elevating the brand's image globally.

A GLOBAL SPOKESPERSON

With Avon's hunger to become a global powerhouse and not a patchwork collection of individual markets, it was ready to unify its image in the visage of one person who could project all that Avon is about.

In 2004, Avon upped its spending on advertising and took its image-burnishing program to a new level with the naming of Mexican-born actress Salma Hayek as the company's official global spokesperson.

"We were looking not just for a supermodel for the celebrity sake," says Jung. "For us the person had to have a deep, deep belief in the company's vision. Salma has her own personal commitment to women's issues and to the domestic violence cause [which Avon recently adopted as well]."

"She is truly a global face. She has vision and values and a true belief that beauty is not skin deep but really about encouragement," be it to become independent or to prevent domestic violence. Adds Jung, smiling, "You can't imagine the response from our Latin American markets."

Hayek first appeared on the cover of an Avon brochure in the fall of 2004 and is being used to promote the new fragrance trilogy

Today, Tomorrow, and Always. She is also helping to relaunch the Avon Color cosmetics collection. Hayek's contract is for two years, with the option for a third.

By signing Hayek, Avon joins a lineup of beauty companies that have been filling their stables with name brand actresses and celebrities. Chanel has Nicole Kidman; Revlon has Halle Berry, Susan Sarandon, and Julianne Moore. Cover Girl has Molly Sims and Queen Latifah. Estée Lauder's American Beauty has Ashley Judd; the Estée Lauder brand itself has Elizabeth Hurley. And that's just to name a few.

Most of Avon's advertising has focused on its products and the personal service provided by its representatives. But way before Sunny, Serena, and Salma, Avon was sprinkling some famous faces into its ads. Actresses Helen Hayes, Irene Dunne, and Claudette Colbert had all appeared in Avon advertisements.

Long before he was touting Mr. Coffee, baseball legend Joe DiMaggio was a promoter of Avon. A print advertisement from 1949 shows a portrait of DiMaggio wearing a blue suit superimposed over a scene at a baseball stadium on the upper half of the page. On the lower half is a smaller photograph of the slugger with Avon representative Dorothy Wills, the two looking over a selection of men's toiletries. The ad copy (supposedly a quote from DiMaggio) read: "On the road or at home, I'm an Avon fan!" Actor Jimmy Stewart was also pictured in a 1951 ad pouring over Avon's men's toiletries, while his wife was shown picking out cosmetics.

Additionally, Avon heralded successful women in a series of wartime advertisements in the 1940s. Ads extolled the contributions of anthropologist Margaret Mead, Martha Washington, and Dolly Madison, along with Nancy Hanks Lincoln, Abraham Lincoln's mother. A bit more recently, Cher stumped for Avon to promote her namesake fragrance, as did actor Billy Dee Williams and the fashion designer Louis Feraud.

A DISTINCT MODEL

Avon's business model is a departure from almost all of the companies with which it competes, notes William Susetka, senior vice president of marketing. In a classic consumer products company, like Procter & Gamble, all the focus is on building the brand. What the brand is, what it offers, and what it symbolizes has to be made clear to the consumer.

By contrast, in the direct-selling model, many times the business is just about the channel. It is not about building the brand and increasing outside awareness of the brand. As notes Neil Offen, president of the Direct Selling Association, some direct-selling companies operate more as buying clubs, whereby people sign on because they want to buy the products for themselves, rather then selling them to others. "Avon is a hybrid, and it is the best of both worlds," Susetka says.

Because of its unique structure, Avon has to act like a consumer products marketer as well as a retailer. While the company does engage in consumer research, "We don't do marketing research to the same level that other consumer products companies might," says Susetka. "We place a greater premium on product development to excite and delight [customers] every two weeks through our representatives."

Avon's mission, says Susetka, is to give a competitive advantage to its representatives by creating superior products and building brands. As previously noted, Avon has outlined a long-term brand building program, with products that customers will want to come back and buy repeatedly.

"We are a company that is about making dreams for women come true, and doing it through the essence of one of the great consumer brands of all time," says Susetka, who is clearly proud of the Avon name. Avon, he enthuses, is "an emotional brand and a community brand. We really do have a relationship and our own set of values. We want to be part of the community and we do develop pride in the Avon community." Susetka maintains that Avon's high quality products at good prices have been one of the company's greatest underpinnings throughout its 119-year history.

What makes a brand or company truly standout, Susetka adds, is if it didn't exist, there would be a void in the world. He cites pharmaceutical companies as examples. If a drug company making a critical medication were to go out of business, it would be devastating to the millions of patients who rely on it.

For very different reasons, he says, the same is true for Avon. "If there were no Avon, there would be a big void," says Susetka. "That's why I believe this model will live forever. There will always be a need for economic empowerment. There will always be someone to say, 'I need a second income. I need a career.'"

DESIGNING THE STORE

With Avon acting as both a product marketer and a retailer, the company develops products and creates advertising to entice consumers. It must then bring all the elements together in its "store," which is its catalog.

Just like any other sophisticated retail operation, the way the catalog is put together is part strategic calculation and part creative flair.

There is nothing casual about Avon's brochures. They are not haphazardly designed, and every inch of space is precious. What products get in, where they are placed, and how they are priced are matters hotly contested for each and every edition. Space allocations and placement in the brochure are carefully calculated and controlled.

Traditional retailers assess shopping habits and store traffic patterns. They know, for instance, that women tend to turn right when they enter a store. There are firms like ShopperTrak and Envirosell that have made businesses out of uncovering these interesting and essential facts. Avon takes the same pains to try and create just the right shopping atmosphere in its catalogs.

Robert Briddon, group vice president of marketing for North America, explains, "We look upon the brochure exactly the same way as a retailer. We put a lot of credibility to where things are."

As previously discussed, the front cover is used to draw consumers into the brochure, like a storefront window. Products that are expected to be popular, or fast movers, are placed in the front, middle, and back pages, since everyone naturally tends to go there. However, how this happens is the result of a complex process.

Within Avon, there are "category houses"—that is departments that work on skin care, color cosmetics, bath and body products, and so on. "The category houses will fight to get their product [in a prime spot], like the front cover," says Briddon. Everyone essentially lobbies for their product and presents the reasoning behind why their product should be the lead item, rather than being relegated to another section. It is all very tactical.

Space in Avon's brochure is so precious, the company had an internal battle a few years ago over whether or not it should take away selling space to create a table of contents page. Providing a contents page is the same as a retailer providing a directory for what is on Floor 1, Floor 2, and so on, Briddon points out.

"The debate is that you can sell off that page," he explains. People opposed to the idea thought it was a waste of real estate that would be better used to present products. But Briddon was behind it. "I overruled and said it helps get consumers through the store. It helps them navigate."

Avon has continued to freshen and modify the look of its brochure over the years, sometimes slightly changing the size and shape or going with a different typeface or page construction. The latest version, introduced in 2004, has shorter, wider pages and features color-coded tabs on the edges of pages to make finding sections easier.

Throughout the brochure, another goal is to "try to mix up the price points," says Briddon. Color cosmetics are usually placed at the front of the book. "It has the highest participation level, but it tends to be [dominated by] low ticket [items]," he explains. Following might be a page with a higher priced item, say a $22 Anew product, in an effort to trigger a larger order.

Avon will never present the entire Anew line in the first few pages of the book. Prices for this line range from $32 for Anew Clinical to $25 for Retroactive. If such relatively expensive items were too prominent, shoppers might be put off by what seems to be a catalog filled with pricey products. "A customer would get to page six or so and say 'I am outta here,'" says Briddon. "So we do mix the price points up so it doesn't appear expensive."

In a fall brochure that included holiday gifts, the opening item was priced at $24.99. On the next double-page spread were items for $19.99 and $9.99, followed by products selling for $29.99, $4.99, $5.99, and $9.99.

In another brochure, the first 10 product pages presented cosmetics ranging from $2.49 to $4.99, before advertising the Anew Luminosity Advanced Skin Brightener face cream, which was on sale for $14, down from $25. On the succeeding pages were other Anew face items for $14 to $32. Whatever the order of presentation, variety in terms of product and pricing are essential.

"Reps hate us to put a lipstick on the front cover," notes Briddon. "A lipstick at $4.50 is sufficiently high priced to be just that one purchase [a customer makes]. They worry that by having a lipstick only on the front cover, it could be dangerous and tend to bring about a lower average order for the customer."

The first 12 pages of the book are called *the platform*. These pages are a key part of the brochure. They must achieve a certain dollar value, which changes depending on the time of the year. Indeed, every section of the brochure has a sales target, including the center and back cover.

Avon also carefully counts the precise units it sells, "because that reflects customer transactions," says Briddon.

There are occasions when Avon will sacrifice selling space to devote a page or two to an image-building message. In campaign 20 in 2004, it devoted space to introducing Salma Hayek as the new face of Avon.

REACHING MULTIPLE CHANNELS

In the United States alone, Avon produces 26 core brochures a year. In addition, it publishes brochures for mark and *M: The Men's Catalog*. Avon has seven or eight editions of the core brochure in play at any given time. From start to finish, each brochure's development cycle is 12 weeks.

There are several factions within Avon that contribute to this process. The category houses, representing different products categories, suggest what products to sell and at what prices. The creative team handles the photography and other artwork necessary for the brochure. The campaign group, essentially the store managers, ultimately decide what gets into the brochure and where it is placed. This group also determines how much each offer should deliver in terms of sales.

The campaign group evaluates all submissions from the category houses to make certain there is no duplication of offers, such as gifts with purchase. For instance, Avon doesn't want to offer two products for sale that both come with a free umbrella. "They look to make sure the range of price points is fine and the merchandising ideas are fresh," Briddon explains. They have a powerful authority. "They have the role to take space from one and give it to another. It is just like at Wal-Mart or Target, the merchandiser who takes the products from the manufacturer and decides what goes into the store, what to do with it and where to put it. It is a bit of a relay race in terms of passing the baton on to the next group."

PLANNING AND TESTING

The process starts with a three-year planning cycle. There is an annual plan that starts being laid out in June or July for the following year. There are also quarterly plans, along with separate meetings for each campaign. "In September, we will plan for the second quarter of next year," says Briddon.

The size of Avon's brochure will vary anywhere from 120 to 160 pages, with the largest catalogs issued in November in time for holiday purchases. The smallest brochures come out in January. This is dictated by representative count and expected sales volume. "The nice thing about Avon is we can vary the size of our store, so you are not driven by bricks and mortar," Briddon points out.

Avon doesn't just depend on its own judgment. It heavily tests catalog pages to see how consumers respond to different offers and images.

Donna Loyle, editor-in-chief of *Catalog Success* magazine, says Avon is very much considered to be a part of the catalog industry. While it's selling method is more one-on-one than traditional catalog firms like L. L. Bean or Lands End, "They really do an excellent job. They have a long track record and are well respected."

Loyle, speaking as both an industry professional and Avon customer, says about the brochure, "They do a fabulous job. It is well-designed, from the cover to the photographs to the page layout."

Besides making its pocketbook-sized pamphlet appealing, Avon wants to ensure it prompts customer purchases. The company tests all aspects of its brochures to determine how consumers will likely respond, a practice that Loyle agrees is common among catalog companies. But Avon goes a little deeper than most.

As far back as 1979, the company was involved in scientific research to gauge how consumers physically respond to its brochure pages. Perception Research Services (PRS) of Englewood Cliffs, New Jersey, designed a research project to assess the value of eye movement information. The firm monitored eye movement of participants as they looked through a sample brochure. The data was compared against what study participants said they would buy. The point was to see whether body language could be used as an accurate means of measuring purchase intent. PRS hypothesized that using the two forms of data together would be more reliable than either measure alone. "The study was successful in confirming that eye movement data can be useful in diagnosing the differing strengths of alternate brochure advertisements," according to a report on the study.

Suzanne Grayson, founding partner of Grayson & Associates, an industry consultant, says Avon is one of the most sophisticated marketers around. One thing the company does well that traditional retail can't is it introduces a rotating array of fringe and niche products. "Avon has been able to fill out their line with products people needed that would have gotten lost elsewhere," says Grayson, naming some Avon niche items over the years like leg makeup and acne products. "That is one of the great virtues of Avon's store. You can find everything and you can see products that you didn't know existed."

CREATING STANDOUT CAMPAIGNS

Every once in a while a single marketing ploy gets a lot of attention. For Avon, one such historic effort was the Operation Smile campaign in 1978. Avon's goal was to get Avon lipstick on as many lips as possible. Doing so would increase the number of customers representatives served for each campaign. It would also get more women to abandon other products they were using in favor of Avon's.

The Operation Smile campaign entreated women to turn in a competitor's lipstick. That, along with 35 cents, got them a new Avon About Town lipstick that was regularly priced $2.25. The campaign was a phenomenal success, moving some 20 million lipsticks.

For Briddon, the jury is still out on whether the program was "good news or bad news." When talking to people about the Operation Smile campaign, "You get different replies," he says. While it "generated a lot of transactions, it was actually at a loss. So it depends on how you measure it. Was it a campaign loss? Or did it bring customers into the business?" It's a dilemma every marketer faces when offering such loss leader promotions.

Avon still occasionally pits its products up against a competitor's, as in a recent brochure where it challenged women to compare one of its mascaras to Maybelline Great Lash, the country's best-selling mascara and one that's popular among makeup artists.

"If we honestly believe the claims and testing that [show] we have parity or superiority, we will make a claim just to bring a punch to something," says Briddon. "If we do too much [to hype the product], people will disregard it."

Assessing Avon's marketing initiatives overall, Briddon insists the company has "really invented a lot of the merchandising which you see out in stores now, such as the buy one, get one and buy two get one strategies." However, the complexity of marketing strategies has so evolved, says Briddon, that a program like Operation Smile probably wouldn't work nearly as well today. "It is hard to get a real 'Wow!'"

Avon is now looking out toward the horizon to see what its next strategy will be, and to keep its merchandising and marketing original. Among other things, Avon is investigating the possibility of entering into more joint ventures with other companies. "It is still a work in progress," says Briddon. "You have to be far cleverer [in product development and presentation], rather than just giving stuff away at a very low price."

MAKING THE CONNECTION

The ultimate point of any marketing or advertising program is to connect with the consumer, which Avon has done so well over the years. It's challenging to find a woman in the United States, and now increasingly around the world, who doesn't have a personal story or two about Avon. Says the company of its ubiquitous brand, two out of every five women in the world at least tried using an Avon product in the past year, and 86 percent of all women in the United States have purchased an Avon product at some point in their lifetime.

Debra Earl is one of them. The 44-year-old from Middlesex, New Jersey, vividly recalls receiving Avon gifts from her mother's close friend at work as a young girl. Aunt Joan, as Earl called her, would buy Earl and her two younger sisters, Kathleen Power and Carole Ann Capuano, such items as little pieces of jewelry and stocking stuffers. Aunt Joan bought them from an Avon representative who came to the doctor's office where she and Earl's mother worked. To this day, Earl still gushes that, as a teenager, a friend's brother once told her she looked like Sunny Griffin, Avon's spokesperson at the time. When she finally saw a picture of the gorgeous Griffin for herself, Earl declared, "I wanted to marry" the youth who offered the compliment.

Today, Earl is a stay-at-home mom of three boys. She still shops the Avon brochure during her Wednesday morning bowling league. "It's not just makeup anymore," Earl observes. "It is little nightgowns and jewelry, and all the ladies there go crazy buying things for their daughters." For her family's needs, Earl tends to mostly buy the Skin-So-Soft and Bug Guard products.

Upon learning that Salma Hayek was Avon's new spokesperson, Earl, fair skinned with hazel eyes, was intrigued. "So Avon is going for a multicultural dimension," she immediately responded. Thinking back to the blonde, blue-eyed look of Sunny Griffin, adds Earl, "Salma is different for Avon. That is kind of cool."

At a summer barbecue, recalling their days together at Wallington High School in New Jersey, schoolmates from the class of 1979—Lisa Taher, Jana Contreras, Dawn Van Tuyl, and Margaret Rosa—said they all remembered Sweet Honesty, Avon's popular teen fragrance first introduced in 1973. The shared experience came to light when one of the women casually mentioned in a conversation about perfume that she had used Sweet Honesty, to which Rosa retorted, "We ALL wore Sweet Honesty!"

Taher's mother, Dolores Blondek, said Avon's Here's My Heart scent, introduced in 1946 and reintroduced in 1957, had long been a favorite of hers. Blondek's now deceased aunt sold Avon and brought the new book with her when she came to visit on Sundays. Remembers Blondek, "She [my aunt] loved her Avon."

"I'm not sure exactly what drew me to Avon," says Jodi Stubbe of Allen, Texas, who is now a Leadership representative. She had not used Avon products before she started selling them two years ago. "I had just been laid off from my job," explains Stubbe, "and was looking for something to put groceries on the table for awhile." Since then, Stubbe has become more knowledgeable about the differences among cosmetics items and shares that information with her customers. She found another full-time job, but has stayed with Avon anyway. "I like it," she says, even though she never fancied herself an outgoing salesperson before. "I had been in communications and always behind a cubicle."

Although Stubbe hadn't used Avon products before, a lot of her customers had. Most of the women she approaches, she says, "have heard of Avon. There is not much explanation needed."

Cindy Schroeder of Batavia, Illinois, has only been selling Avon for a few weeks. Already, the 31-year-old has found that just by handing out brochures, people will readily self-select products. "So far I've just been passing out books and it pretty much sells itself," says Schroeder, who has a full-time job as an accountant and spends four to five hours per week on Avon. Her customers are reaching for facial skin care items and the holiday items that come in decorative packages, she says.

"Some people have ordered the perfume after they saw the commercial [with Salma Hayek] on TV," says Schroeder. "I'm not sure if they bought it because of Salma or because they just saw the perfume. Also, people have said they saw the Avon fashion show on *The Apprentice*. That kind of put [Avon] into people's heads again."

And it's not only the company that's constantly looking for new and creative ways to get its message out. So are its innovative representatives.

CHAPTER 11

GET CREATIVE

The meeting room at the Westbury, New York, Holiday Inn on a gloriously sunny September afternoon was only partially full for Lisa Wilber's "The Winner in You" presentation. That's no reflection of the interest in the topic. The reality is many women have school children to pick up. The evening session was completely sold out, with some 150 area Avon representatives paying $25 each to listen to one of their own—and most successful—share experiences and marketing tips on how to build their business.

Despite the light turnout for her 1 P.M. talk, Wilber, a once divorced and now happily remarried 41-year-old from Weare, New Hampshire, easily held the attention of the 30 or so women clustered in the front rows of the long, narrow hall. With a casual and humorous, yet compelling, manner, she told how her income, through Avon's Sales Leadership program alone, would exceed $300,000 in 2004. In addition, she would draw an additional commission of at least $20,000, and her 3,000 strong Downline group would ring up a remarkable $10 million in sales.

In case there were any doubts of her trajectory, Wilber held up and jubilantly rocked from side to side, a poster-sized copy of her IRS form 1099 showing earnings from Avon of more than $283,000 in 2003.

Wilber is the highest ranked representative in Avon's U.S. Northeast division and one of only 75 senior executive unit leaders in the country. She entered the Sales Leadership program warily in 1993

185

with doubts about the legitimacy of the multilevel venture. The first year she earned a respectable $12,000 in sales bonuses. The next year she upped that to $32,000.

To ensure everyone understood the theme of her presentation from the start, Wilber kicked off the event with a little game. "Look under your seats," commanded the full-figured, pleasant faced woman, who had passed on wearing makeup that day. "I taped a $1 bill to one of them." Obediently, the ladies stood up and felt around the underside of the folding chairs until the dollar was found and waved in the air.

A few seconds passed as the dubious group waited for the point of the silly exercise to be revealed.

Just as patience was growing thin, Wilber won them back, bursting out gleefully, "You have to get off your duff to earn a buck!" She is officially off and running, and the next two hours fly by.

Like any instructive marketing session, Wilber gives real world tips on what representatives can do to increase their visibility in their communities and, in kind, their sales. Her students scribble furiously into notepads.

What works for Wilber and suits her mischievous personality might not be right for everyone. Even she realizes that. The women are encouraged to choose among her suggestions. After all, they are independent contractors.

For years Wilber has been driving around with her phone number and Avon sign printed on her vehicles. First it was a subcompact car with the information on the doors. She has since upsized to a white cargo van with a lighted sign attached to the roof, bought from a pizza driver. "I need people to remember me differently," explains Wilber, one of 15 Avon representatives in her small town of 6,000. "Yes, I am the one with the car."

Taking a cue from realtors, a covered box is affixed to the sidewall carrying brochures. Business cards are key and should be left everywhere, she insists. Wilber also sponsors a girl's softball team, adopted a section of a New Hampshire highway, and doesn't hesitate to call the local media if there is an occasion, good or bad, that could get her name or Avon affiliation in the paper.

Bumper stickers containing phone numbers and Avon information are also encouraged. "At Wal-Mart you can buy stock stickers and make or print your own," she advises. Getting an 800-number is a "necessary business tool and not that expensive." Wilber notes, "I look at what other companies are doing to get ideas for my Avon business."

She has also been known to wear empty Skin-So-Soft bottles as earrings and construct a three-foot-high cardboard cutout of a Skin-So-Soft bottle for a lawn ornament. Her mailbox is decorated with Avon, too.

"In this business, I think the motto should be 'relentless self-promotion,'" says Wilber. "Don't kid yourselves, men do it all the time." Her latest antic is to run for state government. Her slogan is: "Put an Avon Lady in the House." Should she win, Wilber thinks it will further her toward another goal: being the first sales representative on Avon's board of directors. "I don't have a degree from Princeton or Yale [although she does have two associates degrees from a junior college], but I think being a New Hampshire state representative is a good credential."

For enlightenment on the ways of the business world, the audience is told to read *Rich Dad, Poor Dad* and *The Millionaire Next Door*. Additionally, tables set up in the back of the room offer a host of buttons, T-shirts, and other inspirational books for sale such as the *The Credit Diet* and *Eight Proven Secrets to Smart Success*. Wilber has three books of her own including *Marketing Ideas for the Wild at Heart* and an instructive audiotape.

She emphatically urges against the "D" word. Avon products, she admonishes, frequently show up at flea markets at lower than suggested retail prices. "No discounting. I am in this to make money," she proclaims. "This *is* a business."

"It doesn't have to be about the makeup, unless you want it to be," remarks Wilber. "It is about the money. It is about a business opportunity."

But the money-making schemes need to have a meaningful point. "You have to have a big hairy goal," is how Wilber plainly puts it. Hers was to become a millionaire by 40. She has made it. Together, her assets do stack up to more than $1 million. She and her husband own their new house outright and as a special treat put in an oversized bathtub the two can relax in. "Our goal was to have a paid-for life," she says.

Day-to-day living wasn't always so refined for Wilbur, who lived in a trailer for 15 and a half years. It was a 1972 single-wide that for a good portion of the time had a bum heating system requiring someone to sit guard all night. "We would sleep in four-hour shifts," she remembers. "I drove a Yugo and ate macaroni."

Wilber had been dabbling in Avon when she lost her $20,000-a-year office clerk job in 1987. While trying to console her, her husband absently remarked, "Why don't you try doing that Avon thing full-time." With that little push of encouragement, she took up the challenge.

The success doesn't come easy. Even now, says Wilber, "There are days that I just want to quit, but I tell myself, 'If I do work today, I'll be one step closer to my dream.'" She has put together a graphic collage depicting some of the things she wants. She already has the house. Her next goal: Meeting country singer Garth Brooks, a man whose work ethic she admires. Plus, she coos, "Don't you think he's cute?"

MAKING IT A FAMILY AFFAIR

No one had to convince Vondell McKenzie, a senior executive unit leader from Los Banos, California, that there was value in Avon's Sales Leadership program. The 67-year-old grandmother was the first person to sign onto the program in 1991 at the urging of John Fleming, vice president, U.S. Sales Leadership, whom she knew previously from Tupperware.

Having worked for other direct-selling operations, McKenzie was familiar with multilevel marketing programs. Fleming's presentation was enticing. However, she did seek a higher blessing before deciding to accept it. "I seriously prayed over whether it was something that would work for me or not," recalls McKenzie.

Today, McKenzie, whose soothing voice and calming manner make it easy to understand why those in her Downline affectionately call her "mom" and "grandmom," is the matriarch of an Avon family of some 3,000 representatives. Within that "family" are three members of her natural family—a daughter, daughter-in-law, and even her 26-year-old grandson, who is making a full-time job of Avon, too.

Her group, dubbed Nova, is expected to rack up sales of $9 million in 2004. Along with Lisa Wilber, McKenzie is among Avon's top ten earning Sales Leadership members nationwide. Although she prefers not to say exactly how much she makes, it is in the six figures. Her personal sales are also in the $20,000-plus range.

Nova, she explains, "is a bright star and that is how we see every representative. It is important to us and we tagged ourselves that. We say we are 'history makers and record breakers.'"

A high turnover has always been a problem for direct sellers. Avon is no exception. To help stem that flow, McKenzie has created "Grand Openings," a promotional event for Avon representatives. After a new representative goes through their string of family and friends, many get stumped on how to take the business to the next level.

"We are very serious about working toward keeping more of our representatives," says McKenzie. "Sometimes they don't have the chance to build their business the way they would like to. We want to be closer to that."

As with any other business, McKenzie's Grand Openings formally introduce the Avon representative to the community. The representative invites people to her home "to let them know they are opening an Avon business." There is a presentation and the representative tries to find out from guests what their needs and interests are and how they want to be served. "Someone in the upline [a more senior member of the Nova team] will do the demonstration for them," explains McKenzie. "The product purchases, or whatever happens, belong to the representative."

Nova also runs "Boot Camps," where representatives receive additional training to support McKenzie's theme of "no representative left behind." At the camps, says McKenzie, "we talk about how to build our business and how to get people started properly." There are breakout sessions for groups to discuss topics such as how to do the Power of Three and how to set goals to reach the next sales level.

A recent overnight Boot Camp in California drew 75 Nova members from all over California, Washington, and Arizona. A fee of $20 covered expenses.

Nova also holds "Beauty Bashes." "It is like a party where you show people how to apply skin care products and how to use product and how to apply makeup," says McKenzie. "We have so many people [representatives] who really didn't use a lot of makeup. She [the instructor] was able to show them how to put on a foundation and how to go on to do the eyes and lips."

When McKenzie started out, her husband, Terry, stood side by side with her in the business. Since he passed away six years ago from cancer, she has continued to push forward on her own. Some 14 years into her Avon career, she feels she is just getting going.

Her two-room home office is about to be expanded. A goal of McKenzie's is to also own an oceanfront place. "I love the ocean and want to be able to go and just spend some time there," says McKenzie who sings in her church choir and likes to garden in her free time. "I would like to have a place for my Leadership [team members] to come."

McKenzie, who says she was a shy person when she started out in sales years ago, also wants to be a member of Andrea Jung's council—that is a group of sales representatives with whom the CEO meets to discuss issues.

When McKenzie was a girl, her father's auto repair business burned to the ground. As an adult, then living in Cincinnati with her family, she watched as their home went up in flames, too. She felt as if she had lost everything. Then, someone, whom she now sees as "an angel," pointed out that her husband and children were safe. The experiences made McKenzie cherish her memories. "It gives me an understanding of what is important. Material things can always be replaced. There are things you think that are precious to you," she says. "It is important to understand what is really important in life."

GOING WHERE THE RECRUITS ARE

Maria Tirotta will go just about anywhere to sign up a representative. The 54-year-old senior executive unit leader from East Rockaway, New York, took a junket recently with two others in her Downline to Tampa. She is a hard woman to turn down. It's not because she is intimidating. She is just so joyfully involved with Avon, she thinks everyone else will be, too. Her enthusiasm is contagious, causing even the most doubtful of candidates to at least believe they have a shot at success.

To spread her message of Avon, Tirotta places advertisements in newspapers around the country—some 50 a month—wherever she thinks there might be fertile ground to extend her network. She insists her first appointments with potential recruits be face-to-face. Tirotta will hop a plane or get in her car to meet them. "Basically, I will go to wherever I have to go," says the round-faced, dark haired woman who makes a New York accent sound sweet. Her representative base has branched beyond New York and now has strongholds in Florida, North Carolina, and Pennsylvania.

Her husband, Donald, has evolved into her business partner. The couple adhere to Avon's "Power of Three" credo, making certain to speak to at least three random people a day about either buying or selling Avon. Waitresses and hotel clerks have been prime candidates. Tirotta takes new recruits and goes door-to-door to train them.

Financially supporting the business is essential. "I try to reinvest about 30 percent," notes Tirotta, an energetic sort who arises every day by 5 A.M. That money covers brochures, newspaper ads, samples, and even full-sized products that Tirotta likes to give as gifts with her orders.

If there is a new test kit or selling concept Avon is offering, Tirotta will snap it up. She was one of the first to buy a professional-style makeover kit. The metal suitcase contains cosmetics brushes and implements and makeup items for makeovers. She also has the new Party in a Box, a kit for at-home demonstrations that contains a selection of top-selling items, a bag for a raffle, along with samples and product testers. She and her husband have both completed the Beauty Advisor Training program, although it may be awhile before Donald, a former bank accountant, actually does a makeover, he sheepishly acknowledges.

Tirotta's Honda Accord with the MARIAVON vanity plate is parked in her driveway. The garage is filled with products, brochures in English and Spanish, samples, and Avon bags in both plastic and paper for packing orders. She always puts two brochures with each order, hoping the extra will be passed onto a new customer. She buys ahead on some of the most popular items like Skin-So-Soft, Bug Guard, and Retroactive—but not too much because the products all have expiration dates.

Tirotta handily navigates Avon's computer software and calls the new Downline Manager program that can give her an instantaneous read on almost every aspect of her business and the performance of her recruits "her friend."

A generous spirit, Tirotta has a penchant for giving out personal bonuses to deserving Downline members who have been performing well or may just need a little boost. You get the impression that Tirotta is probably known in the neighborhood for giving out really good candy at Halloween.

Her earnings through Sales Leadership have steadily climbed, more than doubling from $43,877 in 2001 to $89,370 in 2003. She entered the Sales Leadership program in 1995 earning $2,762 in her first go round. She will exceed $100,000 in 2004.

Additionally, her personal sales reached $70,000 in 2003, though she scaled back to between $30,000 to $40,000 in 2004 to focus on Sales Leadership to develop the careers of others. She now has three executive unit leaders in her Downline of about 1,000 representatives.

As a couple, Maria and Donald Tirotta now rank 30 in the country in sales and earnings. "I want to be in the top 10," says Maria with a grin. "I think it will take five years."

Off to a good start, in the fall of 2004 the Tirottas signed a lease for office space about a mile from their home and are in the process of moving the operation there. Already Maria says, "I want to open a second training center."

Tirotta likes to wear an Avon pin or shirt with a logo for credibility and thinks many women do not realize how much money they can make from selling Avon. As she points out, the absolute minimum commission is 20 percent and it rapidly goes up from there.

Building and maintaining a successful Downline depends on cultivating a mutually beneficial relationship. "If your group doesn't perform, you will lose your group," says Tirotta on why ongoing training and encouragement is so important.

The mother of two grown daughters hadn't planned on a career with Avon. She started out selling as a one-time fund-raiser for an

Italian-American Club she was a member of 13 years ago. "I was the only one who sold!" recalls Tirotta, who had been working as a bank manager and eventually left to continue with Avon full-time.

"When I first started I wanted to be in the President's Club," Tirotta notes of her initial modest expectations.

Like Lisa Wilber and Vondell McKenzie, Tirotta outlines her goals. One was to buy a vacation home in Lancaster, Pennsylvania. In October 2004, the Tirottas happily crossed that off their list.

Tirotta has an impressive Downline group. At least two members of the group have two master's degrees each, and one recently left a 20-year career in health care. "I wasn't seeing my children and the hospital was threatening layoffs," explains Jackie Kalage, 42, on her decision to focus on building an Avon business. "This is very different. My father asked if I was having a nervous breakdown." But, she continues, "I didn't accomplish what I wanted to accomplish in health care and I needed to do something to make more money for my family." After seeing what Tirotta accomplished with Avon, Kalage hopes she can enjoy the same good fortune.

Another of Maria's recruits, Linda Rose Hanik, a former teacher of the deaf, was downsized at her school. She has found a ripe selling opportunity with women at assisted-living facilities. "I wanted my customers in a concentrated area," she says. Hanik is thrilled with some of Avon's new advertising, particularly the message at the end that directs customers "to their Avon representative," she says. Hanik, who is developing her own Downline, has set a goal to sell $4,000 every campaign.

When it comes to recruiting, Tirotta has learned "you can't pre-judge anybody." Roseanne Fogarty, 35, of Westbury, New York, also a member of Tirotta's group, notes that they will sign up any one, even people who can't pay the $15. "We will let it go," says Fogarty, quietly. "I know we are not supposed to. But we do." She says she has always been repaid after the first order.

"We all feel we can make a difference in someone's life," explains Fogarty. Tirotta who recently signed up a woman who must keep her new job a secret from her abusive husband, adds, "We can help you make your life better. One of my goals is to have enough money to help people get a fresh start."

DOING IT YOUR OWN WAY

In Alida Tracy's living room sits a $7,700 organ purchased with her Avon earnings. It has enabled her to practice for her role as organist at the town's Hope Reformed Church. "I keep my Avon money separate from my house money," says the white haired lady from Clifton, New Jersey, who has been selling Avon for more than 39 years.

The table in the dining room doubles as her business office. Along the walls, there are two curio cabinets filled with Avon awards. One possesses some 35 Albees—20 painted statuettes and the rest in gold and silver. The other case contains teacups with matching saucers. There is also a large Mrs. Albee doll kept securely in a protective box. All are testaments to Tracy's sales achievements. Tracy consistently has ranked in Avon's top sales groups, starting with the President's Club, then the Honor Society. She has also maintained membership in the Rose Circle for many years.

"I would set little [sales] goals for myself. If you set them too high you can get disappointed," says Tracy, now a sprite 81, on how she has been able to keep at it all these years. "I did not push my customers. They bought what they wanted to buy."

Long before Avon began to promote its Sales Leadership program, Tracy had developed her own. "At one time I had 22 subsellers," says Tracy, who due to health reasons has scaled back her operation and is down to a mere "12 helpers." She pays them 25 percent of what they sell. "On clothing, I get 25 percent, so they get 10 percent. The same with toys and watches."

She used to have her own sales area and did go door-to-door. But Avon stopped assigning territories a couple of decades ago. "Now you can sell anywhere. Most women are working and we sell to them in their offices."

Tracy learned for herself the importance of branding. Avon representatives can package their goods in any type of sack, but Tracy has always purchased Avon's official logo-laden bags. "I don't use bags I can buy in the supermarket."

She also over samples her customers. "I put something extra in every bag, no matter what," says Tracy. "I put at least three samples in each order. Even if the manager [Avon's district manager] was buying."

She calls in her order on Monday and it arrives Friday morning. Then she sorts and bags. "I am up at 6 A.M. and not finished until about 6 P.M.," she says, adding that she probably puts in about 30 hours a week on the business. The deliveries go out to her personal customers and her subsellers on Saturday morning. Her orders typically range from $5 to $60 on average, and some products like the Anew line "go like crazy. I sell all of it." Other hot items with her customers are deodorants, bug sprays, colognes, and Skin-So-Soft.

Tracy says to make it work, "you have to be consistent." In disbelief, she recalls being at an Avon meeting, "where a woman said she didn't deliver last campaign's order." That is not acceptable to someone as diligent as Tracy.

Tracy started with Avon when her son was young and her husband preferred she not work out of the home.

When she was laid up because of a broken shoulder for two and a half months last year, her son and daughter-in-law filled in and serviced her customers. "They didn't want me to lose the business," says Tracy. "But they said they wouldn't do it again because it was too much work."

SPEAKING IN RUSSIAN

Natalia Shevchenko is a 45-year-old Avon manager in Moscow, Russia. She spends her days distributing products and issuing invitations to Russian women to either join Avon or buy the products.

She says she approaches, on average, 100 women a day to discuss opportunities at Avon. When she joined the company seven years ago, Shevchenko, speaking through an interpreter, says she was shy and withdrawn. "The catalog arrived at just the right time in my life," says the one-time utility company worker who now plies her Avon business full-time. "It is day and night," she laughs.

To get the business started, she would present the brochure to security guards at business offices and ask them to pass the books on to the office workers. Going out and meeting with the public made Shevchenko feel "revived," she says.

In Russia, women are contacted in public or places of employment. The door-to-door method isn't suitable for the culture. "People won't open their doors," explains a marketing manager in Avon's Moscow headquarters. Avon has identified Central-Eastern Europe as an area for vast expansion and Russia is one of its fastest growing markets within the region. The sales cycle in Russia is every 24 days and there is no $15 startup fee like in the United States.

Under Avon's business model in Russia, Shevchenko earns a commission on the sales of the 100 or so representatives that report to her, as well as on her own personal sales. Her total earnings for the year are equivalent to about $15,000. That is a healthy step above the average income for middle class Russians—about $3,900, according to a recent report by the U.S. Commercial Service in Moscow.

"A person has to be very sociable to sell a lot," notes Shevchenko, who advises, "It is important to be brave and be active and not feel shy or confused or scared because there is no shame in making money."

To entice women to Avon, Shevchenko stresses that it costs nothing to get started and they can benefit from a discount on the products. She also tells them, "It is interesting work where they can meet new friends and acquaintances. It is very involving." Then she adds, "And they don't have to ask husbands for money."

Irina Stotskaya is among Shevchenko's group of representatives. She joined Avon five years ago after receiving an invitation to attend an Avon "open days ceremony," an event that introduces women to the opportunities at Avon. The 45-year-old Moscow resident holds a full-time job in a children's health care clinic. She does most of her selling to women there.

Some of the most popular items for her customers are Avon cosmetics, the Naturals collection, and children's products. Additionally, comments Stotskaya, there is a big demand for the accessories such as scarves and gloves. Throughout Russia, lipsticks, Anew skin care, and Solutions creams are some of the bestsellers.

Stotskaya earns approximately 100,000 rubles (about $3,300) through Avon. Plus, this year she won a new camera for her sales achievements. But there are other, equally valuable, rewards.

"Avon enables me to expand my social circle and improve communications and relationships with my coworkers," says Stotskaya, who takes pleasure when her customers are pleased with their purchases. "When I deliver their cosmetics and beauty products, it raises my mood when they like it."

DEVELOPING A SKIN CARE BUSINESS IN INDIA

Swati Sharma, 48, of New Delhi, India, made her way into Avon in 1996 the way many women do—through someone they know. In her case, it was a cousin.

Eight years later, Sharma is a manager who oversees some 500 sales representatives. "I am helping them to build their business and in that way my business is also growing," she says. She is one of India's top two distributors and on average earns between 25,000 to 30,000 rupees a year. In U.S. dollars that is only $545 to $655. But in India, where the average annual income is $460, according the country's Department of International Development, Sharma is doing well. "I net out pretty comfortably and I am able to lead a comfortable life," says the former restaurant manager. "I definitely make more money than before."

The salary is better but so are the working conditions. By working from home, Sharma has eliminated a several-hour commute from her day. "If I had been working anywhere else 9 to 5, it would have taken 12 hours. Here I am sitting at home, doing my work where I maintain an office."

Sharma spends a lot of time on training and product demonstrations. Currently she is working to develop more interest in skin care. "Skin care is just starting up now," says Sharma. "I keep talking and educating my group on how they should do it [apply products], how it will help them, and what are the best products."

For Indian shoppers, lipstick is among Avon's most popular items, notes Sharma. Many of her representatives aren't actively selling but are buying products for themselves, spending "400, 500, and 600 rupees on orders." The customers are of all ages, but the majority are younger, between 18 to 35, she notes.

Samita Jana, 54, is one of Sharma's team members. She sells Avon, not as a career, but to improve her personal life. Jana earns about 1,000 rupees a year. "I wanted to be more social and it absolutely makes you interact with people of all kinds of backgrounds," says Jana, who has a full-time job in information technology. "It started with workplace contacts. I don't go to homes or anything like that. People now know that I sell it and for anybody who wants it. I'll send a brochure, then they call me back."

MAKING A COMMITMENT

As you can tell, being a successful Avon representative takes ingenuity and a more than a dose of tenacity. Some members of Avon's corporate executive team who have tried their hand at sales have come away somewhat humbled by the experience and awed by what some of these women do to make the sale.

Take Harriet Edelman, for example. In her role as chief information officer for Avon, she is instrumental in developing systems to keep the two-, three-, and four-week campaigns on track. To do that, products have to move smoothly from supplier to distribution point, and she must correctly forecast sales. When she actually tried selling Avon herself for six months a few years ago, she learned firsthand how daunting the two-week turnaround time for U.S. representatives can seem.

"I had always understood and supported the cycle, but when you are on the receiving end, it comes around really fast," says Edelman, exhaling as she recalls the experience. "The regularity of the cycle does call for a high amount of self-discipline."

"My role models are Avon representatives," says chairman and CEO Andrea Jung, who also signed on as a representative in the mid-1990s when she was head of global marketing for Avon. "I am inspired by their self-sufficiency and how incredibly bright business women they are."

As part of her corporate job at the time, Jung oversaw the design of the brochure. In her role as a sales representative, a customer had asked her to find a Skin-So-Soft item. "I realized how difficult it was to find some of the products. I had been flipping through the pages and couldn't find what I was looking for," recalls Jung. "We changed that brochure on Monday."

Jung went knocking door-to-door in her Manhattan neighborhood. She says she might do it again in the future to remind herself of the challenges the representatives face daily. "It is one of the toughest jobs. You have to be self-motivated. It's not like you go to work and someone tells you what to do. You have to get up everyday and create your own business plan. You are truly independent."

The job, "requires motivation and a work ethic and drive that is second to none," says Jung who admits that her own sales as a representative were not all that stellar. "It is daunting. It is intimidating. You do learn fast that it is a human relationship business."

CHAPTER 12

MAKEOVERS CAN BE A THING OF BEAUTY

When Andrea Jung first came on board as a consultant in 1993, she knew that Avon was getting a little worn around the edges. There was nothing desperately wrong with the company. It continued to issue new products regularly, recently had a major breakthrough with Anew Perfecting Complex for Face (the first alpha hydroxy acid product for the mass market), its international business was building, and even U.S. sales were creeping up. But Jung felt Avon could be doing far better.

The 100-plus-year-old brand was losing appeal with younger consumers. To a large degree, it was consigned in the public's mind as something of a dependable and serviceable brand, but hardly one that was modern. Such a mind-set didn't bode well for the company's future. Avon wasn't the lipstick that makeup artists were pulling out of their cases at fashion shows, and high school girls weren't talking about the company anymore. Young women instead were trolling department store counters and shopping mall specialty shops like Bath & Body Works and the Body Shop. They barely knew about Avon, especially since the average age range of Avon customers was between 40 and 55.

Avon has consistently produced solid quality products at modest prices, but that didn't mean it had to be stodgy. Why couldn't it project style and operate like a world class company, too, Jung wondered? A retail veteran, despite her relative youth, she thrived on turnaround projects. When Jung became Avon's chief executive officer in 1999, she was ready to take on the challenge and start redirecting an exciting new course for the company.

Just a year earlier, Jung had a mighty hand in crafting a striking new global symbol for the company. A narrow, yet prominent, storefront on the corner of 57th Street and Fifth Avenue in Manhattan became a constant public reminder of how Avon wanted the world to see it now. And that was only the beginning of her plans for a complete makeover of the company.

A PUBLIC FACE

New York's bustling Fifth Avenue shopping district is home to such elite retail nameplates as Bergdorf Goodman and Tiffany. The world famous area draws visitors from around the globe.

In a momentous break from its 113-year-old tradition, Avon opened its first store ever in the United States in November 1998, taking up residence in Trump Tower, one of Manhattan's most exclusive properties—and a prominent Fifth Avenue fixture. The skyscraper presents a mix of retail stores and residences. It is occupied by the rich and famous, including Donald Trump himself, who is also the site's landlord. With its sparkling gold facade and larger than life Trump signage, the building is a noted New York City tourist destination.

Avon leased 20,000 square feet of space across four floors. On the first and second levels there is a 2,000 square foot boutique showcasing Avon products. The floors above are home to a state of the art spa, salon, and meeting space. The interior was designed using soft, muted colors and comfortable furniture to make it warm and inviting. It is luxurious, but not intimidating. The company took pains to make certain it didn't project a clinical feel. Avon has always prided itself on being an inclusive, not exclusive, brand.

Construction costs were a reported $5 million. The company viewed the store as a major advertising buy. "It is an investment in awareness," Jung said at the time.

Avon had long been laying the groundwork for this moment. Its color cosmetics line had been repackaged, and Anew skin care was relaunched into a cohesive collection in order to make a more powerful statement to consumers. The advertising themes from 1995 to 1997 of "Just Another Avon Lady" and "Dare to Change Your Mind About Avon" were starting to break away, fading old stereotypes about Avon. The company upshifted its message to "Claim Your Beauty," a theme meant to embolden women to embrace their individuality.

TAKING A STAND

With the opening of the Avon Center, the company all but shouted out loud that it was shifting its stance from defensive to offensive.

The Avon Salon and Spa aligned itself with beauty industry celebrity hair colorist and stylist Brad Johns, who first made a name for himself by coloring wide patches of hair that led *Vogue* magazine to dub him the "Father of Chunking." He is now the Artistic Director of Avon's Salon and Spa. Johns has called Avon home since August 1999, when he closed his own shop to make the jump. Famous faces frequenting the salon have included Brooke Shields, Natasha Richardson, and Johnny Depp.

Avon was also on top of the trend when it came to the eye brow shaping craze that swept across the country, snatching Eliza Petrescu, a famed Romanian esthetician noted for her eyebrow work. To get an appointment with Eliza at the Eliza Eyes salon you have to wait several weeks. The price for a first time visit: $100.

Beyond that there is a wide menu of available treatments and services—from manicures and massages to seaweed wraps and a variety of spa packages.

BRANCHING FURTHER INTO RETAIL

Once it had upgraded the product line and started to polish its image, Avon wanted to get more women to try the brand again. Direct selling would always be the company's core strength. After all, Avon learned the hard way from its failed diversification attempts in the 1980s that straying too far from its original model may not be wise.

However, in addition to erecting the Fifth Avenue store as a billboard to the world, Avon wanted to have little poster-sized shops dotting the country as well. So, that same year, the company began leasing mall kiosks and opening up Avon counters, as a way to increase visibility of the Avon brand. These locations also provided an alternate way to buy Avon for those without a representative.

The kiosks started out as corporate-owned businesses. Avon then began franchising them to its own representatives. That way there would be no conflict with the sales reps. Instead, the kiosks provided another option for sales representatives to sell Avon.

The operation never quite caught on in mass. There are now about 100 Avon stores and kiosks throughout the United States. Given the considerable startup costs involved—such as a inventory and the monthly premium mall rent—they never became as popular as originally thought.

Still, a handful of women have found the kiosks to be extremely rewarding and have moved beyond the center court to permanent inline mall stores, which generally carry minimum leases of 5 to 10 years.

MOVING BEYOND RETAIL

There are a group of consumers referred to by Avon as the "channel rejecters." These are women who want to buy Avon products, but do not want to go through an Avon representative. In the past the company historically just turned those potential customers away.

James Preston, who retired in 1999, remembers the company's philosophy had always been that if it isn't sold through the representative, it shouldn't be done. "That was one of the toughest fights—opening up the channel," says Preston. For more than 100 years, "there was only one way to buy Avon and that was if you had a representative."

Studies showed there was a sizable percentage of the population that loved the product and loved the price value, but didn't want a representative. "And we said," recalls Preston, "Too bad, you can't buy our product."

The fear was that the company would alienate its representatives, and that business would suffer as a result. Avon ultimately came to the conclusion that "a rising tide lifts all ships," says Preston. Avon tried to stress that the more people that buy its products, the more money the company will have to "promote its products and reinvest to help you, the representative, with your business," Preston adds.

In 1991, the company began running advertisements for the first time with an 800 number for customers to call to place orders. In 1992, it introduced its "Four Ways to Be Beautiful" campaign, that offered women four ways to order Avon products: by phone, fax, catalogue (using an order form that could be mailed in), or through a representative.

While Preston says Avon made the first break during his tenure, Jung took it to the next level. "We kind of cracked it and she [Jung] said the door is open."

Today, you can buy Avon through representatives, over the Internet, or by dialing 1-800-CALL-AVON, as well as through one of the representative-run kiosks. It is also still possible to send an order in by mail or fax, although sales through these avenues still constitute a very small percentage of Avon's overall business.

In the spirit of offering more avenues of access, Avon again differs from such competitors as Mary Kay, Nu Skin, and BeautiControl. None operate e-commerce operations. Orders via the Web constitute only a small fraction of Avon's sales, but it is still one of the most visited beauty sites on the Web. For Avon, the goal is to ensure that consumers have access to its products when, where, and how they want.

The preferred method, of course, is still through the representative. On its homepage, Avon presents an icon to click directing shoppers to a representative in their area if they so desire. If not, they can shop themselves on the web site.

If you dial 1-800-CALL-AVON, the first thing the customer service associate asks, is "Can I refer you to an Avon representative?" If you don't want to be referred, then someone in the department will take your order over the phone. In either case, you will not be turned away.

Not surprisingly, there has been some representative furor over Avon initiatives from time to time. Avon made the perilous mistake once of putting the 1-800 number on its brochures, making its sales reps very angry. The company quickly corrected that.

One thing is for sure: Avon representatives don't miss a trick, something Avon is still learning. For instance, in late 2004 the company apparently presented some special offers and promotional events on Avon.com that were not being made available in the brochure. Through an e-mail message in early December, sales representatives were alerted that Avon.com would honor their wishes and eliminate exclusive online promotional offers, promising that in the future online promotions would mirror those in the core brochure.

"You have told us that these promotions sometimes compete directly with offers featured in the brochure," wrote Angie Rossi, group vice president of U.S. sales and customer care. "Our goal for Avon.com has always been to reach new and stranded customers with an option for those who prefer an alternative to our direct-selling channel. In the future, only promotions that support both your direct-selling business and our online objectives will be considered."

Obviously, the subject remains a sensitive one.

BECOMING A RETAIL BRAND

Throughout its history, Avon has always considered broadening its reach. In the late 1980s when the company had acquired several prestige fragrance brands such as Giorgio and the Parfums Stern business, it wasn't equipped to fully develop its own retail operations. As discussed in Chapter 2, Avon was distracted by its own financial troubles and takeover attempts, and these outside retail pieces were ultimately sold off.

Ten years later, however, things were moving smoothly again. Jung was a CEO with a progressive outlook. She was looking for ways to augment the slow-growth beauty business in the United States, and Avon was ready to experiment.

As the 1990s drew to a close, retail sales accounted for about 90 percent of the total beauty market. To double the size of Avon from a $5 billion to a $10 billion company—the goal at the time—stepping into the retail world was a logical move. But with the specter of sales representative wrath hovering, Avon opted not to take its core brand into other retail venues, aside from its representative-run counters.

Instead, the company would create a new brand—a more exclusive line with higher priced products that could be leveraged in the moderate department store channel and be considered a cross-over or masstige brand. The line was to be known as beComing.

Several beauty companies play in multiple fields. L'Oreal, for instance, sells Lancome in department stores, along with Maybelline New York and the L'Oreal Paris brands in drugstores. Procter & Gamble produces both Cover Girl and SK II, one of the priciest skin care lines around.

Nevertheless, Avon's new beComing venture had challenges from the start. First of all, representatives expressed mixed feelings about the project. One faction felt that presenting a brand at retail stores could elevate the awareness level of Avon and positively spill over to their businesses. Another group, however, resented that the new brand was being designed as a "premium" line. Internally, it was referred to as "Avon Gold," leading one representative to question whether the core was "Avon Tin." A standard Avon lipstick was priced at $3 to $4, while a beComing lipstick would be $6 to $8.

The beComing collection was designed to come out with a splash. Avon was not going to timidly enter the retail market. The brand would possess six distinct product categories, and the collection would be merchandised in a commanding store within a store layout complete with multiple shelving units and a checkout counter. There would be some 400 items to start across color cosmetics, skin care, mother and baby products, aromatherapy, fragrances, and jewelry. It would be the centerpiece of the store's beauty department.

Avon's first retail partners were to be Sears and JCPenney, and those selections surprised industry observers. Neither retailer had a strong reputation in the beauty business. Avon's beComing would be the lynchpin used to develop their cosmetics departments. A few years earlier Sears developed a proprietary line called Circle of Beauty with an attractive wooden fixture and green accents. It even introduced some innovative products—particularly skin care regimens and novel cosmetics kits. With beComing, Sears hoped to pull in a younger customer.

Plans were being set to introduce beComing into 150 to 200 Sears and JCPenney stores in the fall of 2001. Avon would spend

$10 million to $15 million on advertising and promotions to kickoff the launch.

Then, just two months before construction was to get underway, Sears did an about face. Not only was it not going to take on the beComing brand, it was eliminating the beauty department in its stores altogether. It was an awkward moment for Avon. The company ended up not losing any money on the deal because there was a multimillion dollar settlement with Sears that more than compensated Avon for its startup costs.

The beComing line was therefore introduced at half the original plan with some 92 JCPenney stores. The lighted fixtures of the beComing displays enlivened the look of JCPenney's lackluster beauty sections. Avon claimed sales were building month upon month, yet the operation was running deep in the red.

In another unforeseen twist, less than 18 months after beComing was introduced, JCPenney also decided to yank color cosmetics out of its stores. The centerpiece beComing products fell victim once again.

Like Sears, JCPenney's has kept its fragrances and bath and body products, but ousted skin care and color cosmetics entirely from its stores. JCPenney's used the space to expand its accessories categories instead. Avon immediately issued a press release stating it was repositioning beComing as a brand that would be sold through its core channel. Today, beComing lives on as a premium brand that is only sold through Avon representatives who have completed Beauty Advisor training, so as to keep up its exclusive image.

Jung is philosophical about the episode. "I'm still glad we did it. I think we learned a lot," she says in retrospect. Retail ventures have been put on the backburner in the United States for now. "It's not never, but it is not a high priority, given that I am extremely pleased with the direct selling initiatives and the franchise kiosk opportunity."

Says Jung, "It was probably the wrong partner. If we did it again, we would do something longer and put in more resources over a longer period of time."

William Steele a financial analyst who has been covering Avon since 1993, contends that what beComing didn't deliver in sales it delivered multiple times in good will and awareness for the company.

"People talk not too highly about that, but if you look at the amount of positive press Avon got from 1999 to the present, versus 1995 to 1999, it is dramatically different," Steele points out.

Steele says all of the press Avon gets about its new programs—from beComing to the reformatted advertising campaigns—boosts the morale of the sales force. They get excited each time they hear and read about new projects at the company. "In some respects Avon is a sales and momentum organization," Steele shares. "When reps are jazzed about being Avon reps, lots and lots of good things can happen. This chipping away at the brand's challenges created a lot of positive press and they felt jazzed about that."

Along with beComing, Avon has generated a trendier brand mark, introduced its first global advertising campaign, and has worked with tennis pros Serena and Venus Williams, singer Jewel, and most recently Salma Hayek (its latest spokesperson).

To make everything run smoothly, Avon also wanted to ensure the right systems were in place to support its expansion plans.

REFINING INTERNAL OPERATIONS

While the Avon Center projected the image of a sophisticated global brand, Avon wanted to operate as a world class company that took advantage of its international scope. So, in 1997, Avon introduced a streamlining program called Business Process Redesign (BPR) to start taking a closer look at refining Avon's operations and elevating consumer awareness of the brand. This included looking into every aspect of the business to see where money could be saved and best reallocated to foster growth. By mid-2001, the company said these initiatives had wrung out approximately $400 million in cost savings and helped increase operating margin by 3.2 percentage points. Additionally the BPR initiatives enabled Avon to invest more than $100 million in customer growth strategies annually. That money was applied to boosting Avon's advertising programs, including doubling the U.S. advertising budget. It also beefed up sampling programs to get more consumers to try Avon items.

From 1999 to 2001, Avon's emphasis was on strengthening the core business and restoring business fundamentals. Now it was intent on flexing its muscle to build strategies for the future.

TAKING MAJOR STEPS

The next phase was more aggressive. By mid-2001, Avon began to formally call its initiatives the company's *Business Transformation*. With the fundamentals in place, Avon outlined steps it would take from 2002 to 2004 to accelerate top and bottom line growth.

As Susan Kropf, president and chief operating officer, has said, Avon's new focused approach to globalization was a huge change from the way the company used to operate.

With Avon's team-spirited culture, says Kropf, "We have all driven this story of alignment. We will tolerate a lot of things, but we will not tolerate a lack of alignment across our management team."

It wasn't always that way. Avon used to operate in a much more compartmentalized fashion. Today, "There is a clearly articulated vision and we communicate, communicate, communicate," says Kropf. "There is more clarity of our strategy and our expectations. Not just this year, but for next year and three years out. Everybody knows where they are expected to be."

The company, she says, was sophisticated in its own right in prior years in keeping with the times. "But now," she says, "it is [sophisticated] in a more disciplined and maybe more efficient way than perhaps we found ourselves a number of years ago."

The company has been through many transformations. "I do think this one has been more sweeping and far reaching than anything ever undertaken before because it is both top-line and bottom-line oriented," Kropf assesses. The approach Avon has applied is much more "holistic." It goes beyond simply ringing out expenses to improve operating margins.

From 2002 to 2004, Avon's bold steps included nurturing growth in beauty sales, planting seeds for new businesses, expanding geographically, streamlining the supply chain, expanding Sales Leadership, and implementing tax strategies (which have reduced its effective tax rate from 35 percent to 31 percent).

Several elements have contributed to this transformation process. A key area of focus has been Avon's supply chain. In July 2001, Avon named Lou Mignone to the newly created position of group vice president of the North America supply chain. Mignone joined a team led by John Kitchener, senior vice president of the global supply chain. Avon poached Mignone from competitor Colgate-Palmolive, where he had been vice president of the supply chain. He integrated and streamlined Colgate-Palmolive's supply chain in the United States and was credited for generating a substantial cost savings.

Avon has since taken a strong hand in leveraging its supply chain, by implementing better programs within manufacturing, sourcing, and distribution. "There is a lot of money in the supply chain of a company this size and that has been a huge contributor" to Avon's savings, says Kropf.

First, the company regrouped its business units into clusters to eliminate the duplication of services. It then further reduced those markets into four operating regions: North America, Asia-Pacific, Latin America, and Europe.

Other specific actions have included the realignment of its manufacturing operations. In Europe, the company phased out a plant in Northampton, United Kingdom, and moved those activities to an expanded facility in Garwolin, Poland. In the United States, Avon eliminated manufacturing operations in Suffern, New York, and consolidated those functions with its more modern Springdale, Ohio, plant. (Avon's research and development center remains in Suffern.) The company's manufacturing site in Montreal was phased out, and those operations were consolidated into the Springdale, Ohio, and Morton Grove, Illinois, facilities.

There were other difficult decisions made in streamlining the supply chain. Avon reduced the number of its vendors by half. "I was personally involved in a number of very difficult conversations with suppliers who had been important to us and had actually done a good job," recalls Kropf. Avon had accumulated more suppliers than it needed. "It was really in the best interest of the business to pare down."

Since 2002, Avon has churned up some $312 million in savings from its Business Transformation initiatives, with $200 million coming out of the supply chain. Of that $200 million, $96 million was derived from better sourcing, $57 million from order fulfill-ment and logistics improvements, and $47 million from manufac-turing realignments.

The company has taken some of this savings and applied it to targeted consumer spending, such as advertising and sampling, spending for which has increased $230 million annually since 1999. That, notes Kropf is "to make sure we are driving the top-line."

Another aspect of the transformation is that Avon has become more disciplined and strategic when deciding where to allocate scarce resources. The company considers geography and product categories when determining where to spend advertising money. "That is not a small thing," says Kropf. "That is something we hadn't done before."

POSTING WINNING RESULTS

From 1999 to 2004, Avon's sales grew from $5.3 billion to $7.7 bil-lion. Its operating margin expanded from 9.8 percent to 16 percent and its annual cash flow almost doubled from $449 million to $883 million. It has upped spending on consumer promotional programs such as advertising from $300 million to $530 million annually. The result to Avon shareholders has been a rise in earnings per share from 55 cents in 1999 to $1.77 in 2004.

"Avon is fundamentally a different company now than it was ten years ago," says William Steele of Banc of America Securities. "It was a little bit of a boom-and-bust company. One year they would make their numbers and the next year they would fall short. Since promoting Andrea [Jung] to CEO in 1999, it delivers double-digit earnings per share growth every year."

From Steele's vantage point, he has watched a company that would vacillate between focusing on the brand and focusing on the channel. What has helped Avon stabilize and grow in the past five years, he believes, is that Jung "seemed to have the perfect combina-tion with having a respect for the channel, but really talking about the brand." The company's biggest challenge had been its brand. "It was on the cusp of becoming Grandma's brand," says Steele.

There were two options presented. One would have been to "take a big swing and hopefully turn it around. That also equates to risk," says Steele. "The other avenue was to chip away at the brand to improve it. To me that is what she [Jung] did." He points to the global advertising campaign, the beComing and mark brands, and the new celebrity spokeswomen as examples. "There were several initiatives that all helped to push the brand forward. None were high risk and high reward. There is nothing that she bet the farm on."

As an analyst who follows Procter & Gamble and Gillette as well, Steele says he has learned "not to underestimate leadership. She has just done a phenomenal job, setting a strategy, understanding the challenges and really leading the organization," he says. "A lot of good things have happened at Avon."

PLANNING THE NEXT PHASE

From the company's perspective, it is just getting started. At a year-end conference for financial analysts in 2004, Avon presented valiant plans for the next three-year phase of its transformation to becoming a seamless global behemoth. Executives refer to it as Avon's "Coming of Age" period.

Avon expects to see a continuation of its Business Transformation Plan objectives, along with global expansion and new product and technology initiatives, to reap some stellar rewards. Company executives have also hinted that some acquisitions could be in Avon's future.

The company projects that net sales will increase 10 percent annually, reaching $10 billion by 2007. Along with that, operating margins are expected to widen to between 18.5 and 19 percent, for an operating profit of $1.9 billion. Cash flow is projected to rise to a robust $1.5 billion, while generating earnings per share of $1.95 to $2 by 2007.

This financial good fortune won't only accrue to Avon's executives and shareholders. The company is also determined to use it to make the world a better—and healthier—place in which to live.

CHAPTER 13

GIVE BACK

A von is a company of many missions. As expressed throughout its corporate credos and public statements, it is dedicated to finding ways to empower and enrich the lives of women around the world. Part of that means offering a way for them to achieve financial independence. But the company now also has hearty aspirations for giving back to those who have helped make it so successful. It wants to develop its public charity arm, the Avon Foundation, into the largest nonprofit organization anywhere exclusively dedicated to serving the causes of women.

"That is our vision," emphasizes Andrea Jung, chairman and chief executive officer, "to have the largest foundation for women, not just for breast cancer, but other women's issues, too." Says Jung, "At Avon, we measure our accomplishments in two ways—in what we achieve as a business, and in our commitment to what we can do for others."

Jung says that being heavily involved in philanthropic efforts is part of Avon's DNA. Nevertheless, the company's philanthropic work is not considered to be a factor in driving its business, nor are its programs undertaken with the goal of directly impacting sales.

A company spokeswoman notes that, while it may be possible to quantify awareness levels of Avon's programs, business generated as a result of all this charity work is not measured. There's no question, however, that being aligned with a cause gives Avon's representatives another reason to engage in a dialogue with their customers, and it only increases their loyalty to the company.

For some shoppers, the social programs a company supports may be a determining factor in deciding whether to buy their products. "It is like being ecologically friendly," comments one drugstore cosmetics buyer. "There are those who'll only buy from companies with a cause . . . and they are fiercely loyal."

Many companies have integrated cause-related marketing and fund-raising programs into their culture. While altruism is usually at the heart of these initiatives, there can be an upside for the business as well. Researchers have found many large corporations do take into consideration what the potential upside for the company could be depending on the charity it becomes involved with. "We've seen much more focus on corporate giving where the company is looking at a return on their investment," says Dwight Burlingame, associate executive director at the Center On Philanthropy at Indiana University in Indianapolis.

Even if a company isn't looking for a business return on its contributions to society, an added benefit is often the perception that the company is a good place to work, Burlingame adds.

A HISTORY OF PHILANTHROPY

David Hall McConnell set this philanthropic tone for the company from the very start. It began with his support of community programs and churches. In his writings, McConnell expressed his feelings about the fundamental connection between society and business. In the Suffern, New York, area, the McConnell family contributed money for scholarships, donated land for parks, and financed a local middle school football field (which is still called McConnell Stadium). McConnell also permitted the local Boy Scout troop to use a company building for its meetings.

The commitment, "To meet fully the obligations of corporate citizenship by contributing to the well-being of society and the environment in which it functions," is listed among the seven "Principles that Guide Avon," originally developed by McConnell and under which the company continues to operate.

McConnell would also personally lend a hand and a dollar to those in need. His secretary, Ann Meany, wrote about an employee who tended the wood stove at the company's first offices at 126 Chambers Street. The man had a dream to equip his five sons with uniforms and instruments, and then corral them into a drum and bugle band. One day, the boys strode into the office playing instruments and wearing matching outfits. Where did they get them? Meany said that some of McConnell's friends stopped by about the same time, and while it was never said, she concluded that McConnell must have bought the instruments for the boys and invited his chums over to watch the show.

Several years after his death, McConnell's daughter, Edna McConnell Clark, continued in her father's tradition. In 1955, she established a private foundation that still exists today. Two of her grandsons remain as board members. One, H. Lawrence Clark, says that while his grandmother was a student at Smith College she was "interested in outreach" and worked as a volunteer in New York City. "She was also very interested in Africa and helping people suffering from hunger and disease," he adds.

Edna married Van Alan Clark, a Cornell graduate and chemist, who took a job at Avon beginning in 1920 and stayed there until retirement. Clark vividly recalls his grandparents being grateful for their fortunes in life and wanting to somehow give back. "One of the things I absolutely remember is my grandfather saying they have three sons and they have all been in harms way during the war [World War II]. They were all very active on the war front in the Navy, and unlike a lot of their neighbors and friends, all three of their sons came home," Clark says. With the safe return of their sons, they felt as if they had been given every blessing they could have asked for, recalls Clark, "and they started a formal foundation. For years it was run basically by the family and a lawyer friend."

As time went on and his grandparents got older, the value of Avon stock—and, in turn, the foundation—grew to where they felt it was time to turn it over to professional managers. Today, the Edna McConnell Clark Foundation is based in Manhattan and funds educational and development programs centered on improving life prospects for young people from low-income backgrounds.

THE AVON FOUNDATION

The Avon Foundation was created in 1955 as a private foundation. Its goal: improving the lives of women and their families—with an emphasis on education and job training. Now a public charitable organization, it adheres to its heritage with scholarship programs, particularly for the economically disadvantaged in areas where Avon operates.

Over the past decade, the Avon Foundation has elevated the breast cancer cause as its premier area of focus and has made an astounding impact through aggressive fund-raising efforts. Through its Breast Cancer Crusade, Avon issued millions of dollars in support of awareness, care, and research programs. Points out Kathleen Walas, president of the Avon Foundation, "Over the last 10 to 15 years, we have redefined what we stand for since our philanthropy was formalized in 1955."

Beyond the work Avon did with breast cancer, there was a belief that Avon was ready and able to take on another cause. "We wanted to know," recalls Walas, "are there opportunities to look at beyond scholarships and work programs? How could we narrow our focus in the area of economic empowerment?" Any project considered, of course, would have to fit in with Avon's culture and belief system, and be embraced and supported by its sales representatives.

After fully evaluating the landscape, including a commissioned report by McKinsey & Co., Avon recently added another pillar to its platform: domestic violence. Over time, the company pledges to pursue the cause as vigorously as it has with the Breast Cancer Crusade. "It would be nice if we didn't have this kind of cause to support," Walas admits. "But the reaction from the representatives has been overwhelming."

Because of the one-on-one relationships Avon representatives have with their customers, they have a personal insight into their lives and a window into the struggles that can go on in homes behind closed doors. Looking to improve domestic violence problems is a natural matter for Avon to address.

Avon is gingerly entering the realm of domestic violence, says Walas, with a modest $1 million initial investment to begin an awareness campaign titled "Speak Out Against Domestic Violence." The effort will focus on education and prevention.

"It will start small like we did with the Breast Cancer Crusade—to get the word out—and then we will identify and partner with the best organizations," Walas notes. "The Avon Foundation is not a check-writing philanthropy. We are going out and creating our programs together with [existing] programs in those communities."

Avon has already learned that its educational literature on the subject needs to be presented in a pocket-sized form that can be easily hidden if handed to a woman in public. It is a sensitive problem and one that needs to be addressed in a gentle and cautious manner.

To help draw attention to the issue, Avon's new spokesperson, actress Salma Hayek, will be lending her voice. "Salma and her own personal commitment to women and the issue of domestic violence was very, very strongly considered when we thought about a spokesperson," says Jung. Hayek has already leveraged her marquee name, turning her latest movie premier with actor Pierce Brosnan into a fund-raising event.

THE BREAST CANCER CRUSADE

For now, however, it is in the arena of breast cancer programs where Avon is putting its full global heft. The current Avon Foundation Breast Cancer Crusade beneficiary list in the United States alone is five typed pages long. Avon is now funding similar programs in at least 50 countries around the world. The emphasis has always been on programs that treat and educate medically underserved, low income, and minority women—those with the most limited access to health care.

The program actually started out as a public education and awareness campaign in the United Kingdom. It has now advanced into one of the single most comprehensive charitable funding initiatives for the breast cancer cause. Breast cancer remains the most commonly diagnosed cancer among women worldwide. In the United States, it's the second most deadly cancer after lung cancer.

Jung has a personal connection to breast cancer, which makes the cause especially close to her heart. Her maternal grandmother died of the disease when Jung was 14. At that time in society, there was more mystery surrounding the disease. It is a term that still sends shivers through patients and families. In Jung's household, as in many others back then, cancer was a condition talked about in whispered tones and referred to as the "c" word. In Jung's home, she recalls, there was also a fear that it was contagious.

Since coming to the helm of Avon, Jung has energized Avon's breast cancer cause with personal zest and passion. To date, the Breast Cancer Crusade has raised and distributed an incredible $350 million. This money is awarded to clinical care, research, and community-based outreach and support programs worldwide. Most of this money has been accumulated through fund-raisers, such as the noted Avon Walk for Breast Cancer, along with the sale of dedicated Pink Ribbon products through sales representatives. There are also other events such as the annual Avon Kiss Goodbye to Breast Cancer Awards gala, held in New York, the most recent of which had performances by Harry Connick Jr. and Vanessa Carleton and raised $2.3 million. Since its inception in 2001, the annual awards gala has brought in $8 million.

"My mother lost her battle to cancer when I was a young boy, and I know personally how the disease affects everyone, not just women," Connick said. "It impacts families and friends, and shatters lives, and with three daughters I have a special interest in eradicating breast cancer."

While there are fund-raisers now around the world, the bulk of the financial support still comes through efforts in the United States where the culture is acclimated to and supportive of corporate philanthropy.

PINK RIBBON PRODUCTS

The Avon representatives themselves are walking talking breast cancer crusaders. Some are also survivors. Each year Avon offers dedicated Pink Ribbon products for which the proceeds are used to benefit Avon Foundation Breast Cancer Crusade programs. Representatives do not receive a commission on these items, because of the fund-raising component. What's more, sales of these products can cannibalize their regular orders for the month, since customers are not likely to buy both a Pink Ribbon lipstick and a traditional lipstick at the same time. But the reps feel it's worth it, given where the money goes. "We do it from the goodness of our hearts," says Dottie Randall, a Sales Leadership representative and breast cancer survivor.

The first Avon Pink Ribbon products were sold in the United Kingdom in 1992. It was the first time that Avon raised money for the cause through external sales. By the following year, the Pink Ribbon products were being sold in the United States, the first item being a pin that cost about $3.

The Pink Ribbon products are most highly visible during October (National Breast Cancer Month) and in May near Mother's Day, although they are available year round for purchase. Each comes in a pink box with literature on breast cancer resources.

The U.S. brochure now devotes some front covers and considerable space inside to Pink Ribbon products, because of the importance to the company's charitable work. Pink Ribbon items are never featured in Avon's paid advertisements, however, because it is not a commercial enterprise.

Information on Avon Foundation news and Pink Ribbon products go out to representatives via e-mail messages and through Avon's bi-weekly *Representative Times* newspaper. There are also breast cancer seminars for the sales reps.

Pink Ribbon items have included a pink rhinestone pendant on a silver tone chain for $7.50 and a heart-shaped locket with a key chain for $5. Net proceeds on these items range between 50 percent to 87 percent, depending on the item. Avon has also sold celebrity-endorsed beauty items, such as a recent nail polish collection. Six shades of Avon Nailwear polish were each named after a celebrity. They included Cybill Shepherd with Cybill's Strength, Tracee Ross with Tracee's Passion, Ali Landry with Ali's Faith, Leah Remini with Leah's Courage, Sharon Stone with Sharon's Heart, and Salma Hayek with Salma's Hope. The nail enamel is $3 with 80 percent, or $2.40, going to the cause for every bottle sold. So far, some $65 million has been raised through the pink ribbon sales.

THE WALKS

Avon started its charitable breast cancer walks seven years ago. Today, the Avon Walk for Breast Cancer events generate the largest proportion of the Foundation's funding. Begun in 1998 as a three-day event, Avon relaunched the fund-raiser as a two-day program in 2003. "We are a year-round focus," Walas points out, "not just in October for Breast Cancer Month."

The walkers pitch two-person tents and camp out overnight. Avon staff members often participate in the walks, too. Brian Connolly, executive vice president and president of Avon North America, personally raised $25,000 in the most recent New York walk. Sales associates who participate are clearly identified by the special green "Team Avon" hats they wear.

To commemorate the Avon Foundation's 50th anniversary in 2005, the Avon Foundation organized a major worldwide awareness and fund-raising effort, including the "Walk Around the World for Breast Cancer" event in the fall orchestrated in some 50 countries around the world.

WHERE THE MONEY GOES

For the first several years of the Crusade, proceeds were used exclusively to fund screening and awareness campaigns, transportation to and from treatment centers, and other support and counseling measures. By 2000, Avon became more actively involved, and for the first time began funding research, taking a lead role in fostering medical initiatives with the goal of finding a cure.

With the foundation's heightened level of involvement, it announced major grants in the amount of $10 million and more to several leading U.S. medical institutions beginning in 2000 to help support research and a variety of other breast care programs. The recipients included Herbert Irving Comprehensive Cancer Center at the Columbia Presbyterian Medical Center in New York; Massachusetts General Hospital/Harvard Comprehensive Cancer Center in Boston; Robert H. Lurie Comprehensive Cancer Center of Northwestern University in Chicago; the Sidney Kimmel Comprehensive Cancer Center at Johns Hopkins in Baltimore; the Winship Cancer Institute of Emory University School of Medicine and The Grady Health System in Atlanta; and the University of California's San Francisco Comprehensive Cancer Center with the San Francisco General Hospital.

Avon also gave an unprecedented $20 million grant to the National Cancer Institute.

JOHNS HOPKINS SIDNEY KIMMEL CANCER CENTER

The world renowned Johns Hopkins health institution in Baltimore will shortly unveil the Avon Foundation Breast Center as part of its Sidney Kimmel Comprehensive Cancer Center. The new facility is possible thanks to a $10 million grant the medical center received from the Avon Foundation in October 2003. "We have been the happy recipient of over $12 million from Avon in the last several years," says Dr. Nancy E. Davidson, director of the breast cancer program at Johns Hopkins. Construction on the new building is at a moderate pace because it is being done around the existing facilities. Notes Davidson, "Daily patient care activities need to continue to take place."

When completed, the new center will enable women to receive all of their treatment and care under one roof, rather than having to wind their way from one floor to meet with an oncologist to another for a CT scan, and possibly even another for the film to be read. "It will help us to streamline the process and make it more efficient for the patient to receive treatment. That is very big to us," Davison says. The facility will bring together experts from prevention and detection through diagnosis, surgical treatment, and postoperative care.

The grant will also enable Johns Hopkins to pursue startup research projects. As Davidson explains, many initiatives are challenged to find funding. Large grant organizations like the National Institute for Health (NIH) tend to support projects that are fairly mature. "Avon has been very good about allowing people to use funds early in the research process and get it to a point where they can then request additional funding," she observes.

One area now being investigated is the use of immunio-therapy—that is the development of a treatment to prevent breast cancer. This work is being done in conjunction with the Fred Hutchinson Cancer Research Center in Seattle, Washington, also a recipient of Avon funding.

"The grant allows us to bankroll new scientific projects in areas that other people have not been willing to fund," Davidson says. "Avon has allowed us to continue work on some of these seedling ideas."

In addition to the work with Hutchinson, Johns Hopkins researchers are looking into cancer prevention methods as well. The Center has been able to expand its staff through the Avon scholar program.

A portion of the funding has been allocated to the Avon Foundation Access to Breast Health Initiative, an outreach program for low-income and minority women in the Baltimore area. Through already established partnerships, the Kimmel Cancer Center experts work with community centers to reduce disproportionately high incidence and death rates from breast cancer.

Even for leading medical centers like Johns Hopkins, Davidson says it has been more difficult to find sources of funding to support programs. "It is very hard to get funding and it is getting worse in this economic environment. The NIH is dropping back on its funding and other philanthropies have had reductions too," she says. "We are very appreciative to Avon."

UCSF COMPREHENSIVE CANCER CENTER

Avon's relationship with the University of California's San Francisco Comprehensive Cancer Center, in conjunction with San Francisco General Hospital, began in 2000 with a $2.2 million grant that was to be spread among several programs. The focus was on funding research delving into the causes and possible cures for breast cancer, along with areas related to clinical care access and prevention programs for underserved women in the community. Dr. Frank McCormick, director of the UCSF Comprehensive Cancer Center, and Avon worked together to get the program started.

According to Dr. John Ziegler, director of the cancer risk program at the UCSF Comprehensive Cancer Center, Avon came back with an additional award of $10 million for a total of $12.2 million in grants as of January 2004. That was followed by another $500,000 stipend.

"Avon wanted to increase the gift and support for the hospital to upgrade all the aspects of care for underserved women in the area of breast cancer," says Ziegler. One result was the creation of the $3.6 million Avon Foundation Comprehensive Breast Center, a 4,500 square foot building that opened in May 2004. It has enabled the hospital to improve access and diagnostic testing to women in the area who are most in need.

The building's architect, Ignatius Tsang, said the design explores healing and dialogue, and the layout is said to be child-friendly with a healing garden designed by landscape artist Topher Delaney as a centerpiece. Before this center opened, the hospital had two mammogram machines that were constantly in operation. With the expanded capability, twice the number of patients—about 10,000 a year—will be served. Before, there was a large backup and many were not being reached for early detection. "It just has made a huge stride forward to meet the needs of these women," Ziegler says.

For more than one-half of the hospital's patients, English is a second language. Thanks to Avon's help, the center has been able to fund a program providing "Patient Navigators," multilingual staff members who help patients through the maze of the hospital system, assisting with paperwork and explaining the proper handling of medications.

Additionally, San Francisco now boasts a genetic testing program for women with a strong history of breast cancer and who are seen as high risk. As far I know, says Ziegler, "this [service] has not been done before in any public hospital."

Avon Foundation money is also funding a new support group for women with cancer and their family members to "help them through the process of treatment and rehabilitation."

"It is a very, very generous contribution to our effort," says Ziegler, noting that Avon's endowment departs from standard gifts in both size and in the freedom of how granted money can be used. "This is an unusual philanthropic thrust and a very welcome one I might add."

Public health centers, Dr. Ziegler points out, "are strapped for cash and are always responding to a greater need and greater demand than they can provide." These public centers serve the region's indigent, homeless, and unemployed. "With those relatively unrestricted funds that the Avon Foundation gave to the hospital, it has made it possible to fill in a lot of gaps and meet the needs of these women in effective ways."

WINSHIP CANCER INSTITUTE OF EMORY UNIVERSITY

At the Winship Cancer Institute of Emory University, there is now the Avon Foundation Breast Cancer Research and Care Program. There is also the Avon Foundation Comprehensive Breast Center at Grady Memorial Hospital in Atlanta. African-American women in the Atlanta area have a breast cancer mortality rate 10 percent to 15 percent higher than the national average for African-Americans. A grant from Avon has enabled Winship to hire a trained health care professional to head a community outreach program to educate women on the importance of early diagnosis and preventative care. Funding has also provided for research initiatives through the Avon Scholar program. Winship now has seven Avon Scholars, whom are named on its web site.

"We have been really blessed by Avon's philanthropy," says Dr. Jonathan Simons, director of the Winship Cancer Institute. For one thing, he says, the impact of a grant to Grady Hospital, "has been overwhelming."

It is estimated that more than 17,000 women have participated in the community advocacy health fairs. Those women come from 40 housing projects in some of the most underserved and poorest areas of metro and urban Atlanta. "It may be one of the largest outreach programs ever for the underserved, particularly for reaching Hispanic and African American women," says Simons. "Among those women, less than one in three had even had a mammography in the last 10 years. There has been an enormous community impact."

Avon's funding has touched many programs, but another huge impact has been in the area of research, Simons notes. Three of the researchers in the Avon Scholar program have turned the initial $150,000 research awards into new federal grants, enabling them to continue the work started with Avon Foundation money. Explains Simons, "We were given research awards to test new ideas and the ideas have been so promising they have been able to leverage the initial data to obtain much larger research grants. Avon has provided the bench money to very gifted young researchers and turned it into more research. It has been enormously powerful.

"We have taken a lot of pride in the association [with Avon], and we have taken the stewardship of these funds very seriously," Simons adds. "We think the return on the investment has been enormous."

THE CHARLES B. WANG COMMUNITY HEALTH CENTER

There are smaller scale programs funded by the Avon Foundation, too.

The Charles B. Wang Community Health Center in the Chinatown section of New York City has been serving the needs of the area's Asian population for more than 30 years. The majority of the center's clients are low income, uninsured or underinsured Asian immigrants with nowhere else to turn for basic health care. To effectively reach these local residents, the center recruits and trains bilingual health care providers.

Within the center is a dedicated women's health segment to address a broad spectrum of primary and specialty services. Avon has been lending a hand there for six years by funding research and community outreach programs, says Rebecca Sze, executive director of the center. "We are trying to collect age and demographic data on the women in the community that we screen for breast cancer, and tie into that the results of tests," Sze explains. The research is helping the center find common links among Asian women and breast health.

"Before starting to receive the Avon grants, we were very limited in scope," says Sze. "We didn't have the sophisticated database to capture all of the information." Now the center is also able to generate and mail reminders to women to come in for breast cancer screenings. "The reminders are helpful," Sze insists. "Sometimes it's not that they don't want to have the screening, but they tend to overlook it because they are busy. It enhances our case management. We have been able to learn more about the breast health of Asian women. Before, we were running a very small scale program.

"The center now supports close to 800 to 1,000 women a year," Sze says. "These are uninsured women and they really feel that health care is so inaccessible to them because they can't afford it."

OTHER AVON BREAST CANCER CRUSADE BENEFICIARIES

The list of the Avon Foundation grant recipients is very long. It has provided more than $350 million to the breast cancer cause in 50 countries.

Since the Breast Cancer Crusade began, Avon has distributed more than 200 million free educational brochures worldwide. In addition to the aforementioned beneficiaries, Avon has funded dozens of programs large and small across America. The Olive View UCLA Medical Center in Los Angeles used monies from the Avon Foundation to expand its Mammography Clinic and add new equipment to better reach more minority women in the greater San Fernando Valley. The Jewish Hospital in Cincinnati used its Foundation funding to buy a new mobile mammography unit, provide a patient assistance program, and pay for mammograms for women in Northern Kentucky without access to other forms of financial assistance. Through the Y-ME National Breast Cancer Organization in Chicago, an Avon Foundation grant enabled the area's underserved Latina, Chinese, and Vietnamese women to receive proper follow-up care after receiving abnormal screening results. In Denver, The Children's Treehouse Foundation has obtained money for a support group for children whose mothers have breast cancer. It will be expanded to other U.S. cities in the future.

A $4 million gift from the Avon Foundation, along with additional funding from the National Cancer Institute, will support a clinical trial to evaluate the role of ultrasound as a supplemental screening tool in women with dense breast tissue who are at high risk for breast cancer. The research is being headed by the American College of Radiology Imaging Network.

Then there are programs like the one at the University of Colorado Cancer Center, which has developed a new cancer exercise program with the help of Summit Cancer Solutions and the Denver Parks and Recreation Department—all funded by the Avon Foundation. The point of the program is to aid in the recovery of patients by improving general fitness during and after cancer treatment. Exercise, it has been shown, can improve the immune system and fight depression. In the Colorado area, the Avon Foundation has further supported conferences such as the Avon Latina Breast Cancer Survivorship Conference.

INTERNATIONAL PERSPECTIVES

Similar philanthropic initiatives are happening internationally. Hortensia Orozco Romero of Guadalajara, Mexico, a 46-year-old Avon representative, has been treated for uterine cancer that was diagnosed two years ago. "The support I have received from the company has been marvelous," says Orozco Romero. "I always wear the ribbon of hope so people notice. I want them to see that I could survive cancer and continue working."

She says she "would love" Avon to organize a fund-raising walk in Guadalajara, "so I could take part in it." In the meanwhile, she says, "I do always support this cause and I am very committed to selling the products in order to help the fight against the disease."

Her colleague, 57-year-old Agustina Alvarez Diaz, who lives in the State of Mexico, says she always tries harder when the campaign brochures offer pink ribbon products to raise money. "I make a special effort to sell more," she says. "My customers tell me that the Avon Crusade is a very noble cause."

Swati Sharma, a leading sales representative in New Delhi, India, says that her district recently held a fund-raiser and used the proceeds to donate an ambulance for cancer patients to a local hospital. Meantime, Natalia Shevchenko, 45, of Moscow says while that fund-raising events such as those in the United States don't exist in Russia, representatives there do sell special pink ribbon products to raise money. She notes that twice during the year, "We go to the streets and distribute brochures to talk to women about the illness."

Around the world, Avon has funded programs in at least 20 countries in Europe and Africa; 15 countries in its Latin America regions; and 13 countries in its Asia/Pacific territory.

A sampling of those efforts include new mammography equipment for the Dominican Republic; education and prevention programs in Ecuador; and medical exams and treatment for women in El Salvador, Guatemala, and Honduras. Venezuela has received 13 mammography machines and three mobile clinics, while Avon has supported a new breast cancer clinic in Mexico and paid for more than 6 million clinical examinations for women in 360 cities.

In Europe, Avon funded 10 medical scholarships and medical research in Italy. It also paid for 80 research scientists and 15 nurses, plus provided funding for a new health clinic in the United Kingdom. In Africa, a breast cancer study is being led by a female researcher in the United Arab Emirates.

Furthermore, Avon has initiated a national mammography program for poor women in Thailand, complete with mammography machines and six funded regional cancer centers. In China, the company has funded treatments, lectures, and education for women through 2,000 health volunteers.

SETTING A GOOD EXAMPLE

Avon is not alone in its efforts to raise funds for women's health issues. The breast cancer cause has been adopted by several other beauty companies—Estée Lauder, Revlon, and Mary Kay, among them. L'Oreal has been holding fund-raisers to support the Ovarian Cancer Research Fund. Even Target has opened a special store stocked with only pink merchandise to raise money to support breast cancer awareness.

The Five Star Fragrance Company has just introduced Red Dress, from which 100 percent of the proceeds will go to the American Heart Association's Go Red for Women program. The program is designed to teach women about the risks of heart attack and stroke.

Through these efforts companies garner positive media coverage and hopefully consumer loyalty, while also providing for worthy organizations.

The number of companies hoping to do well by doing good has continued to grow. The stunning sales of the Lance Armstrong Foundation's Live Strong yellow rubber bracelets are supportive of the notion that consumers like to combine a purchase with a good cause. To-date, the bracelets have raised $8 million to benefit cancer programs.

Retail consultant Wendy Liebmann cautions that companies must be committed to the cause they are raising funds for. "It has to mean something and has to be marketed with legitimacy as opposed to just branding," she says. "It has to have credibility like MAC [and its AIDS fund-raising] because the consumer is smart and will figure out when you're just doing it to be purely promotional."

AT THE HEART OF THE EFFORT

If there is a living embodiment of the Avon Breast Cancer Crusade it is Dottie Randall. The 55-year-old resident of Newark, Delaware, is a 27-year veteran Avon representative—and now a breast cancer survivor.

Randall was diagnosed seven years ago after she detected a lump in her breast. Only a few months earlier, a mammogram came up negative. Randall now returns to her doctor annually for testing to make certain her system is still clear. "The shadow is always there," she shares. "I could be a ten year survivor and I go in for a yearly checkup and be told the cancer is back." The emotional tug and never-ending uncertainty of the outcome is what makes cancer so difficult to bear, she maintains. The side effects of radiation and chemotherapy treatments that can bring on weakness, nausea, hair loss, and a host of other unusual side effects can be devastating.

Now Randall's younger sister has been diagnosed with breast cancer and is undergoing treatment. It surprised both of them because their family had no prior history of the disease. Since her experience, Randall has become a personal crusader for the cause. During her treatments she befriended other women going through the same thing. A few have not been as fortunate as Randall. "Some of these women were at a stage more advanced than mine," Randall notes. "Some of them made it and some of them didn't." Randall says she learned there was "such a need out there. Early detection made such a big difference."

Randall recently retired from her day job as an administrative assistant at a school and began expanding her Avon business. She has also become involved in several breast cancer programs in her area. "When I was going through my treatment I wasn't involved in any of the organizations that I am involved with now," she says. "I never thought it would hit me."

Randall speaks out on behalf of Avon's Breast Cancer Crusade and works with the Breast Cancer Coalition and Sisters on a Mission. "We teach women about mammograms and how to do a self-examination," she says. "We have molds of a breast made of silicone with five knots in it of different sizes. We ask women to tell us how many knots do they feel. No one ever feels all five. It really makes them aware." She also helps organize educational workshops in local churches and community centers.

Randall recently sold $1,000 worth of Avon pink ribbon products. But that is the tip of the iceberg for what she wants to achieve. "I really want to get into the corporate world with pink ribbon items because they buy all the time for their employees and customers." In addition to helping the cause, she adds, "they could use it as a tax write off."

Randall thinks she can rapidly multiply her sales of pink ribbon products that way. "If I can get into the corporate world, my goal would be $50,000." Avon, of course, hopes that Randall and others won't be called upon to sell pink ribbon products indefinitely.

"The Avon Foundation will continue to champion the [breast cancer] cause until we have reached our goal," says Walas. The goal: "To make the Crusade obsolete because we have eradicated breast cancer."

EPILOGUE

Every fall, Art Goodwin organizes an Avon alumni cocktail party at a restaurant on Manhattan's East Side. Anywhere from 80 to 130 people turn out for the annual gathering, which has taken place for the past 10 years. Goodwin, who retired as Avon's director of sales promotions 12 years ago, sends out invitations to former employees in places as far flung as Europe and the Far East.

"The company has a very interesting loyalty factor," Goodwin, a retiree, comments. The party is an opportunity, he says, "to renew old friendships and for networking. Many of Avon's alumni have moved on to become CEOs or chairmen of other companies, both major and minor." But for the most part, the get together is held because, Goodwin says, "we just have fond memories to share about Avon."

Like Goodwin, several executives interviewed for this book who have made lifelong careers at Avon remarked that they were given ample opportunity to move into new positions throughout the company. By doing so, they grew professionally and never got bored.

But while those inside the company may be sold, in the elitist beauty industry, Avon hasn't always projected such a prestigious image to outsiders.

"There was a time when it was harder to attract top talent," admits Robert Briddon, Avon's group vice president of marketing for North America. That changed as the company's image began to be burnished and modernized over the past few years. "We started getting hot," Briddon boasts.

Even though the company and its current CEO Andrea Jung regularly make front-page news these days, the internal corporate culture at Avon has retained many of its old fashioned ways. While it operates at a brisk pace and fully embraces technological advancements, there remains a degree of civility in how things are accomplished.

"There have been people come through here who are very aggressive," Briddon shares. "It just doesn't work. They don't get things done. The atmosphere doesn't respond to that."

The company's distinct culture is said to be replicated in its offices around the world, be it in New York, Asia, Europe, or Latin America.

When hiring, the company looks for people with a passion for success, but not at the expense of others. "We talk about an Avon person. We look for someone who will be comfortable and supportive of the whole culture here," says Briddon.

Possibly because of its somewhat reserved nature, Avon's mammoth business has frequently gone unnoticed by the competition. The fact that the company owns a predominant share of the mass fragrance market globally is not mentioned often. Despite a well-oiled publicity machine that regularly issues news releases, in some respects, the heart of Avon's operation has remained the beauty industry's best-kept secret.

That Avon has not been on the competitive radar screen has, in some respects, played to its favor and kept it from being subjected to aggressive attacks. Procter & Gamble and L'Oreal, for instance, go head-to-head with each other in attempts to bite off a piece of the other's retail market share. If one has a new product coming out, the other may try to rush a similar item to market first.

"To me it is our competitive advantage that people aren't aware of how powerful and large we are," says Briddon. "Therefore, they are not watching us." Although, note several Avon executives, it can be frustrating when the company doesn't get the credit it deserves.

Frequently, when newspapers and magazines write about fragrance sales, Avon's scents are not even mentioned because they don't come up on lists provided by industry tracking firms such as NPD Beauty and Information Resources, which collect sales data on department and mass stores, respectively.

As a result, of being virtually invisible, few are out there knocking off Avon's products. If Skin-So-Soft, now more than 40 years old, had been sold in retail stores, you can be assured there would be several copycat bath oil items crowding the shelves today.

Because it operates in a different venue, Avon is able to slyly copy others without anyone really paying attention. But there is a downside to not being so showy. "What is least known and least perceived about Avon," says Angie Rossi, group vice president U.S. sales and customer care, "is that we have great product."

Under Jung's leadership, Avon's sales have jumped 45 percent and the company's stock has more than doubled since 1999. Its future growth is being predicated on international expansion. The company is also counting on the Sales Leadership program to help stabilize its revolving sales force and entice more women seeking lucrative career opportunities who wouldn't have considered Avon before.

If Avon has learned anything from its past, it's that it must respond to market demands and shifting consumer trends quickly in order to stay viable. With its U.S. business softening, the company has already put into play a series of actions designed to stabilize its largest market and restore it to a growth track by 2006.

To buttress slumping U.S. sales, Avon has recently added a new section within its brochures dubbed "Beauty on a Budget" to showcase lower priced items—everything offered in the category is under $10. Cheaper skin care and personal care collections are also being introduced to meet the needs of consumers.

The move is patterned after a retail trend that has gained wide acceptance in the past few years. Several retailers—Wal-Mart, Eckerd, CVS, and others—have added special budget sections presenting an array of beauty and cosmetics items (typically in travel sizes) at lower prices to compete with the growing dollar store market.

For the first time since its introduction, Avon also integrated its Wellness product selection into its core brochure in 2005. Before, these items had been presented in a separate catalog, which representatives were required to purchase separately.

Additionally, Avon may have hit a price ceiling with its fragrance customers, having increased prices to an all-time high of $29.50 for the Today, Tomorrow, and Always trilogy. Avon will therefore make sure it presents a balanced selection to customers in future brochures with fragrances in a range of prices, ensuring there will be something affordable for everyone.

At the same time, the company is expected to continue to ramp up its successful skin care business and has just released two major new products in the Anew Clinical line—Lift and Tuck Professional Body Shaper and Laser System.

As Avon tweaks and modifies its business, it has every intention of sticking to the tenets laid out by its founder, beginning with a dedication to its sales representatives and a commitment to delivering high quality, fairly priced products. The company has learned that those basic concepts have served it well for more than 100 years. Company executives are already talking about how to deliver on those same promises for the next century.

BUSINESS LESSONS

Through examining Avon's operations and leadership principles, a number of lessons emerge about how to successfully build and run a global company. These are valuable strategies that can be applied to building just about any kind of business—large or small—in almost every industry:

- *Never forget who is responsible for your success.* From the outset, Avon founder David McConnell recognized that his sales force—the legions of women representatives—were the heart and soul of his operation. Then as now, the company wastes no energy in supporting the troops with educational materials and various rewards to motivate and inspire them.

  When existing rewards are no longer relevant, Avon creates new incentives to appeal to changing tastes. For instance, mark representatives have a chance to earn individual trips to the Caribbean, as opposed to having to go on a group cruise like the older core representatives.
- *Keep up with significant industry trends, but stick to your values.* A major reason Avon initiated the Sales Leadership program

was that it saw itself falling behind the compensation structures offered by other leaders in the direct-selling industry. Nearly every other company gave its independent contractors a multi-level marketing payment plan, including Mary Kay. To ensure Avon would be able to continuously recruit new saleswomen and not lose them to other companies, it fell in line with the way the market was moving. It was a hard move. Avon had always been a single level firm. But the action created a program that allowed the company to continue to adhere to its core principles of maintaining a close relationship to each representative.

- *Remember what business you are in.* Avon almost came apart in the 1980s when a new management team that didn't understand the company's fundamental philosophy tried to dismantle and reconfigure Avon into something it was never intended to be—a health care provider. Once leadership was restored to the hands of a team that had faith in Avon's primary business—beauty products and direct selling—it was able to refocus, modernize operations, and breathe life back into the business.

- *Maintain a consistent message.* Avon has been successful around the world by using the same person-to-person selling method and increasingly selling the same core Avon products. It also organizes fund-raisers and supports breast cancer charities in nearly every one of its markets. Put simply, women around the world know that, at its core, Avon is a beauty company that empowers women and supports the breast cancer cause.

- *Let your independent contractors do it their own way.* Avon has put few restrictions on how its sales representatives promote, market, advertise, and or operate their individual businesses. As a result, millions of Avon representatives around the world have been able to customize their own businesses to fit their lifestyles and economic goals. This freedom has also given women the chance to be as creative as they want to be when selling Avon products. While everyone offers the same Avon items, each business is unique. When company representatives refer to their Avon businesses, it is not uncommon to detect a cheerful possessiveness. You frequently hear representatives unconsciously refer to the business activities as, "Doing my Avon."

- *Create and nurture your image.* Avon learned early on what a few breakthrough advertising and marketing campaigns can do. Avon was a company with saleswomen who went door-to-door. Its association with the doorbell, initiated through the company's 1950s "Avon Calling" advertising campaign, has stood the test of time. While Avon has modified its message as society and the culture have changed, it has stuck to stressing its personal approach. Advertisements continue to tell consumers to call their Avon representative. It has remained a high touch company, providing individualized service to women. Reps may not be ringing doorbells unannounced any longer, but every sale is still hand delivered.
- *Use available tools effectively.* Avon has not hesitated to employ developing technologies into its business practices. It could be an automated lipstick manufacturing line, the development of online educational programs, or the implementation of a global software package that opens a window into all of its activities like never before. After weighing the rewards versus the expenditures, Avon has always readily invested in its future.
- *Build systems that support your business cycle.* Avon has never tried to squeeze its square peg system into a round-hole solution. All of the departments within Avon are geared toward supporting its one of a kind operation—with marketing, advertising, product development, and manufacturing all designed to support the company's quick-spin selling cycles. With no other operation like it, Avon's systems have been finely tailored to match its unique needs. A prime example is its product development arm. Not only does Avon produce more than a thousand new beauty products annually to feed the demands of the brochure, its scientists know to search for ingredients that will enable it to create effective products at modest prices.

AN AMAZING REACH

One of the most extraordinary things about Avon is the number of women who have come through its sales system over the years. More than 40 million women worldwide have sold Avon products since the company's founding. In the current year, Avon representatives around the world will earn some $3 billion in commissions. The reach of the company and its brands is nothing less than phenomenal, considering it has achieved this one individual sale at a time.

Avon employs some 47,000 people worldwide to run the company and serve its 4.9 million representatives. The company has been lauded in numerous circles for its commitment to ensuring equality for both women and minorities.

Because of its dedication to maintaining a positive work environment, Avon has been cited by *Fortune* magazine as one of the 50 best companies for minorities, by *Latina Style* magazine as one of the 50 best companies for Latinas, and by *Working Woman* magazine as one of the best companies for female executives. In addition, *Computer World* called Avon one of the best places to work in information technology, and *Business Ethics* magazine listed Avon among the top 100 most ethical companies. And that's just a small sampling of some of the company's more recent accolades.

Kathleen Walas, president of the Avon Foundation, says that being a good corporate citizen remains a central mission for the company. She is currently overseeing a global company survey of whether Avon is doing all it could and should to be socially responsible throughout the organization. That includes everything from environmental concerns and equal employment opportunities to ethical practices with its business partners.

In the meantime, Avon persists with its core duty of providing employment opportunities for women worldwide, while encouraging and assisting them to succeed. As one former company executive says "Avon was always the American dream. No matter what your background, you could be somebody at Avon. Whoever that is would only be limited by the size of the dream." This same dream is now being delivered to women around the globe.

At a time when people are searching for meaning in their lives, Avon continues to make good on its promise of helping women everywhere belong to something—and build businesses—that are much bigger than them.

TIMELINE OF SIGNIFICANT EVENTS IN AVON HISTORY

1886 The California Perfume Company is established at 126 Chambers Street in New York City by David Hall McConnell, a bookseller. Mrs. Persis Foster Eames Albee of Winchester, New Hampshire, is the first sales representative. The startup collection includes five fragrances: violet, white rose, heliotrope, lily of the valley, and hyacinth.

1897 The first permanent laboratory is built in Suffern, New York. The three-story wooden building measures 3,000 square feet. The company records its first $500 day.

1901 The California Perfume Company records sales of $200,000, with the sales agents earning a total of $80,000 in commissions. There are now 6,100 representatives.

1902 The number of sales representatives reaches 10,000.

1905 *Outlook,* a magazine for sales representatives offering advice and company news, is introduced.

1909 Company's home office moves to 31 Park Place, New York, New York.

1914 Company's first office outside the United States opens in Montreal, Canada.

1915   California Perfume Company wins the Gold Medal Award at the Panama-Pacific Exposition in San Francisco for quality and packaging.

1916   California Perfume Company is incorporated in New York State.

1920   California Perfume Company sales exceed $1 million.

1922   Mission Garden fragrance line is introduced.

1926   Home office relocates to 114 Fifth Avenue, New York, New York. Sales reach $2.2 million.

1928   California Perfume Company introduces the Avon name on a handful of products, including a toothbrush, cleanser, talc, and vanity set.

1929   The Avon brand name is now applied to a cosmetics line that includes the first Avon logo. It features a sketch of Anne Hathaway's cottage.

1931   The Good Housekeeping Seal is awarded to 11 California Perfume Company products. The award was subsequently extended to the entire line.

1932   Company shifts to three-week brochure campaigns, from monthly campaigns. There are now more than 20,000 representatives.

1934   The Cotillion fragrance line is introduced.

1936   Company's first national advertising campaign begins with *Good Housekeeping*. Sales reach $3.6 million. Representatives now number 23,000.

1937   California Perfume Company founder David Hall McConnell dies at his home in Suffern, New York, at age 78. His son, David Hall McConnell Jr., becomes president of the company.

1938   Company sales climb to $5 million.

1939   The name of California Perfume Company is officially changed to Avon Products, Inc. on October 6, 1939.

1941   Sales reach $10.8 million.

1942   Company's Suffern, New York, plant devotes 40 percent of its capacity to manufacturing military supplies such as gas masks, canisters, and insect repellent.

1944   David Hall McConnell Jr. dies at age 42 at his summer home in East Hampton, New York. John A. Ewald becomes president. Sales hit $14.2 million. A district manager plan is introduced that calls for staff managers to oversee regional sales territories. It remains a point of distinction for Avon among other direct-selling companies.

1946   Stock in Avon is offered to the public on the over-the-counter market for the first time. Here's My Heart fragrance line is introduced. Sales climb to $17.2 million.

1948   Sales exceed $21 million.

1950   Avon's sales reach $31.2 million. To a Wild Rose fragrance line is introduced, including the first cream sachet.

1952   Sales hit $40.7 million.

1953   The Latin American division is established. Television advertising is launched. Avon is the first beauty company to do so.

1954   Sales climb to $55 million. The company opens divisions in Puerto Rico and Venezuela, its first international markets outside the United States and Canada.

1957   Sales reach $100 million, with more than 100,000 representatives worldwide.

1958   Avon enters Mexico. Sales increase to $120 million.

1959   Avon enters the United Kingdom, Brazil, and Germany (West).

1961   John A. Ewald is named chairman of the board, succeeding W. Van Alan Clark. Russell Rooks becomes president.

1962   Russell Rooks dies on January 31, less than two months after being named president. Wayne Hicklin becomes president. The Teenage Good Grooming program is instituted. The educational campaign is introduced in schools throughout the United States. Sales reach $210 million. Skin-So-Soft bath oil is introduced.

1963   Avon enters Australia.

1964   Avon Products, Inc. is listed on the New York Stock Exchange.

1965   Sales reach $351 million, with 250,000 representatives worldwide. Hays Clark is named president of international. The Unforgettable fragrance line is introduced.

1966   Avon enters Italy, Spain, and France. Sales reach $408 million. John A. Ewald is named chief executive officer.

1967   John A. Ewald retires as chairman of the board and chief executive officer, but remains as chairman of the board's executive committee. Fred G. Fusee is elected president.

1968   Two-week selling cycles begin testing in Pasadena, California, and Springdale, Ohio. Wayne Hicklin becomes chairman of the board.

1969   Two-week selling cycles are extended to all U.S. locations. The new plan is called The Better Way. The idea is to give more frequent service to customers and provide representatives with a greater sales and earnings opportunity. Sales reach $656 million.

1970   Avon enters Argentina. Sales hit $759 million, with more than 450,000 representatives worldwide.

1972   Sales reach $1 billion, with more than 600,000 representatives worldwide. Avon's headquarters move to 9 West 57th Street in Manhattan. Selling begins in The Netherlands. David W. Mitchell becomes president and Fred G. Fusee is named chairman of the board. Avon begins selling jewelry.

1973   Wayne Hicklin, chairman of the board, retires. Avon begins voluntarily listing ingredients on packages and develops a computer program to store ingredient formulations. A Corporate Responsibility Committee is formed.

1974   Automatic lipstick assembly factory begins operating in Suffern, New York. Sales now recorded at $1.2 billion, with 750,000 representatives worldwide.

1975   Avon enters Guatemala. *Outlook* magazine changes its name to *Avon Calling*.

1977   Avon enters Chile, Malaysia, and Paraguay. David W. Mitchell is named chairman of the board. William R. Chaney becomes president. Sales climb to $1.6 billion, with 650,000 sales representatives worldwide.

1978   Avon enters Thailand, The Philippines, and New Zealand. Sales exceed $2 billion, with more than one million representatives worldwide. The first Avon International Women's Marathon is held in Atlanta, Georgia. With the start of this program, Avon helps women's running become an Olympic event.

1979   Avon acquires Tiffany & Co. The company participates in the Pasadena Tournament of Roses Parade for the first time.

1980   Avon Products enters Honduras. David Hall McConnell's childhood home in Southwest Oswego, New York, is dedicated a New York State historic site.

1981   Avon agrees to buy Mallinckrodt, Inc., a health care company.

1982   Avon enters Taiwan, Peru, and Portugal. Sales reach $3 billion, with 1.3 million representatives worldwide. Fifth Annual International Women's Marathon takes place in San Francisco. Races are held in 19 countries.

1983   Avon enters the Dominican Republic. David W. Mitchell retires as chief executive officer, but continues as a board member. Hicks B. Waldron is elected chairman, president, and chief executive officer.

1984   Avon enters Austria, acquires Foster Medical Corporation, and sells Tiffany & Co. to a management-led investment group. Sales decline to $2.6 billion from a high of $3 billion in 1982.

1985   Sales continue to slide to $2.47 billion. John S. Chamberlin is named president and chief operating officer. Avon sells Mallinckrodt to International Minerals and Chemical Corporation.

1986   Avon acquires Retirement Inns of America and the Mediplex Group. The company announces a turnaround in its beauty business after a six-year decline. Sales inch back up to $2.8 billion, with 1.3 million representatives worldwide. Avon celebrates its centennial: 1886–1986.

1987   Prestige fragrance company Giorgio, Inc. and Parfums Stern are acquired. Foster Medical Supply is sold.

1988   The Avon Color brand is rolled out in the United States and the company announces that an international introduction will follow. John S. Chamberlin resigns as president. James E. Preston becomes president and chief executive officer. Hicks B. Waldron, chairman, retires. The Mediplex Group is sold.

1989   Avon Products enters Indonesia. James E. Preston assumes the additional post of chairman. Sales climb to $3.2 billion, with 1.5 million representatives worldwide. Avon sells Parfums Stern and Retirement Inns of America. Avon fights off three hostile takeover attempts, including separate groups involving Mary Kay and Amway. Avon becomes the first major cosmetics company to ban animal testing.

1990   Avon enters China, Hungary, and Germany (East). Sales reach $3.4 billion, with 1.5 million representatives worldwide.

1991   Avon enters the Czech Republic, Panama, Ecuador, Bolivia, and Russia. Hays Clark retires from the board. He is the last descendant of company founder David H. McConnell to be associated with Avon.

1992   Anew Perfecting Complex for Face, the first alpha hydroxy acid skin care product for the mass market is introduced. Avon enters Poland.

1993   Avon enters Slovakia, Ireland, and Turkey. Sales hit $4 billion.

1994   The Giorgio fragrance business is sold to Procter & Gamble for $150 million.

1996   Avon enters South Africa, India, and Nicaragua. For the first time, Avon becomes one of the official sponsors of the Centennial Olympic Games in Atlanta. Avon establishes an Internet web site.

1997   Avon enters the Ukraine, Romania, and Croatia. The company's sales reach $5 billion.

1998   Avon enters Uruguay. Charles Perrin is named chief executive officer and chairman. Andrea Jung becomes president and chief operating officer.

1999   Andrea Jung becomes Avon's first woman chief executive officer. Avon enters Hong Kong, Lithuania, Slovenia, Bulgaria, and Latvia. Company launches its first global advertising campaign with "Let's Talk." Signs tennis stars Venus and Serena Williams as spokespersons. James Preston retires.

2000   Avon enters Singapore and South Korea. Sales are now $5.6 billion. Andrea Jung is elected chairman.

2001   Avon enters Greece and Morocco. Susan Kropf becomes president and chief operating officer. Sales rise to $5.9 billion.

2002   Avon sales reach $6 billion.

2003   Avon sales grow to $6.8 billion, with 4.4 million representatives worldwide.

2004   Avon enters Vietnam. The company introduces Mexican-born actress Salma Hayek as its new global spokesperson. The Avon Foundation adds domestic violence as a cause. Sales reach $7.7 billion.

2005   The Avon Foundation celebrates its fiftieth anniversary with the "Walk Around the World for Breast Cancer" fundraiser. The event is held in 50 countries around the world.

ACKNOWLEDGMENTS

The making of this book was an extraordinary group effort that couldn't have happened without the work and support of numerous people.

First, I must express my appreciation to the Avon sales representatives worldwide. You invited me into your homes, took my phone calls, and responded to e-mails. All business leaders should be as warm and forthcoming! I hope this account does you justice.

Without the support of Avon's corporate leadership, this story would not have been possible. Thanks to Nancy Glaser, Victor Beaudet, Debbie Coffey, Sharon Samuel, and Kate Babb for opening those doors and for your invaluable help throughout the process. Separate thanks to all of Avon's executives who appear in this book for their time and willingness to talk, not only about the company's business, but to share their personal stories as well. Additional gratitude to Andrea Jung, Susan Kropf, and James Preston for providing context no one else could have.

For the historical perspective, I'd like to express warm appreciation to H. Lawrence Clark, the great grandson of founder David Hall McConnell, for sharing accounts of his family. Additionally, I'd like to recognize the assistance of Lynn Cantanese, Marge McNinch, and Steve Shisler at the Hagley Museum and Library; Gardner and Josephine Watts of Suffern, New York; Pastor Allen Kemp of the Suffern Presbyterian Church; the Oswego Historical Society; the Suffern Public Library; the Conant Public Library; and the Historical Society of Winchester, New Hampshire.

Seven years at *Women's Wear Daily* prepared me for this assignment, and I thank editors Pete Born, Ed Nardoza, Dianne Pogoda, and Jim Fallon for their steady support over the years. I also must recognize my *WWD* "beauty pod" colleagues past and present for sharing the journey with me, with special recognition to my WWD writing partner, Faye Brookman, for her sage advice. What's more, I'd like to acknowledge the WWD financial team for all of their help. Additional thanks to Roy White, Marianne Wilson, Dr. Stanley Blondek, and Melanie Best for their professional insights.

For their constant encouragement, I thank my brothers, David Klepacki and Anthony G. Klepacki, and wonderful friends for whom I am ever grateful.

All of this would have been for naught had it not been for the enthusiasm of executive editor Debra Englander at John Wiley & Sons who helped get this project off the ground. I'd also like to thank Kim Craven, Joan O'Neill, Michael Freeland, Peter Knapp, Mike Onorato, Colleen Scollans, Jesica Church, and Lissa Brown at Wiley for their efforts in publishing and promoting the book.

Finally, I'd like to express deep appreciation to Kirk Kazanjian of Literary Productions for trusting me with his story concept and patiently guiding me through the editorial process of constructing a book. Even when information seemed hard to find, deadlines loomed, and I was uncertain about the outcome, you made the project fun.

In closing, may this book serve as a tribute to my late parents, Anthony J. and Rena Klepacki, who gave me my first typewriter and blank journal to take notes in.

NOTES

All quotes and interviews featured throughout the book were obtained firsthand by the author unless otherwise noted.

CHAPTER 1   Give Them What They Want

p. 7   *When he set out as a young man to seek his fortune, McConnell said that his hardy up bringing gave him a "positive advantage" over others with less life experience.* David H. McConnell, Sr. "A History of the California Perfume Co.," Avon Corporate Archives, from 1903.

p. 8   . . . *"gave me good insight into human nature."* McConnell.

p. 10   *". . . to build up a permanent and well-established trade."* McConnell.

p. 11   *"But there were many things that were not pleasant."* McConnell.

p. 11   *". . . 'to make ends meet.'"* George DeMaas, "Avon Calling: My Uncle Mac," *Twenty-Sixth Publication of the Oswego County Historical Society,* 1963, p. 19.

p. 12   *". . . it was a beautiful house,"* Jan Sevene, "Persis Albee of Winchester first to ring bells of success," *The Banner,* August 17, 2001, p. 1.

p. 12   . . . *"unfailing integrity."* George Beauregard, "Avon Calling," Winchester Historical Society Archives. Winchester, NH.

p. 12   *". . . She helped those who helped the business prosper,"* Jan Sevene, "Persis Albee of Winchester first to ring bells of success," *The Banner,* August 17, 2001, p. 1.

p. 12   *". . . put in practical operation by Mrs. Albee."* David H. McConnell, Sr. "A History of the California Perfume Co.," Avon Corporate Archives, from 1903.

p. 14   *. . . by a resident vote of 206 to 19.* "Suffern: 200 Years 1773–1973. An Historical Account," Prepared by the Bicentennial Committee, p. 36.

p. 14   *. . . no formal police or fire protection.* Ibid.

p. 15   "*. . . Our rouge is now ready for delivery.*" "Outlook," Avon Corporate Archives from 1905.

p. 15   "*. . . charged with the heinous crime of vanity.*" Ella Adelia Fletcher, "The Woman Beautiful," Brentano's (New York, 1901), p. 1.

p. 16   *. . . the region's largest provider of jobs.* Louise Zimmerman, Editor, "Rockland County Century of History," Historical Society of Rockland County.

p. 19   "*. . . a difficulty that cannot be overcome.*" David H. McConnell, "A History of the California Perfume Co.," Avon Corporate Archives from 1903.

p. 20   *. . . "One of [the] Community's Outstanding Men."* "D. H. McConnell, Prominent Local Citizen, Passed Away at Suffern Home Wednesday," *Ramapo Valley Independent,* January 22, 1937, p. 1.

CHAPTER 2   Stay Focused

p. 23   *. . . 40 percent of the total.* "Avon a Chronological History," Public Affairs, March 1993, Avon Corporate Archives.

p. 31   "*. . . and far less profitable business,*" Hicks Waldron, "A Letter to Shareholders," Avon Products, Inc., Annual Report, 1988.

p. 31   *. . . failed health care operations.* Robert W. Pratt, from a speech presented to Avon management, January 23, 1989, from the personal holdings of James Preston.

p. 35   "*. . . there can be no major surprises.*" Robert W. Pratt.

p. 35   "*. . . a dollar that can go toward debt reduction,*" James Preston, Presentation to Avon Management, September 26, 1988, from the personal holdings of James Preston.

p. 37   *. . . 6.5 percent of the company's stock.* Jeffrey Tractenberg, "Group Acquires 6.5% of Avon Common Stock—Purchase by Gordon Getty, Mary Kay Aide, Fisher, Could Put Firm in Play," *Wall Street Journal,* November 14, 1989, p. 1.

p. 38   *. . . 9.1 percent of Avon common stock.* Jeffrey Tractenberg, "Avon Holder Plans to Seek Four Board Seats: Analysts Are Disappointed Chartwell Doesn't Make More Aggressive Move," *Wall Street Journal,* February 9, 1990, p. A2.

CHAPTER 3 Hire the Best Man (Or Woman) for the Job

p. 43 *". . . value diversity in the workplace."* James Preston, speech presented before the American Woman's Economic Development Meeting, February 20, 1988.

CHAPTER 4 Empower Your Sales Force

p. 65 *"This is what I try to get across to new recruits."* Tanya Alina Gingerich, "A Beautiful New Life," *Avon Dreams,* Summer 2003, p. 28.

CHAPTER 5 Incentivize the Troops

p. 92 *". . . image-enhancing program,"* Neil H. Offen, speech presented at the Direct Selling Association's Annual Meeting, Boca Raton, Florida. June 9, 2003.

p. 92 *". . . guise of direct-selling companies."* Neil H. Offen, speech presented at the Direct Selling Association's Annual Meeting, Boca Raton, Florida. June 9, 2003.

p. 92 *". . . show respect for our sales people."* Neil H. Offen, speech presented at the Direct Selling Association's Annual Meeting, Boca Raton, Florida. June 9, 2003.

p. 92 *". . . very powerful growth engine,"* Nanette Byrnes, "Avon Is Calling Lots of New Reps," *Business Week Online,* June 4, 2003.

CHAPTER 6 Constantly Innovate

p. 107 *. . . Marshall Field's department stores.* Julie L. Belcove, Cara Kagan and Soren Larson, "Beauty Companies Ride the Acid Wave," *Women's Wear Daily,* March 18, 1994.

p. 108 *. . . Avon's skin care lab in Suffern.* Barbara Woller, "Stabilizing Vitamin C," *The Journal News,* March 28, 2003.

p. 108 *". . . You feel like a trailblazer."* Barbara Woller, "Stabilizing Vitamin C," *The Journal News,* March 28, 2003.

p. 109   . . . *what women want in a lipstick.* Laura Klepacki, "Avon Delivers Fresh Twists," *Women's Wear Daily,* May 7, 2004.

p. 113   "*. . . saltwater and (fresh water) fisherman."* Jim Binns, "Keep Those Bugs Away," *Bass Fishing and Fly Fishing Magazine,* August 6, 2004, p. 2.

p. 113   "*. . . product for bug repellency."* Kim-Van Dang, "Sun Care With Repellent: Catches the Bug," *Women's Wear Daily,* March 21, 1997.

p. 115   "*. . . great items, that are very adaptable,"* Caryn Monget, "Avon's Newest Call—Casual Sportswear by Von Furstenberg," *Women's Wear Daily,* February 2, 1995.

CHAPTER 7 Keep Up with the Times

p. 117   "*. . . to do a lot of corporate appearances."* Laura Klepacki, "Pennington Adds a Play: Avon," *Women's Wear Daily,* April 16, 2004.

p. 128   "*. . . no favors and no exceptions."* Bryn Kenny, "Making My Mark," *WWD BeautyBiz,* February 2004, p. 43.

p. 129   . . . *as essential to feeling good.* "Women's Well-Being Merchandising Strategies," A Study by the General Merchandise Distributors Council, Colorado Springs, Colorado, 2001.

p. 129   . . . *compared to a year ago.* "Introducing and Merchandising New OTC Whole Health Products," A Study by the General Merchandise Distributors Council, Colorado Springs, Colorado, 2002.

p. 129   "*. . . overall sense of wellness."* "Women's Well-Being Merchandising Strategies," A Study by the General Merchandise Distributors Council, Colorado Springs, Colorado, 2001.

p. 131   . . . *24 percent of the U.S. population.* "Population Growth will Foster Demographic Shifts," *CNNfn Online,* March 31, 2000.

CHAPTER 8 Speak in Every Language

p. 134   "*. . . other Latin American countries,"* Avon Products, Inc., Annual Report, 1954.

p. 134   "*. . . and England were costly,"* Avon Products, Inc., Annual Report, 1959.

p. 134   *". . . unlimited opportunities for Avon."* Avon Products, Inc., Annual Report, 1965.

p. 135   *". . . superior products at reasonable prices."* Avon Products, Inc., Annual Report, 1965.

p. 135   *. . . before approving the venture.* George White, "Avon Will Go Calling on China Despite Political Controversy," *Los Angeles Times,* June 18, 1990, p. 3.

p. 135   *". . . China and Avon's shareholders."* George White, "Avon Will Go Calling on China Despite Political Controversy," *Los Angeles Times,* June 18, 1990, p. 3.

p. 136   *". . . treated like a queen, like a film star."* Amelia Hill, "Real Life: Avon Calling," *Observer* magazine, June 15, 2003, p. 25.

p. 137   *". . . to represent the company."* Amelia Hill, "Real Life: Avon Calling," *Observer* magazine, June 15, 2003, p. 25.

p. 137   *". . . selling lipsticks from tent to tent,"* Amelia Hill, "Real Life: Avon Calling," *Observer* magazine, June 15, 2003, p. 25.

p. 137   *". . . what am I going to do with a chicken?"* James Brooke, "Who Braves Piranha Waters? Your Avon Lady!" *New York Times,* July 7, 1995, p. A4.

p. 137   *. . . had a total of 10 cars.* Mandalit Del Barco, "Avon Ladies on the Amazon," *All Things Considered,* May, 29, 1999, p. 1.

p. 137   *". . . And, so here I am."* Mandalit Del Barco, "Avon Ladies on the Amazon," *All Things Considered,* May 29, 1999, p. 1.

p. 137   *. . . 20 pounds of flour for a cologne.* Mandalit Del Barco, "Avon Ladies on the Amazon," *All Things Considered,* May 29, 1999, p. 1.

p. 139   *. . . $3.5 billion in 2000.* Jill Jusko, "Avon Calling On Russia," *Industry Week,* December 2003, p. 48.

p. 140   *. . . $18 billion annually within 20 years.* Jill Jusko, "Avon Calling On Russia," *Industry Week,* December 2003, p. 48.

p. 141   *. . . brought in from China.* Margot Cohen, "More Than a Pretty Face," *Far Eastern Economic Review,* April 1, 2004, p. 36.

p. 141   *". . . opportunities to build their brand."* Margot Cohen "More Than a Pretty Face," *Far Eastern Economic Review,* April 1, 2004, p. 36.

p. 142   *. . . that country's army and navy.* Bernice Kanner, *Pocketbook Power,* McGraw-Hill (New York, 2004), p. 67.

p. 142   *"That has created a market."* Miriam Jordan, "Knock Knock: In Brazil, an Army of Underemployed Goes Door-to-Door," *Wall Street Journal Eastern Edition,* February 19, 2003, p. A1.

p. 142   *". . . to get consumers to buy."* Miriam Jordan, "Knock Knock: In Brazil, an Army of Underemployed Goes Door-to-Door," *Wall Street Journal Eastern Edition,* February 19, 2003, p. A1.

CHAPTER 9   Embrace Technology

p. 156   *. . . predicted within 10 percent accuracy.* Mary Jo Foley and Tom Steinert-Threlkeld, "The Ultimate CRM Machine," *Baseline Research,* October 29, 2001, p. 6.

p. 158   *. . . fell far short of the number ordered.* Mary Jo Foley, "Demands of Forecasting," *Baseline Research,* October 29, 2001.

p. 158   *. . . impact of an adjacent product.* Mary Jo Foley, "Demands of Forecasting," *Baseline Research,* October 29, 2001.

p. 160   *. . . "corporate nervous breakdown"* Mary Jo Foley and Tom Steinert-Threlkeld, "The Ultimate CRM Machine," *Baseline Research,* October 29, 2001, p. 4.

p. 161   *. . . a women-centric Internet service provider.* Mary Jo Foley and Tom Steinert-Threlkeld, "The Ultimate CRM Machine," *Baseline Research,* October 29, 2001, p. 3.

p. 164   *. . . compared to $1.50 for the paper forms.* Mary Jo Foley and Tom Steinert-Threlkeld, "The Ultimate CRM Machine," *Baseline Research,* October 29, 2001, p. 2.

CHAPTER 10   Connect with Your Customers

p. 170   *". . . went straight into the curb."* Amelia Hill, "Real life: Avon Calling," *Observer* magazine, June 15, 2003, p. 25.

p. 170   *. . . ding dong sound alone.* Amelia Hill, "Real life: Avon Calling," *Observer* magazine, June 15, 2003, p. 25.

p. 171   *. . . desire for Avon products and services.* Avon Print Advertising Collection, Avon Corporate Archives.

p. 172   *". . . plan to turn up the volume."* Kim-Van Dang, "Avon Launches Last Phase of Corporate Revamping," *Women's Wear Daily,* February 5, 1997.

p. 176   *. . . women tend to turn right when they enter a store.* Bernice Kanner, *Pocketbook Power: How to Reach the Hearts and Minds of Today's Most Coveted Consumers—Women* (McGraw-Hill, New York), p. 182.

p. 180   "*. . . alternate brochure advertisements,*" Joan Treistman and John P. Gregg, "Visual, Verbal and Sales Responses to Print Ads," *Journal of Advertising Research,* August 1979, p. 41.

CHAPTER 13   Give Back

p. 216   "*. . . and they are fiercely loyal.*" Faye Brookman, "A Lip Balm and Fundraiser in One," *Women's Wear Daily,* January 17, 2003.

p. 216   "*. . . where the company is looking at a return on their investment,*" Ann Meyer, "Corporate Philanthropy With a Personal Touch," *Chicago Tribune,* December 13, 2004, p. 3.

p. 231   "*. . . you're just doing it to be purely promotional.*" Faye Brookman, "Critical Mass," *Women's Wear Daily,* December 17, 2004, p. 8.

INDEX

16309918R00150

Made in the USA
Lexington, KY
16 July 2012